CHAUCER STUDIES V

CHAUCER'S BOCCACCIO

CHAUCER'S BOCCACCIO

Sources for *Troilus* and the *Knight's* and
Franklin's Tales

Translations from the *Filostrato,*
Teseida and *Filocolo*

N. R. HAVELY

D. S. BREWER

First published 1980 by D. S. Brewer
Reprinted in paperback 1992

Transferred to digital printing

ISBN 978-0-85991-349-2

D. S. Brewer is an imprint of Boydell & Brewer Ltd
PO Box 9, Woodbridge, Suffolk IP12 3DF, UK
and of Boydell & Brewer Inc.
668 Mt Hope Avenue, Rochester, NY 14620, USA
website: www.boydellandbrewer.com

A CiP catalogue record for this book is available
from the British Library

This publication is printed on acid-free paper

Contents

Introduction

(i) *Boccaccio and Naples*

'How many famous cities there are in this country – how many magnificent castles, how many bays, harbours, ports, lakes, curative springs, forests, woods, pastures, pleasant retreats and fertile fields! Moreover, what multitudes of common people there are and what numbers of illustrious nobles! Indeed, it would not be easy to describe what great wealth exists there and what abundance of all that life requires.'[1]

This was how, later in life, Boccaccio described the Kingdom of Naples, where his earliest works had been written. These works themselves reflect in several ways the strength of his loyalty to the place. Several of his early lyrics evoke and idealize the activities and atmosphere of the Neapolitan court.[2] His first longer poem, the *Caccia di Diana* presents a number of named Neapolitan ladies, who are summoned from the city to serve the goddess of the hunt.[3] At the beginning of his first major prose narrative, the *Filocolo,* the work itself is shown to have a local habitation in Naples, and its hero visits 'the noble city of Parthenope' twice.[4] And the social life of Troy in the *Filostrato* and the festivities and rituals of Athens in the *Teseida* have discernible roots in the court and town that Boccaccio grew to know during his formative years as a writer.[5]

The Kingdom of Naples as a whole was, despite Boccaccio's description in *De Mulieribus Claris,* not very densely populated by comparison with the rest of the peninsula, and its capital was by no means the largest of the Italian cities.[6] But having been part of the Kingdom of Sicily until 1282, its culture had been influenced by a variety of prestigious ruling families,[7] and the Angevins, who had held the throne for over half a century before Boccaccio's birth, were one of the leading dynasties of Europe. Charles I had chosen Naples rather than Palermo as his capital when he added the kingdom to his French possessions in 1266, and the impression the Angevins made on the city's visual appearance was probably most marked during the reign of his successor, Charles II (1285–1309).[8] Yet Robert I (1309–43), with whose court Boccaccio was so closely associated, also made several major contributions to its architecture. The Franciscan Church of Santa Chiara, in which he is buried, was completed in 1328, and bears witness to the alliance between the Angevin kings and the Minorite Order.[9] A chapel there, and a hall and chapel in the royal palace, the Castelnuovo once had frescoes by Giotto, who was employed by the King from 1328 until 1332 or 3.[10] Robert also laid out two royal gardens which Boccaccio may well have had in mind when he came to describe the settings for several of the courtly gatherings in the *Filocolo*.[11]

For projects such as these, for Robert's extensive diplomatic and military ventures,[12] and for the repayment of the crown's considerable debt to the Papacy[13] funds had of course to be raised; and careful management was needed, for the kingdom was, as Caggese says, no longer 'the garden of the Hesperides.'[14] Yet it does not, on the other hand, appear to have been in a state of desperate economic decline. Several of its provinces, such as Campania, were considered particularly fertile and wealthy, and the king was a shrewd and frugal administrator.[15] Expenditure was usually modest and carefully documented,[16] and in the later years of the reign the royal budget seems even to have shown a surplus.[17] Robert was therefore able to conduct his fiscal affairs without recourse to violent measures such as had been adopted, for example, by Philip the Fair of France.[18]

His ability to do so, however, was in large measure due to his dependence upon foreign financiers. Venetian and Genoese merchants, among others, had long been active in the kingdom, but by the early years of the fourteenth century their influence had considerably declined. By that time a position of financial and commercial dominance had been established by the Florentines.[19] Indeed, the power of what Dante called the *maladetto fiore* (the accursed florin)[20] had supported the foundation of the Angevin kingdom in the first place, to such an extent that a recent historian has spoken of Charles of Anjou's venture in 1266 as a 'sound investment' for the bankers of Florence.[21] The returns on this investment were certainly high,[22] and by the time of Robert's accession, Caggese concludes, 'not only had the fortunes of the Florentine companies, and particularly the three most powerful [the Bardi, Peruzzi and Acciaiuoli] been securely guaranteed, but he knew from his own experience that it was not and would never be possible for him to take any political or military action without the help of the Florentines . . . The finances of the kingdom were in their hands.'[23] The range of these companies' activities in Naples included the manufacture of clothes and weapons, the running of shops and the provision of luxury goods for the Court; and as merchants they dealt in the main commodities that the country produced.[24] But it was as bankers to the Court, the Church and individuals that the Florentines were most active, and the larger companies also very efficiently farmed the kingdom's taxes.[25] Their crucial importance in this respect was reflected by the measures the King took to protect their interests.[26]

Many Florentines also held public offices and positions at Court during Robert's reign,[27] and a royal document of June 2nd 1328 names as 'counsellor and chamberlain'[28] one Boccaccio da Certaldo, usually referred to as Boccaccino, the father of the poet. Boccaccino had shortly before been made an associate of the largest of the three Florentine companies, the Bardi, and had been sent to Naples in the later months of

1327, at a time when Robert was much in need of funds to defend his kingdom in the face of threats from several quarters.[29] He was joined, probably at this time, by his fourteen year old legitimized son, Giovanni,[30] who was subsequently to undergo four years of apprenticeship as a banker in the Bardi office there.[31]

It was thus Robert's financial dealings that brought the young Boccaccio with his father to Naples. The King's concern to remain solvent under difficult circumstances may have been what led the poet later to describe him as miserly.[32] Yet while such writers as Boccaccio, Villani and Dante all rehearse this charge, they also in various ways acknowledge the extent of Robert's reputation for learning. At the opening of the *Filocolo*, which he wrote in Naples, Boccaccio describes the King as reigning 'with the aid of Pallas' (I, 1, par. 14). Even when he later denounces him as 'Midas' in the *Comedia Ninfe* (1341–2), he still describes him in the same sentence as one who is 'plentifully endowed with the gifts of Pallas' (XXXV, par. 32); and towards the end of the *Genealogia Deorum Gentilium* (c.1350–c.1360), which was written some time after Robert's death, he speaks of him as 'a King whose superior in learning men have not seen since Solomon' (XIV, 9), and as 'a shining example of all virtues . . . a distinguished philosopher, an eminent teacher of medicine, and an exceptional theologian in his day' (XIV, 22).[33] Many others, including Villani,[34] praise Robert's wisdom and learning in terms that cannot easily be dismissed as mere flattery.[35] And even Dante, hostile as he was,[36] has the King's elder brother, Charles Martel, pay him the somewhat back-handed compliment of suggesting that he ought to have been a preacher (*Paradiso* VIII, 147).

By the standards of his time Robert indeed seems to have been a 'noble preacher'. He wrote large numbers of sermons for various occasions, and a tract on poverty – relating to the conflict within the Franciscan movement – was a product of the years he spent at Avignon.[37] Modern opinions concerning his ability have been somewhat divided. Caggese, his main biographer, considers that his 'wisdom and knowledge . . . did not go beyond the limits of mediocrity',[38] whilst Léonard, the leading historian of the dynasty, argues for a more generous estimate of his capacities – pointing out that much of his work has been lost, and inclining to trust the verdicts of contemporaries, including Petrarch who chose to be judged by Robert before receiving the laurel crown in 1341.[39] There appears, moreover, to be general agreement that, whatever his own intellectual gifts may have been, he was an exceptionally good judge of such qualities in others – and even Caggese goes so far as to allow that he was 'in some sense a humanist'.[40]

One way in which such judgment was manifested was through his patronage of the university in his capital. The *studium generale* at Naples had been founded by Frederick II in 1224. Its privileges had subsequently been confirmed by the first two Angevin kings and by Robert himself, and included exemption from taxes, with direct dependence upon the authority of the Chancellor of the Kingdom, who was also Rector of the University.[41] Its teachers were nominated by the King and usually paid directly by the Court. Amongst the distinguished visitors invited to teach there during Robert's reign was the jurist, poet and friend of both Dante and Petrarch, Cino da Pistoia. Cino, although he had earlier been an opponent of the Angevins,[42] was welcomed by a special announcement from the King in August 1330. He remained at the University for only a year, and appears to have left in a mood of some hostility towards it and towards what he called the *regno servile* (servile kingdom) of Naples.[43] Yet during his stay Boccaccio, who by then had ended his apprenticeship with the Bardi and embarked upon the study of canon law, attended his lectures on the code of Justinian,[44] thus probably confirming an admiration for the older poet which was later to be reflected in, for example, his imitation in the *Filostrato* (V, 62–5) of one of Cino's *canzoni*.[45] A rather less volatile academic visitor was the Augustinian friar Dionigi da Borgo San Sepolcro, who had taught at the Sorbonne and came to Naples as professor of canon law in 1338.[46] He is believed to have introduced the young Boccaccio to the work of Seneca and Augustine and to have aided his understanding of Petrarch and other vernacular poets.

Robert's patronage of learning was, however, by no means confined to the University. Andalò del Negro of Genoa – compiler of a treatise on the planets and best known, according to Branca, 'for his endless and confused studies'[47] – received a pension from the King and imparted some of his persistence, and perhaps his confusion, to Boccaccio, who acknowledges later in the *Genealogia* that 'I have frequently cited that noble and venerable old man . . . who was once my teacher of astronomy' (XV, 6).[48] Andalò also appears as a stargazing shepherd, Calmeta, who instructs the fugitive Idalogo in an autobiographical episode in the *Filocolo* (V, 8, par. 16f.).[49]

Among those who held office at Court there were also intellectuals whose interests brought them into contact with both Boccaccio and Petrarch. Two of the most important of these were Giovanni Barrili and Barbato da Sulmona, who both became Boccaccio's friends early in his life and continued to be so.[50] Nothing of Barrili's work now survives and only a little of Barbato's. But Barbato's intelligence, style and learning were much admired by Petrarch (*Sen.* III, 4),[51] and he is referred to a number of times with affection and respect in Boccaccio's letters.[52] One of Barrili's claims to fame and sympathy is that he accidentally missed Petrarch's coronation in 1341.[53] Boccaccio also pays his family the compliment of mentioning it first in the list of nymphs in the *Caccia di Diana* (I, 16–18), and later in the *Genealogia* (XIV, 19)[54] he respectfully refers to Barrili himself as the source for a story about the composition of Virgil's *Georgics* and *Aeneid*.

Barbato and Barrili are thus among those figures associated with the Court who are of some significance for the early history of renaissance humanism. The literary and cultural interests of these scholars do not appear, however, to have been directly sustained by the teaching of Greek or the translation of classical Greek texts, such as Boccaccio attempted to encourage later in life.[55] The mixed culture of the kingdom still indeed contained a living strain of Greek, and a number of its monasteries possessed important collections of Greek texts,[56] as did the library of Charles I;[57] moreover, translators from Greek were employed at the courts of both Charles II and Robert. But their work mainly served those Kings' theological, scientific and, particularly, medical interests;[58] and they thus

4

appear to have coexisted rather than actively collaborated with the early humanists of Naples.[59]

Yet humanists and translators alike undoubtedly shared the resources of the Angevin Library, and King Robert was certainly no miser when it came to endowing this collection. He is said to have paid an associate of one of the Florentine companies sixty ounces of gold for a *corpus iuris*[60] – five times as much as the pension he paid Giotto for his services in 1332.[61] Items in the royal treasury accounts before and during his reign cover payments for the copying and purchase of books;[62] and in addition to copiers and translators from Greek, Hebrew and Arabic the King also employed experts to search for further material.[63] On the whole, therefore, he seems to have been quite as dedicated and energetic a bibliophile as his English contemporary, Richard of Bury.

Acquisitions during the reign substantially reflect the King's interest in theology,[64] but the Library also by this time included collections of medical texts and works on canon and civil law.[65] Among the hundred or so volumes it contained by 1341 only three classical items are listed,[66] but of these the Seneca that was copied in that year probably reflects the special interests of Boccaccio's friend Dionigi da Borgo San Sepolcro. And a classical scholar whose name is very closely associated with the Angevin Library during Boccaccio's years in Naples was another of the young poet's friends and guides, the royal librarian Paolo da Perugia.[67] As Boccaccio himself shows in the *Genealogia* (Preface and XIV, 8) there is some evidence of contact between Paolo and the Greek scholars of the time, such as Abbot Barlaam of Calabria – but as with Barbato da Sulmona his surviving work does not indicate that he actually knew Greek. Boccaccio, however, regarded him as one of the leading classicists of his time, 'a man of the highest authority', and at least one more recent scholar has acknowledged his 'vast and varied culture'.[68] His main work on pagan mythology, the *Collectanea*, was lost shortly after his death, but it may well have inspired Boccaccio's own long labour on the subject, the *Genealogia*, in which Paolo is cited on about ninety occasions.[69] His surviving work, including a commentary on the satires of Persius, gives some indication of the range of literature to which he could have introduced the poet,[70] and from his example, Torraca suggests, Boccaccio might have learnt 'the practice of taking notes and transcribing texts and the sound habit of working patiently and methodically that remained with him constantly throughout his life.'[71]

Paolo thus seems to have been one of the major influences upon Boccaccio's intellectual growth during this period – facilitating his acquaintance with classical Latin writers, and with mythographers especially – and fostering the development of the encyclopaedic tendency that characterized his work both then and later. The *Caccia di Diana* (1334?), for example, although it fulfils a largely social function as a *sirventese*, clearly displays an interest in the symbolism of metamorphosis[72] that is to be more fully developed in certain passages of the *Filocolo*.[73] On the other hand the *Filostrato* (1335?), which is probably the second of Boccaccio's major Neapolitan works,[74] does not follow in this direction, and its rhetoric and narrative style are for the most part closer to the vernacular traditions that will be considered shortly. Yet the choice here of a romance with the Troy story as its context still reflects something of the poet's interest in classical legend and its traditions, however much he and others had overlaid this with medieval courtliness. And even here can be found several allusions to classical myths concerning the transforming power of love;[75] whilst a couple of random references to the story of Thebes (VI, 24 and VII, 27) hint at an interest that is eventually to be embodied in the *Teseida*.

It is, however, the two later works of Boccaccio's Neapolitan period – the *Filocolo* (1336–8?) and the *Teseida* (1339–41?) – that display most fully the development and range of his interests in classical myth and literature, and his indebtedness to Paolo, Dionigi and others[76] for the furtherance of these. In the *Filocolo* particularly, although the plot clearly derives from vernacular romance tradition, its treatment reflects the influence of such mentors in a number of passages.[77] By the time he came to write this 'little book' (referred to as such both in the first chapter and some six hundred pages later) Boccaccio had gained some acquaintance with Servius, Boethius and Fulgentius, and Albericus amongst others, probably from Paolo, who refers to them in his Persius commentary.[78] And, as the *Filocolo* epilogue suggests,[79] he was also familiar with the major works of Virgil, Lucan's *Pharsalia*, Statius's *Thebaid*, and – perhaps above all at this stage – 'Ovid of Sulmona', in whose 'sacred book' (the *Ars Amatoria*) the lovers are instructed at an early age.[80] Ovid is also referred to reverentially on a number of occasions throughout the work,[81] and the *Metamorphoses*, as already suggested, provide the model for many of its allegorical episodes.

The *Teseida* which Boccaccio was writing during the last years of his stay in Naples is his first and only thoroughgoing imitation of classical epic, and his most ambitious venture as yet into the world of classical myth. The story of Arcita and Palemone has no ascertainable classical source,[82] although a number of episodes and descriptive passages in the poem are modelled on parts of the *Thebaid*;[83] and in a host of local instances throughout Boccaccio's language bears witness to his reading of Statius, as well as Virgil and Ovid.[84] The influence of classical epic models also has some effect upon the structure of the *Teseida*, which is divided like the *Aeneid* and the *Thebaid* into twelve books and contains (without the introductory sonnets) the same number of lines as the former. In the prologue to the work (as in that to *Filostrato*) Boccaccio alludes to the antiquity of his source, and in its conclusion he claims to be introducing the martial epic into the vernacular (XII, 84) – whilst the accounts of battles in Books I, II and VIII and the catalogue of heroes in VI undoubtedly contribute to what Boitani calls 'the general martial "patina" of the work.'[85]

Ovidian mythology is also much in evidence in the *Teseida*[86] as it had been in the *Filocolo*; but the influence of this and other kinds of lore is more fully incorporated in Boccaccio's own *chiose* (glosses) to the poem. The poet's own commentary on his text reflects the concern with which he regarded the course that his craft somewhat erratically followed through waters no vernacular poet had furrowed before (XII, 85), and the seriousness with which he contemplated the work that was to remain his longest narrative in verse. And the compendiousness of these *chiose*, especially in the mythographic essays on Mars and Venus in Book VII, makes the *Teseida* even more than the *Filocolo* a tribute to those who steered Boccaccio's interests during his years at the Angevin court.

This court also maintained contact in various ways with the native culture of its rulers. Scribes from France along with those of other nations continued to be employed there,[87] and at least one of the major texts that Robert is known to have had copied is in French.[88] And whatever weight is attached to the presence there of a book of romances and poems *gallico scripti*,[89] the French romance tradition is of undoubted importance in relation to three of Boccaccio's four main Neapolitan poems. Benoit's *Roman de Troie* is thought to have been consulted by him,[90] along with other sources, during the composition of *Filostrato*; and the *Teseida* may well have been influenced in certain episodes by the *Roman de Thèbes* as well as the *Thebaid*.[91] And the plot of the *Filocolo* moreover derives from one of the most widely disseminated of all medieval romance stories, that of Floire and Blanchefleur.

Such romance plots also provided material for the verse narratives called *cantari* which were popular in Italy at this time; and indeed a *cantare* version of the Floire and Blanchefleur story exists in a version that is roughly contemporary with the *Filocolo*.[92] The *cantari* have some affinity in style, and to some extent subject-matter, with the English tail-rhyme romances of about the same period. Their characteristic tone is similarly compounded of piety, naïve admiration and seemingly inapposite humour; suffering and disaster are often presented in rather comic or bathetic terms;[93] an atmosphere of mystery is often powerfully evoked[94] (as in the tail-rhyme *Sir Amadace*);[95] and the narrative tends to be bald in presentation and rapid in pace. Their plots draw ultimately upon a wide variety of sources in classical,[96] Arthurian and Christian legend; and their authors are mostly unknown.[97]

Boccaccio followed the example of the *cantari* in employing the octave stanza for both *Filostrato* and *Teseida*,[98] and both his handling of this verse-form[99] and his use of formulaic epithets[100] clearly reflect their influence. Unlike the *canterini*, however, he shows an interest in the personality of his characters, which in Criseida's case, as Branca points out, tends to overpower the effect of such descriptive formulae.[101] Emilia in the *Teseida* is much more akin to the heroines of the *cantari*, for not only is she often described in similar terms, but she also like them displays a tragic awareness of her own beauty as the cause of conflict and suffering.[102] The *Teseida* as a whole reflects, as well as an aspiration towards epic, a greater debt than *Filostrato* to the *cantare* tradition,[103] and it seems hardly coincidental that it should be amongst the works cited by a late fourteenth century *canterino* as major examples of the genre.[104] Indeed it may have been one of Boccaccio's ambitions at this time to become, as Branca suggests, 'the *canterino* for the chivalrous and courtly society in which he lived.'[105]

That society's appetite for stories of the sort that were provided by French romances, Italian *cantari* and Boccaccio himself is to some extent symbolized by the figure to whom the *Teseida* is dedicated – the mythical Fiammetta.[106] The similarity of this lady's literary tastes to those of Dante's Francesca (*Inferno* V) is clearly apparent in the later prose *Elegia di Madonna Fiammetta* (ch. VIII).[107] But her association with the telling of tales is already evident from her initial appearance in the *Filocolo* (I, 1), where the 'little book' is said to have been composed at her bidding (pars. 25–6) – and from her role as 'queen', presiding over the assembly at which questions of love are posed in the form of stories later in the same work (*Filoc.* IV, 19–70).[108]

Fiammetta's importance as a symbolic figure for the love-poet is also acknowledged in the prologue to the *Teseida* and before that in the first chapter of the *Filocolo* (pars. 17–22), where the narrator describes his first sight of her at the church of San Lorenzo in Naples. This latter encounter is presented in terms that obviously owe a great deal to the language of the *dolce stil novo* and in particular to that of Dante's *Vita Nuova*.[109] Such poets were of course far more concerned with portraying the inner state of the soul than the *canterini* were, and Boccaccio shows his respect for them in the *Filostrato* and the *Teseida* by continuing to anatomize the lover's condition in a stilnovistic manner.[110] Furthermore, in the course of Troiolo's lamentations over his loss of Criseida's 'sweet gaze' in Book V of *Filostrato*, the poet, as has already been noted, takes occasion to pay tribute to one of the later stilnovists by imitating one of Cino da Pistoia's *canzoni*.[111]

Cino forms a link not only between Boccaccio and the stilnovist poets but also, more importantly, with Dante. He had been referred to a number of times in Dante's *De Vulgari Eloquentia* as a poet in the tragic style and exponent of the illustrious vernacular,[112] and had exchanged a number of sonnets with him.[113] He wrote a consolatory *canzone* on the death of Beatrice,[114] and his commemoration of Dante in *Su per la costa, Amor*[115] makes even Petrarch's tribute to Cino himself look somewhat perfunctory.[116] For such reasons, if no others, it seems likely that Cino's visit to Naples in 1330–1 would have been a major event in Boccaccio's early life. Boccaccio's own long study of Dante's work, however, had probably begun before that. His initial interest in the poet of the *Vita Nuova* and the *Commedia* may well have been given some impetus by his stepmother who was related to Beatrice's family;[117] and while at Naples he is thought to have met Graziolo de' Bambaglioli, the first commentator on Dante.[118] His years at the Angevin court thus seem to have fostered a devotion to Dante that later produced, among other works, a biography of the poet[119] and a commentary that was Boccaccio's last work in the vernacular.[120]

Such devotion is already apparent in the *Caccia di Diana*, which, like several of his later poems is written in *terza rima*, the verse-form of the *Commedia*, and draws upon the language of *Purgatorio* especially.[121] The references even at this stage suggest that Boccaccio's reading of Dante has been well assimilated – whilst in his second major work, the *Filostrato*, such allusions are deployed to an often ironic effect. Here Criseida appears at times as a rather reluctant Beatrice,[122] and Pandaro as a somewhat disingenuous Virgil;[123] whilst Troiolo is seen as a pilgrim of love whose labours, and those of his guide, serve to bring him from Hell to Paradise, only to plunge him once again into the *cieco mondo*.[124] A more sustainedly successful pilgrim of love is the *Filocolo*'s hero Florio, who describes his quest several times in such terms.[125] He addresses his followers before departure in the language of Dante's Ulysses,[126] and the metamorphosis

8

of the *pellegrino d'amore* into a pilgrim to Rome in the final book may well reflect the influence of the *Commedia*.[127] Allusions to and echoes of Dante are frequent elsewhere in the *Filocolo*,[128] and it is hardly surprising to find the author in conclusion addressing his book as a lowly follower of Dante, who is here placed in the company of Virgil, Lucan, Statius and Ovid.[129]

The *Teseida*, the final product of Boccaccio's years in Naples, reflects the continuing influence of Dante upon the poet's language, together with that of Virgil, Statius, Ovid and the *cantari*.[130] Indeed these sources have by now become so assimilated that it is sometimes difficult to distinguish between them.[131] The poem is thus envisaged in Virgilian, Statian and Ovidian terms – executed in a manner which recalls the *cantari* – and dispatched at the end in response to what has been taken as a demand from Dante.[132] It seems appropriate therefore that the work Boccaccio was completing as he returned to Florence at the end of his apprenticeship should be one that expressed his various ambitions – some more enduring than others – to be an epic poet, an encyclopaedic mythographer, a courtly *canterino*, and one who would follow in the wake of Dante,

'dinanzi all'acqua che ritorna equale.'
Par. II, 15

(ii) *Chaucer and Boccaccio*

'That most remote little corner of the world, England'[1] was in the later fourteenth century by no means isolated from the culture represented by Boccaccio's Neapolitan romances. The court in which Chaucer grew up, by which he was employed and for which he at times wrote had several sorts of connexion with ruling families of Italy[2] and a marked receptiveness to Italian cultural influences.[3] The English kings had also, like Robert of Naples, been heavily dependent upon Florentine finance earlier in the century; in Richard II's time the re-formed Bardi society was the main Italian banking company represented in England, and one of the family, Walter de Bardi, was the king's moneyer.[4] Also of importance to the Crown and the English wool-trade particularly was the community of Luccan and Florentine merchants, who had been active in England since the twelfth century, and with whom Chaucer, as Controller of Customs and Subsidy of Wools, Skins and Hides (1374–86), may well have had to deal.[5]

Whether or not Chaucer was introduced to the Italian language and literature through such dealings, his initial acquaintaince with Italy itself was made in the course of diplomatic business. The late fourteenth century was a period of quite active English involvement in Italian politics;[6] in 1368 a short-lived dynastic marriage took place between Lionel Duke of Clarence (the second son of Edward III) and Violante, daughter of Galeazzo Visconti of Milan, and it is possible that Chaucer, who had been associated with Lionel's household, may have accompanied him to Italy on that occasion.[7] Commercial links were maintained at this time with another of the Northern Italian states, the Republic of Genoa; and it was for that reason that Chaucer was commissioned to undertake his first definitely documented journey to Italy in 1372–3 – a journey that took him to both Genoa and Florence.[8] Diplomatic dealings with Milan, and the prospects of another Visconti marriage, were to also occasion the second of his known visits, in 1378.

Despite the difficulty and expense of the five weeks' journey to Italy,[9] English travellers there were not a rare or restricted class in Chaucer's time. They had come to include not only pilgrims to Rome, like the Wife of Bath,[10] and those on clerical business, like the Pardoner[11] – but also scholars and students like the Clerk,[12] mercenary soldiers such as Sir John Hawkwood,[13] and a few merchants[14] – as well as those who, like Chaucer, were on diplomatic missions between the English court and the Italian states.

Whether Chaucer actually met the elderly Boccaccio during his visit to Florence in the early months of 1373 remains a matter of pure, if appealing, speculation.[15] But, as R. A. Pratt points out, Florentine interest in Dante's *Commedia* was to lead a few months after Chaucer's visit to a petition for the lectureship that Boccaccio was to hold;[16] hence Chaucer's interest in both the subject and the lecturer may have received some additional impetus at that time. During his second visit to Italy, in connexion both with the royal wars and Richard II's projected marriage to Caterina Visconti, Chaucer could have had access to Visconti libraries, such as the one at Pavia. The collection there may then have included works by Dante, Petrarch and Boccaccio (among them the *Filostrato* and the *Decameron*);[17] and the concern of the Visconti for the success of the negotiations could well have prompted them to offer the fullest possible facilities – including those for copying manuscripts – to an envoy who had interests in Italian literature.

The employment of Chaucer on both of these missions itself suggests he had special qualifications, including perhaps a knowledge of Italian; and that was also probably the reason why he was appointed to deal with a problem concerning Genoese merchants at Dartmouth in August 1373, shortly after his return from his first Italian journey.[18] He could well have learnt the language from English travellers or from native speakers who were to be found both in the London mercantile community and at court.[19] And it would have been a distinct advantage for him on his first visit to Italy to be able to communicate more freely both with his Genoese companions on the journey[20] and with those involved in the subsequent negotiations at Genoa and Florence.

It seems therefore that by the time Chaucer came to write *Troilus* in the 1380's he would have had ample scope, as well as need, to improve his knowledge of the Italian language, and would have had considerable opportunity to develop an acquaintance with the work of Italian writers, especially the 'three crowns of Florence'. Hence although it has been suggested that Chaucer consulted a French translation of *Filostrato*,[21] the *Roman de Troyle et de Criseyda* by 'Beauvau', the influence (if any) of this text is not very profound, although it may perhaps have left some mark upon the poem's vocabulary.[22] French culture of course provided a further means by which the Italian poet's importance might have come to be recognised in

England, and Chaucer could well have been influenced by the interest shown in Boccaccio's early romances and Latin works at the Valois court.[23] But the influence of the *Teseida* and of Dante's *Commedia* is already apparent in Chaucer's writing well before *Troilus*, and, so far as is known, no French version of either existed at the time.[24] Ironic analogies between Chaucer's dreamer and Dante's pilgrim are suggested by allusions in both the *House of Fame* and the *Parliament of Fowls*,[25] and in these Chaucer's familiarity with both the *Commedia* and the *Teseida* is further attested by the way allusions to the two Italian works occasionally combine.[26]

The *Teseida* appears to have influenced Chaucer's early poetry not only in these instances, but also in his attempt to combine epic with tragic romance, following Boccaccio's precedent, in the unfinished *Anelida and Arcite*.[27] It also struck a few echoes later on in *Troilus*, especially, the *Legend of Good Women* and the *Franklin's Tale*.[28] But Chaucer's most substantial debt to Boccaccio's last Neapolitan romance is of course evident in the first of the *Canterbury Tales*. Chaucer in the *Knight's Tale* is highly selective in the treatment of his source's plot and characters, expecially by comparison with his tendency in *Troilus* to supplement and substantiate what he found in the *Filostrato*. Such a compressed treatment of the original accentuates its balanced, hierarchical structure of relationships – whilst at the same time reinforcing, and even adding, elements which impose severe strain upon that structure. This paradox is embodied particularly in Chaucer's introduction and portrayal of Saturn, but it is also apparent in his whole approach to the inventive but undisciplined mythography of the *Teseida*.[29]

Chaucer's treatment of pagan mythology both here and in the *Parliament of Fowls* raises the question of whether he knew the commentary to the *Teseida* in which Boccaccio interprets his allusions so extensively. A common assumption, following R. A. Pratt's article on the subject,[30] has been that Chaucer probably used a text of a type that did not have Boccaccio's approval and lacked the *chiose*. More recently this view has been strongly contested by P. Boitani, who disputes some of Pratt's negative evidence and notes correspondences between the *Knight's Tale* and Boccaccio's glosses.[31] [See, however, W. E. Coleman's article in *Medium Aevum* LI (1982).]

There has also been some disagreement concerning the nature and extent of Chaucer's knowledge of the *Filocolo*. K. Young suggested that *Troilus* is influenced by it in a number of cases, including the consummation scene in Book III and the homage to the poet's predecessors at the end of Book V.[32] Such influence was subsequently discounted by H. M. Cummings,[33] but Young's arguments have more recently been supported, at least in the two instances mentioned, by S. B. Meech.[34] Moreover Menedon's story in Book IV of the *Filocolo* is authoritatively regarded as the probable main source of the *Franklin's Tale*.[35] On the whole, it seems very likely that Chaucer had at least a cursory acquaintance with this encyclopaedic romance, and that his interest may have been attracted by the writer's final tribute to his predecessors (*Filoc.* V, 97), as well as the lovers' encounter (IV, 109–25) and the device of presenting stories as a collection presided over and commented upon by a figure of authority.[36]

11

Rather more uncertain is the question of whether Chaucer knew or even knew of the *Decameron*. The attractions of assuming that he did are beguiling enough, and they have been steadfastly resisted by such scholars as Cummings, Farnham, Wright and, more recently, Reiss.[37] The arguments about the lack of both external and decisive internal evidence of influence, and about the pre-eminent reputation at this time of Boccaccio's Latin works and early romances – cannot lightly be set aside. Yet at least four of the *Canterbury Tales* have plots analogous to those of Boccaccio's collection,[38] and some recent criticism, especially of the *Shipman's Tale*,[39] has credited Chaucer with some degree of knowledge of the *Decameron*.

And a further mystery is the absence in Chaucer's work of any reference to the writer whose work influenced him more obviously than that of any other 'grete poete of Ytaille'. Both Dante and Petrarch are mentioned respectfully by him more than once,[40] and the latter indeed is credited on several occasions with work that in fact belongs immediately or ultimately to Boccaccio.[41] It may be that Chaucer is following a fairly common medieval practice in this respect; Boccaccio himself, for example, makes no mention of Statius either in the text or the glosses of the *Teseida*, although the *Thebaid* is an ascertainable source for some of his plot. Chaucer may perhaps have been genuinely unaware of, or confused about, the authorship of some of Boccaccio's works.[42] This seems possible with regard to the *De Casibus* but is rather difficult to credit in all cases. For someone who had visited Italy at least twice and spent some time in Florence, to misattribute one or two of the works may be considered ignorance; but to disregard the authorship of the whole corpus begins to look like design.

It may be, therefore, that while Chaucer regarded Petrarch and especially Dante reverentially as *auctours*, he saw his relationship to Boccaccio more as a working partnership between equals.[43] For both poets by virtue of their origins, career and education had access to mercantile, aristocratic and academic circles. And whether or not Chaucer knew the *Decameron*, one of the attractions of Boccaccio's work for him would very possibly have been its concern to make sense of the relationships between the worlds of the merchant, the courtier and the clerk.

Chaucer and Boccaccio:
Further Reading

The preceding Introduction has attempted to characterize the context of Boccaccio's early work and to indicate some of the ways by which it might have come to influence Chaucer. The following list is intended to provide a selection of further reading about the relationship between the two writers. It has been revised to take account of the considerable amount of work in the area that has been published since this book first appeared (1980).

All the works referred to are (unless otherwise indicated) in English and are listed in chronological order under each heading.

(I) CRITICAL STUDIES:
General surveys:

H. M. Cummings, *The Indebtedness of Chaucer's Works to the Italian Works of Boccaccio* (Cincinnati, 1916, repr. New York, 1965).

R. A. Pratt, "Chaucer's Use of the *Teseida*", *PMLA* LXII (1947), 598–621.

G. B. Parks, *The English Traveller to Italy (I): The Middle Ages* (Rome, 1954).

H. G. Wright, *Boccaccio in England, from Chaucer to Tennyson* (London, 1957).

H. Schless, "Transformations: Chaucer's Use of Italian", in *Geoffrey Chaucer (Writers and their Background)*, ed. D. S. Brewer (London, 1974), pp. 184–223.

E. Reiss, "Boccaccio in English Culture of the Fourteenth and Fifteenth Centuries", in *Il Boccaccio nella cultura inglese e anglo-americana*, ed. G. Galigani (Florence, 1974), pp. 15–26.

J. A. W. Bennett, "Chaucer, Dante and Boccaccio", in *Chaucer and the Italian Trecento*, ed. P. Boitani (Cambridge, 1983), pp. 89–113.

D. Wallace, *Chaucer and the Early Writings of Boccaccio* (Cambridge, 1985).

"Filostrato" and "Troilus & Criseyde":

K. Young, *The Origin and Development of the Story of Troilus and Criseyde* (London, 1908).

C. S. Lewis, "What Chaucer really did to *Il Filostrato*", *Essays & Studies* XVII (1932), 56–75.

T. A. Kirby, *Chaucer's "Troilus": A Study in Courtly Love* (Louisiana, 1940).

D. Everett, *Essays in Middle English Literature* (Oxford, 1955), pp. 115–38.

S. B. Meech, *Design in Chaucer's "Troilus"* (Syracuse, N.Y., 1959).

P. M. Kean, "Chaucer's dealings with a stanza of *Il Filostrato*", *MAe* XXXIII (1964), 36–46.

P. Dronke, "The Conclusion of *Troilus & Criseyde*", *MAe* XXXIII (1964), 47–52.

I. C. Walker, "Chaucer and *Il Filostrato*", *ESt* XLIX (1968), 318–26.

J. I. Wimsatt, "Medieval and Modern in Chaucer's *Troilus and Criseyde*", *PMLA* XCII (1977), 203–16.

G. Morgan, "The Ending of *Troilus*", *Modern Language Review* LXXVII (1982), 257–71.

B. Windeatt, "Chaucer and the *Filostrato*", in Boitani (1983), pp. 163–83.

N. R. Havely, "Tearing or Breathing? Dante's Influence on *Filostrato* and *Troilus*", *Studies in the Age of Chaucer, Proceedings* I (1984), 51–9.

J. Dean, "Chaucer's *Troilus*, Boccaccio's *Filostrato* and the Poetics of Closure" *PQ* LXIV (1985), 175–84.

P. Boitani (ed.), *The European Tragedy of Troilus* (Oxford, 1989), [essays by
Natali and Windeatt].
N. S. Thompson, "Translation and Response: *Troilus* and the *Filostrato*", in
The Medieval Translator II, ed. R. Ellis (London, 1991), pp. 123–50.

"Teseida" and Chaucer's Early Poems:
J. A. W. Bennett, *The Parlement of Foules* (Oxford, 1957).
D. S. Brewer (ed.), *The Parlement of Foulys* (London, 1960), pp. 43–5.
J. A. W. Bennett, *Chaucer's Book of Fame* (Oxford, 1968).

"Teseida" and "The Knight's Tale":
W. P. Ker, "Chaucer and the Renaissance" (Clark Lecture, 1912), repr. in
Geoffrey Chaucer, ed. J. A. Burrow (Harmondsworth, 1969), pp. 104–11.
R. A. Pratt, "The Knight's Tale", in *SA*, 82–105.
W. H. French, "The Lovers in *The Knight's Tale*", *JEGP* XLVIII (1949),
320–8.
H. S. Wilson, "The Knight's Tale and the *Teseida* again", *UTQ* XVIII (1949),
131–46.
J. A. W. Bennett, *The Knight's Tale* (2nd edn., London, 1958), pp. 16–32.
P. Boitani, *Chaucer and Boccaccio* (Oxford, 1977).
W. E. Coleman, "Chaucer, the *Teseida* and the Visconti Library at Pavia: a
hypothesis", *MAe* LI (1982), 91–101 [argues strongly that Chaucer's MS
of *Teseida* did *not* contain Boccaccio's commentary].
P. Boitani, "Style, Iconography and Narrative: the Lesson of the *Teseida*", in
Boitani (1983), pp. 185–99.
D. Anderson, "Theban Genealogy in *The Knight's Tale*", *ChauR* XXI (1987),
311–20.
D. Anderson, *Before "The Knight's Tale": Imitation of Classical Epic in
Boccaccio's "Teseida"* (Philadelphia, 1988).

"Filocolo" (IV, 31–4) and "The Franklin's Tale":
G. Dempster & J. S. P. Tatlock, "*The Franklin's Tale*", in *SA*, 377–97 (esp.
the references on p. 377).
G. Morgan, "Boccaccio's *Filocolo* and the moral argument of *The Franklin's
Tale*", *ChauR* XX (1986), 285–306.

"The Decameron" and "the Canterbury Tales":
R. K. Root, "Chaucer and the *Decameron*", *Englische Studien* XLIV (1912),
1–7.
W. Farnham, "England's Discovery of the *Decameron*", *PMLA* XXXIX
(1924), 123–39.
R. A. Pratt & K. Young, *SA*, 13–20.
M. Copland, "*The Shipman's Tale*: Chaucer and Boccaccio", *MAe* XXXV
(1966), 11–28.
R. Guerin, "The *Shipman's Tale*: the Italian Analogues", *ESt* LII (1971),
412–19.
D. McGrady, "Chaucer and the *Decameron* reconsidered", *ChauR* XII (1977),
1–26.
R. Kirkpatrick, "The Wake of the *Commedia*: Chaucer's *Canterbury Tales* and
Boccaccio's *Decameron*, in Boitani (1983), pp. 201–30.
R. Kirkpatrick, "The Griselda Story in Boccaccio, Petrarch and Chaucer, in
Boitani (1983), pp. 231–48.
C. Morse, "The Exemplary Griselda", *Studies in the Age of Chaucer*, VII (1985),
51–86.

(II) TRANSLATIONS AND PARALLEL TEXT EDITIONS:
(a) *Filostrato:*
W. M. Rossetti (Chaucer Soc., 1873–83) [*Troilus* with corresponding passages
   from *Filostrato* in prose tr.].
H. M. Cummings (1924) [verse translation].
N. E. Griffin & A. B. Myrick (1929) [*Filostrato*, with prose translation].
R. K. Gordon, *The Story of Troilus* (1934) [prose tr.].
B. A. Windeatt (ed.) *Troilus & Criseyde* (1984) [with *Filostrato* in the original].
R. P. apRoberts & A. B. Seldis (1986) [*Filostrato*, with prose translation].

(b) *Teseida:*
B. M. McCoy, *The Book of Theseus* (1974) [for some corrections of this
   translation, see the review by A. K. Cassell in *Modern Language Notes* XCI
   (1976), 164–7].
A text and translation of *Teseida* (by W. E. & E. A. Coleman, for *The Chaucer
   Library*) is in preparation; see *Spec* LIII (1978), 209, and *ChauR* XXIV
   (1989–90), 79.

(c) *Filocolo:*
G. Dempster & J. S. P. Tatlock, *SA* 377–83 [glossed text of Menedon's
   question in IV, 31–41].
H. Carter, *Boccaccio's Thirteen Questions of Love* (1974) [revised version of
   "H.G."'s 16th-century translation of the questions in IV].
R. P. Miller, *Chaucer: Sources & Backgrounds* (1977), pp. 121–35 [translation of
   Menedon's question].
D. Cheney & T. G. Bergin, *Il Filocolo* (1985) [complete translation].

(d) *Decameron:*
J. M. Rigg (Everyman's Library, 1930).
G. H. McWilliam (Penguin Classics, 1972).
[The relative merits of these two versions are assessed by A. L. Lepschy in
   Studi sul Boccaccio VIII (1974), 329–35.]

(e) *Genealogia:*
C. G. Osgood, *Boccaccio on Poetry* (1930) [translation of the Preface and Books
   XIV–XV].

(f) *Other works by Boccaccio:*
Ninfale fiesolano, tr. D. J. Donno (1960); tr. J. Tusiani (1971).
Corbaccio, tr. A. K. Cassell (1975).
Amorosa Visione, tr. R. Hollander, T. Hampton & M. Frankel (1986) [parallel
   text].
Diana's Hunt: Caccia di Diana, tr. A. K. Cassell & V. Kirkham (1991) [parallel
   text].

(III) BIBLIOGRAPHIES:
A. L. Lepschy, "Boccaccio Studies in English, 1945–69", *Studi sul Boccaccio*
   VI (1971), esp. 224–5.
P. G. Ruggiers, "The Italian Influence on Chaucer", in *Companion to Chaucer
   Studies*, ed. B. Rowland (rev. edn., 1979), pp. 160–4.
L. K. Morris, *Chaucer Source and Analogue Criticism: A Cross-referenced Guide*
   (N.Y. & London, 1985), esp. under "Boccaccio" (pp. 220–5).
L. Y. Baird-Lange & H. Schnuttgen, *A Bibliography of Chaucer, 1974–1985*
   (Hamden, Conn. & Cambridge, 1988), esp. pp. 66–73.
J. P. Consoli, *Giovanni Boccaccio: an Annotated Bibliography* (Garland Medieval
   Bibliographies, N.Y., 1992).

This translation: explanations and acknowledgments

The following texts are a selection. They do not include works by Boccaccio that Chaucer might perhaps have known – such as the *Decameron* and the *De Casibus*. And in an anthology of this scale it is not possible even to do justice to both of the works whose influence upon Chaucer is beyond doubt; hence, although a complete version of *Filostrato* is provided, the much lengthier *Teseida* is presented in the form of excerpts.

Yet selection implies interpretation, and some explanation of the procedure is perhaps called for. The complete version of the *Filostrato* and the Appendices represent an attempt to trace some of the main features in the medieval portrayal of Troilus before Chaucer, although they by no means account for all the sources and influences bearing upon *Troilus and Criseyde* itself, as readers of Ovid, Statius, Boethius, the *Romance of the Rose* and Dante (for example) will readily recognize.

The choice of passages from the *Teseida* (amounting to about a quarter of the poem) has been governed by several considerations. It is hoped that the excerpts will give some indication of Boccaccio's avowed ambitions and purposes, as conveyed by his *chiose* and the explicit declarations of intent within the poem. But I have assumed that readers of the *Knight's Tale* would in the first place be more interested in the romance of the marriage of Emilia than in its epic context, and hence the major omissions are of the feats of Theseus in Books I and II, the catalogue of combatants in Book VI, and the details of the battle in Book VIII. On the other hand, I have attempted to provide a fair sampling not only of those episodes and descriptions that appear to have had particular influence upon Chaucer, but also of those that may help to illustrate the two poets' divergences of interest and emphasis – particularly regarding the presentation of courtly idealism, ceremony and ritual, the portrayal of the pagan gods, and the characterization of the four main human figures.

The selection of excerpts from *Filocolo* IV, 31–4 likewise aims, on a smaller scale, to illustrate both the interest in romance idealism and magic that Menedon's question shares with the *Franklin's Tale*, and the ways in which Boccaccio differs from Chaucer in his exposition of the ethical issues in such a story. For these reasons, and because of the more self-contained character of its narrative, Menedon's question has been chosen in preference to other passages from *Filocolo* that may well have influenced Chaucer (for example, the lovers' reunion in Book IV and the tribute to poetic predecessors at the end of Book V). *Decameron* stories that could be compared with the *Franklin's Tale* and other Canterbury tales have been excluded, although the possibility that Chaucer knew them has not – and those interested in pursuing such comparisons will find reliable translations (those of Rigg and McWilliam) readily available.

Amongst existing translations of the texts in this volume the most useful to me has been the parallel-text edition of *Filostrato* by N. E. Griffin and A. B. Myrick. Much important work on establishing the text of *Filostrato* (notably by Pernicone and Branca) has been done since their version appeared, and Griffin and Myrick's prose reflects an earlier generation's taste for archaic diction and syntax. Nonetheless, I have often found it helpful to consider their treatment of cruces in the poem, and the major divergences between our renderings are recorded in the Notes. I have referred at times to R. P. Miller's version of *Filocolo* IV, 31–4 (in *Chaucer: Sources and Backgrounds*) and to R. K. Gordon's selections from Benoit's *Roman* (in *The Story of Troilus*); and I have compared my excerpts from the *Teseida* with the complete translation by B. M. McCoy, but did not think it worthwhile in this case to record my numerous disagreements.

The aims of my own translation have been to assist those attempting to follow the original texts, whilst providing readable versions for those approaching the works for the first time. I have therefore tried to avoid over-simplifying Boccaccio's syntax, and some of the notes on usage will be of interest only to those seeking to ascertain the range of possible meanings in the Italian. On the other hand, it has sometimes been necessary, in the interests of clarity, to divide sentences and repeat proper names where Boccaccio does not do so. My practice with regard to proper names in *Filostrato* and *Teseida* has been to preserve the Italian forms for the central romance 'triangles' of characters (Troiolo, Criseida and Pandaro; Palemone, Arcita and Emilia), but to use the Greek or Latin equivalents (where ascertainable) for the remainder.

The Notes chiefly concern problems of interpretation and give some further indication of the historical and literary context of the works translated. Detailed correspondences with Chaucer's poems have not been noted, since such references would unduly expand the volume of annotation, impose perhaps too much of a pattern of interpretation upon the material, and in any case reduplicate much of the information that is already summarized in, for example, the tables in Robinson's edition (pp. 670 and 813) and Bryan and Dempster's *Sources and Analogues* (pp. 91–2).

In conclusion I must acknowledge a considerable debt to those whose work on these texts has made my own task much easier. The translations of *Filostrato*, *Teseida* and *Filocolo* are mainly based on the texts in the Classici Mondadori series (*Tutte le Opere*, gen. ed. V. Branca), although other editions (by Pernicone, Battaglia, Roncaglia and Ricci) have also been consulted, and emendations proposed by M. Marti (*Opere minori in volgare*, in the Classici Rizzoli series) have sometimes been adopted. The commentaries of Branca, Limentani and Quaglio are particularly informative about the literary context of Boccaccio's work, whilst Marti offers much valuable linguistic guidance in the form of lexical notes and glosses. For the other texts, I have been greatly assisted by the meticulous glossary in L. Constans's *SATF* edition of Benoit's *Roman,* and by the apparatus in N. E. Griffin's text of Guido's *Historia.*

This anthology has also required and received generous aid from a number of friends and colleagues. Professor Elizabeth Salter helped to launch the project, and gave encouragement and advice that proved crucial during its early stages. Expert pilotage past certain rocks and shoals was provided by Prof. Giuseppe Mazzotta of Cornell (for the *Filocolo* excerpts), Dr D. J. B. Robey of Wolfson College, Oxford (for *Filostrato* and *Teseida*), and Dr Stephen Minta of York (for Benoit's *Roman*). Dr Alan Charity and Dr Barbara Reynolds read parts of the *Filostrato* and *Teseida* translations, and their comments and suggestions have had far-reaching effects upon the work as a whole. And on mythographical matters the Notes have benefited greatly from the genial erudition of Meg Twycross. Any errors that remain will of course be at points where I had not thought to seek guidance, and for these I must claim sole responsibility.

The labour of preparing the book for publication has been greatly eased by the efficient typing of Mrs J. Nixey, Mrs P. Wallace and Miss J. Waters; and my only complaint about their work is that its speed deprived me of excuses for delay.

And such delay would have been infinitely prolonged without the presence of Cicely Palser Havely, who has throughout shown the right degrees of patience and impatience with the enterprise, read through the whole translation, shed much light upon its obscurities of thought and expression, and steered the work towards a conclusion. To her the book is dedicated.

> 'E quelle grazie con effetto pieno,
> che render dee il grato pellegrino,
> a chi guidati n'ha, qui rendereno.'

N. R. Havely

Department of English & Related Literature
University of York

IL FILOSTRATO

'*Filostrato* is the title of this book, and that is because it suits the subject-matter supremely well. "Filostrato" in effect means "the man overcome and struck down by love" – as one can see Troiolo was, for he was overcome by love, in loving Criseida so ardently, and continuing to do so until his dying day.'

Prologue

Filostrato sends greetings to his Filomena, whose charms surpass those of other women.

On many occasions now, most noble lady, it has happened that I, who almost from my boyhood until now have been one of the servants of love, have found myself at his court amongst the noble men and lovely ladies who were spending their time there in much the same way as I was; and I have then heard the following question[1] being asked and considered: 'A young man ardently loves a lady of whom Fortune allows him nothing more than being able to see her sometimes, or talk about her sometimes to someone else, or to think about her pleasantly by himself. Which of these three things, then, offers him the greatest pleasure?' Not one of these three choices ever failed to be keenly and shrewdly defended by many speakers – some favouring one of them and some the other. And, since this question seemed to bear closely upon my more ardent than fortunate passions, I recall that being swayed by a false opinion I frequently took part in the argument, asserting and maintaining that the pleasure of being able to think about the loved person at times was far greater than what either of the other two choices could offer. Among the other arguments I put forward was the claim that it was no small part of the lover's delight to make his beloved in his imagination accord with his desires and render her kind and responsive to them, even if such delight lasted only as long as the thought – and that could certainly not be achieved through seeing or talking.

How far such a crass judgment, foolish reckoning and hollow argument were from the truth! Bitter experience, alas, makes that plain to me now. Dearest hope of my troubled mind and sole comfort of my wounded heart, I shall not shrink from showing you how that truth which I in my childish perversity had defied broke in upon my clouded understanding. And to whom but you could I tell this, in the hope of obtaining some alleviation of the penance imposed upon me either by Love or Fortune for the false opinion I had held?

Hence, most beautiful lady, I affirm that, after you had left the pleasant city of Naples for Sannio[2] at the loveliest season of the year and removed yourself from my eyes which are more enamoured of your angelic face than of anything else – then the truth that I should have recognized, but failed to when you were present, soon came home to me far more forcibly when, on the other hand, I was bereft of your presence. And this has caused my spirits such overwhelming grief that I can very clearly understand how great was the pleasure I derived from your graceful and lovely appearance, even though I little realized it then. But in order that this truth may emerge more clearly, let me not shrink from describing, as evidence of my great error, what happened to me after your departure; and I do not wish to leave that out, even though it is portrayed in more detail elsewhere.

In the hope that God may soon, through the sight of your lovely face, restore my eyes to the bliss they have forfeited – I therefore declare[3] that when I knew you had left this place and gone where no honourable pretext could bring me to see you, these eyes through which love brought that most gentle light from yours into my spirit have, many times more than my words could render credible, bathed my face and drenched my woeful breast with a quantity of most bitter tears. And my eyes would not only have aroused wonder because of the amount of moisture rising to them, but would also have inspired pity both in you, whom I believe to be as gentle as you are noble, and even in someone who was my steely-hearted foe. And this does not happen simply at moments when I remember the loss of your charming presence and the grievous consequences of that – but whatever comes before their gaze becomes a reason for their sorrow to increase. Alas, how often, to ease their pain, have they instinctively turned away from gazing at the temples, the arcades, the squares and the other places where they were eagerly and longingly seeking, and sometimes joyfully found, your likeness – and have in their grief made my heart repeat to itself that sad verse from Jeremiah: 'How desolate remains the city that till now was full of people and mistress of the nations!'[4] I shall not of course claim that everything grieves them as deeply as this, but I declare that there is one thing alone which eases their sorrow to some extent as they look around, and that is to gaze towards the countryside, mountains and quarter of the sky amidst and beneath which I indeed believe you to be. My face welcomes every breeze or gentle wind that comes from that direction, just as if it had undoubtedly touched yours. But this relief consequently does not last very long, for just as flames will sometimes be found to flickering over the surfaces of oily things, so such soothing effects are only fleetingly felt within my troubled heart and are soon banished and supplanted by the knowledge that I am unable to see you, although my desire to do so has already been immensely inflamed.

What am I to say about those ardent sighs that the pleasure of love and the sweetness of hope once used to draw from the depths of my heart? I can indeed say no more than this: that, multiplied many times by my deep anguish, they rise from there and are forced violently through my lips a thousand times each hour. And my words also, which were once heard[5] in love-songs and passionate protestations prompted by some secret delight that sprang from your radiant looks, can ever onwards[6] be heard by all at hand, calling upon your most gracious name[7] and upon love to reward my sufferings or death to end them – or transforming – themselves into the most bitter complaints.

This therefore is how I live whilst separated from you, and it does not help me to know how great was the previously almost unrecognized happiness, pleasure and delight that your eyes brought me. Indeed, weeping and sighing have still left me plenty of time to speak of your worth and also to think of your loveliness, your fine manners, your noble dignity and your supremely delightful looks which are always in front of my mind's eyes. And I do not therefore in any way claim that my spirit derives no joy from such speeches or thoughts – but such joy is mingled with a most ardent desire which so inflames all my other desires with the hope of seeing you that I can hardly keep them from overcoming all due propriety and considerations of prudence and bringing me to where you now are. But since I am so determined to set your honour above my well-being, I restrain them, and because I know the way by which I might come to see you again is denied for the reason I have given, I can do nothing but resume my interrupted laments. Alas, what stern schooling and correction of my faults have I always received from Fortune, spiteful and grudging as she is towards my pleasures! Now in my misery I realize, now I feel, now I perceive most clearly how much more happiness, how much more pleasure, how much more sweetness dwelt in the true light of your eyes when mine beheld them than there was in my false and deluded thoughts.

In this way, therefore, glorious light of my spirit, has Fortune, by withholding your loveliness from me, dispersed the mists of error that previously beset me. But indeed such harsh measures were not needed to dispel my ignorance; a gentler chastisement would have set me back upon the right path. So this is how things stand now: my strength, however much I may resent it, cannot resist that of Fortune. And whichever way matters may turn, I have, through your absence alone, been reduced to the state that I have so far described for you – and in the course of this most grievous affliction I have come to acknowledge the truth of what I once doubted and denied.

But now we must come to the purpose for which I have continued writing up to this point – and I declare that, finding myself on your departure plunged into such great and bitter misfortune, I meant at first to keep my misery completely hidden within my sorrowful heart, so that it should not, by being displayed, eventually breed much more. And since I held to this resolve firmly, the moment came when it brought me very close to a miserable end – which indeed, if it had come then, would have been wholeheartedly welcome. But at that point, because of some secret hope of being able, whenever it might be, to see you again and restore my eyes to their former bliss – there arose in me not only a fear of death, but also the desire to live longer, however wretched my existence might be whilst unable to see you. And then I clearly understood that if I simply followed the promptings of the grief that swelled unseen within my breast – then, when it rose up with such immense force (as it so often did), it would inevitably so overcome my already much weakened powers that death would ensue without fail, and I should then as a result not see you. So, beginning to think more positively, I changed my mind and considered how through some dignified form of complaint I might provide the means for my grief-laden breast to be relieved of such sorrow, so that I might live and see you again and remain alive longer for your sake. And this idea had no sooner entered my mind than I at once recognized a way of putting it into effect – and in this revelation, which may have been inspired by some unseen deity, I saw a sure sign of future recovery. And the way to do this was by contriving, through some person prey to passion as I was and am, to tell of my sufferings in verse. I therefore began to study the ancient legends[8] with close attention, to see which one I could convincingly use as a disguise for my secret and passionate suffering. And I could think of no-one more suitable for the purpose than the valiant young Troiolo son of Priam, the most illustrious king of Troy. For if the ancient sources can be credited his life was very like what mine has been in your absence, in being rendered sorrowful by love and the loss of his lady, once Criseida whom he loved above all else had been sent back to her father Calchas. Hence, finding this man's character and fortunes very well suited to my purpose I then in simple verse, in my Florentine tongue and in a very melancholy style, treated[9] both his sorrows and mine in the same terms. And having recited them on one occasion or another I found them to be very helpful, as I had intended in the first place.

It is true that before his most bitter misfortunes a part of the work deals in a similar style with the happiness he experienced – but I did not include this in order to give the impression that I myself can boast of gaining similar happiness, for Fortune has never granted such a favour to me, nor, even should I strive to hope for it, can I ever imagine it would be achieved. The reason for my describing it, however, is that if we witness someone's happiness we shall understand much better the extent and nature of his ensuing sorrow. Yet such happiness nonetheless reflects my experience, inasmuch as I derived no less pleasure from your eyes than Troiolo had from the fruits of love that Fortune yielded him in Criseida.

Hence, noble lady, I put together verses of this sort in the form of a little book, to be for those who will read it in times to come a perpetual testimony to your nobility (which in the guise of another character[10] adorns them throughout), and to my misery. And having put them together I thought it would not be right that the first hands they came into should be those of any other person but you, who have been the only true begetter of them. This, therefore, may be an insignificant gift to send to such a lady as yourself, but nonetheless, since my affection in sending them[11] is very great and full of true devotion, I yet dare to do so – trusting that they will be accepted by you not by virtue of my merits but because of your kindness and courtesy. And if you should come to read them, then wherever you find Troiolo lamenting and grieving over the departure of Criseida, you may clearly recognize my own words, tears, sighs and torments – and wherever you find beauty, good manners and any other praise-worthy feminine features described in Criseida, you may take such things to refer to you. As for the great amount of other material – this, as I have already said, neither relates to me nor is set down on my behalf, but is there because the story of this noble and passionate young man requires it to be. And if you are as perceptive as I believe you to be, you will be able to gather from these verses the extent and nature of my desires, what their goal is, what they seek above all else, and whether they deserve any favour. I do not yet know whether they will succeed in influencing your chaste thoughts if you read them with any degree of sympathy, but I pray Love that he may give them power to do so. And if this happens, I beg you as humbly as I can to hasten your return, so that my life, which hope is barely managing to sustain upon the slenderest of threads, may, when I see you, joyfully recover its former confidence. And if it cannot happen as soon as I should like, then through some sigh or prayer of pity, at least make Love grant some relief to my sufferings – and you will thus ease my confused existence. My long discourse of its own accord seeks to reach an end, and so, as I allow it to, I pray to him who has put my life and death in your hands to kindle in your heart that desire which alone can lead to my recovery.

Part I

(*Here begins the first part of the book called* Filostrato, *which tells what Troiolo endured for the sake of love. Here it is shown how Troiolo fell in love with Criseida, and what passionate sighs and tears there were for her before he disclosed his love to anyone. And first comes the author's invocation.*)

(1) Some writers piously follow the custom of invoking the favour of Jupiter at the opening of their works, whilst others call upon the power of Apollo. I used to pray to the Muses of Parnassus when I needed to, but Love of late has made me change my old-established ways, as the result, my lady, of being in love with you.

You, lady, are the bright and lovely light by which my life is guided through this dark world; you are the pole star that I follow in order to reach port;[1] you are my sheet-anchor and my sole joy and comfort. You yourself are my Jupiter, Apollo and Muse, as I have proved and know.

Because your departure has been sadder and crueller to me than death, I wish to tell how sorrowful Troiolo's life was after the lovely Criseida had departed from Troy, and how she had earlier shown him favour; and I must therefore seek your favour if I wish to be able to complete my undertaking.

Therefore, sweet lady, to whom I have been and ever shall be true and obedient – lovely light of those fair eyes in which Love has set all my delight – sole hope of him who loves you more than himself, and with complete devotion – guide my hand and direct my thoughts in the work that I am about to write.

(5) Your image is so firmly imprinted upon my sorrowful heart that you have more power over it than I. Make my mournful voice speak from there

in such a way as to reveal my own suffering by means of another's – and make it so persuasive as to move with pity all those who listen to it. Let the honour be yours and the labour mine, if what I say should earn any praise.

And I beg those of you who are lovers to attend to what my woeful verses will relate; and if you come to feel any spirit of compassion stirring within your hearts, I beseech you to pray for me to Love who afflicts me as he did Troiolo whilst I remain bereft of the sweetest joy that anyone ever cherished.

(How Calchas fled from Troy, and the occasion and the reasons for it.)

The Greek kings strong in battle had surrounded Troy, and each of them was doing as much as he could to prove how bold, warlike, brave and well-endowed he was, whilst day by day they drew their forces more tightly around the city – united in the common purpose of avenging the outrage and the rape committed by Paris upon Queen Helen.

Then Calchas, whose profound knowledge had already privileged him to hear all great Apollo's secrets, sought to know the truth about the future and whether the Trojans' long endurance or the Greeks' great daring would triumph; and he found out for certain that after a long struggle the Trojans would be slaughtered and their city destroyed.[2]

Thereupon this wise and provident man decided to leave secretly, and having chosen the time and place for flight he made his way to the Greek camp; and from there he found many of them coming to meet and welcome him with expressions of joy, since they expected to obtain the best of advice from him about all unforeseen events and dangers.

(How Criseida went before Hector to exonerate herself from her father Calchas's crime.)

(10) The outcry was great when it became generally known throughout the city that Calchas had fled. This was variously spoken of but condemned on all sides, and he was thought to have done wrong and committed an act of vile treachery. Indeed many people were almost inclined to go and set fire to his house.

Calchas had left a widowed[3] daughter of his in the midst of such dangers, without giving her any warning about them. She was so angelically beautiful to behold that she did not seem to be a mortal being, and her name was, I believe, Criseida. She was as prudent, honourable, wise and well-mannered as any woman born in Troy ever was.

When she heard the fierce outcry that her father's flight had caused she was terrified of the great risks that such disturbances posed, and throwing herself on her knees at Hector's feet in a sorrowful and tearful manner, she pleaded for herself, arousing pity both by her words and her appearance. She condemned what her father had done, and concluded her speech with an appeal to his clemency.

Hector was naturally compassionate, and so when he heard the laments of this woman who was more beautiful than any other creature, he spoke kindly to her and reassured her somewhat by saying: 'Let your father go, and let misfortune follow him since he has wronged us so. But you may remain in Troy, safe, happy and untroubled for as long as you wish.

You may always be sure of receiving from each and every one of us such respect and service as you would look for if Calchas were here; so let the gods render him his due reward.' She offered him many thanks for this and would have continued doing so, but since he would not permit it, she arose, returned to her house and remained there in peace and quiet.

(15) There she dwelt while she remained in Troy, with such a household as her rank obliged her to maintain – and her noble bearing and conduct were to be marvelled at. She had no need to concern herself about sons or daughters, since she was one of those who had never been able to have any; and she was loved and respected by all who knew her.

(During the offering of sacrifices to Pallas in the temple Troiolo mocks those who are in love, and at that moment he himself falls in love.)

The affairs of the Trojans and Greeks went very much according to the way of war; sometimes the Trojans sallied forth boldly against the Greeks – and many times the Greeks, if the account is not mistaken, boldly advanced as far as the ramparts, plundering all around and burning down castles and towns.

And although the Trojans were hemmed in by their Greek foes, this did not mean that their sacrifices to the gods were neglected, for they continued to be observed in each case according to the usual practice of the time. But they worshipped Pallas in every way more reverently and solemnly than any other, and had more regard for her than the rest.

Hence at the approach of that pleasant season which clothes the meadows again with new grass and flowers, and when every animal rejoices and displays its desires in various ways – the Trojan elders arranged for the ill-fated Palladium[4] to be paid its customary honours; and this festival was one that ladies and knights also gladly attended.

Amongst them was Criseida, the daughter of Calchas, dressed in dark clothing – and as the rose surpasses the violet in beauty, so much more beautiful was she than other women. And she on her own lent more radiance to the great festival than did any other lady, as she stood very close to the doorway with a dignified, cheerful and modest bearing.

(20) Troiolo, as is the way with young men, was walking about in the great temple, glancing here and there, and strolling with his friends from one place to another. He would start to praise this woman and that, and then find fault with each of them, as do those who favour no one woman more than another – continuing to rejoice in his freedom.

Indeed if, whilst walking about in this way he saw anyone fix his gaze on a lady and sigh to himself, he would point him out with amusement to his companions, saying: 'That poor soul has renounced with the freedom that so encumbered him, and delivered it into the hands of that lady. You can see just how vain his hopes are.

'What is the point of devoting any kind of love to a woman? For as a leaf flutters in the wind, so in one day their affections change more than a thousand times, and they do not care what pain any lover may feel on their account, nor do any of them know what they want. Happy is he who is not beguiled by their charms and is able to avoid them!

'Through my own great stupidity I have already found out what this accursed passion is like, and I should certainly be lying if I said that Love had not been gracious to me and given me joy and pleasure. But the happiness, all in all, amounted to little or nothing beside the torments and miserable sighs of yearning.

'Now I am free of that and at peace, thanks to him who took greater care of me than I did of myself – I mean Jupiter, the true God and source of all aid. And although I enjoy looking around I still take care to avoid backsliding, and find it pleasant to laugh at those besotted people whom I know not whether to call lovers or scatterbrains.'

(25) How blind men's understanding is, and how often do events turn out quite opposite to our intentions! Troiolo is going about now finding fault with other people and their love-longings, without a thought of what the heavens may be hastening to involve him in; for before he left the temple Love pierced him more deeply than any of the others.

Whilst Troiolo, then, was going about in this way, mocking one man or another and frequently turning his gaze upon this woman or that, it so happened that his wandering glance pierced through the throng and fixed upon the place where the lovely Criseida, in dark clothing beneath a white veil,[5] was standing among the other ladies at that solemn ceremony.

She was tall and her limbs were perfectly proportioned to her height; her face was resplendent with heavenly beauty, and in her looks she displayed a noble dignity. With one arm she had drawn her mantle away from her face, thus making more room for herself and keeping the crowd at some distance.

This action appealed to Troiolo, and so did the way she had wrapped herself up again disdainfully, as if to say: 'They shall not stand here'. And he began to give more attention to her looks, which he thought worth far more praise than any of the others; and he took the greatest pleasure in gazing past the rest to look at her bright eyes and angelic face.

And he who shortly before had been so wisely censuring others did not perceive that Love lurked with his arrows within the beams of those lovely eyes – nor did he remember the insults he had earlier directed at the servants of that god; and he did not notice the arrow that flew towards his heart until the very moment it struck him.

(30) Since this lady in the black cloak pleased Troiolo above all others he gazed from a distance at his heart's desire without saying what object there attracted him so; and without disclosing anything to anyone he went on gazing for as long as the ceremonies in honour of Pallas continued. Then with his companions he left the temple.

But he did not leave it as freely and cheerfully as he had entered, but he left it pensively and more deeply in love than he had believed possible; yet he kept his desire well hidden, both because of what he had said shortly before and for fear that his insulting speeches might be thrown back at him by anyone who chanced to notice the intensity of passion that had overcome him.

(*Troiolo, finding himself attracted to Criseida and dwelling upon her in his thoughts makes up his mind to pursue this new desire, and gives thanks for having fallen in love.*)

After Criseida had left that noble temple Troiolo returned to the palace with his companions and spent a long while there making merry with them. In order more closely to conceal the wounds of his passion he thoroughly mocked those who were in love; and then, claiming that other matters demanded his attention, he told each of them to go where he wished.

And when they all had gone he went off to his chamber along, sat down sighing at the foot of his bed, and began to recall to himself the pleasure he had taken in Criseida's looks and most beautiful features that morning – dwelling upon each of them approvingly in turn.[6]

He much admired her behaviour and the way she had stood there, and from her manner and bearing her considered her to be most noble of heart. He thought himself most fortunate to be in love with such a lady – and even more so if through persevering he could come to be loved by her as much or nearly as much as he loved her – or if at least she did not spurn his devotion.

(35) He imagined that neither trouble nor suffering for such a lady's sake could be wasted, and that if anyone ever found out about his desire they ought thoroughly to approve of it. And the young man thus blithely concluded that his passion would be less likely to be censured if it came to light – though he little realized what woes were in store for him.

Being thus inclined to pursue this desire, he thought of how he might set about it discreetly, resolving from the start that, unless he had to, he would not reveal to any friend or servant the passion that his ardent spirits had already conceived – for he thought that a love that was made known to many people would reap sorrow rather than joy as its reward.[7]

And he also thought of trying a great many other ways either of making his desires known to the lady[8] or of making himself attractive to her. Thus, in high hopes, he joyfully began to sing – firmly resolving to love Criseida alone, and setting no store by any of the other women he had seen or ever found desirable.

And at that moment he reverently addressed Love thus: 'My lord, the soul that used to be mine now belongs to you, and that pleases me, since you have ordained that I should serve one whom I know not whether to call woman or goddess; for no woman in dark clothing beneath a white veil was ever so beautiful as this one appears to me.

'You, my true lord, dwell within her eyes, which are a fit place for your power to reside. Hence, if my devotion finds any favour with you at all, entreat them, I beg you, to redeem my spirit that lies prostrate beneath your feet, struck down thus by the sharp arrows you loosed at it when you showed me the fair face of this lady.'

(*How Troiolo becomes more overwhelmed with passion than he had thought possible, and what he then endured.*)

(40) The fiery flames of love did not spare his royal blood, his mighty spirit or even his nobility – nor did they heed the physical strength or bravery that Troiolo possessed. But like fire that can be kindled in the right sort of material, whether it be dry or wet,[9] they set all ablaze when they touched this new lover.

Thus his thoughts and fancies daily provided more dry fuel within his noble heart; and he thought he might be able to draw water to cool his continual fervour from those lovely eyes; so he keenly sought every

28

opportunity to look at them – not realizing that as a result the fire within him burnt more fiercely.

Wherever he might go, whether walking or even sitting, be it alone or in company, drinking or eating, night and day and in every place he was always thinking of Criseida; and he would declare that her nobility and her exquisite face in every way surpassed both Polyxena's beauty and Helen's.

And nòt an hour of the day went by without him saying to himself a thousand times: 'O bright light that inspires my heart to love, O fair Criseida – God grant that your noble qualities which have made my face lose its colour may arouse some compassion in you. No-one but you can make me happy; you alone amongst women can help me.'

All other thoughts about the great war and his own well-being had vanished, and only that which spoke of his lady's noble gifts was entertained within his bosom; and since he was thus shackled, he concerned himself solely with tending the wounds of love, which took up all his thoughts and energies and gave him all his delight.

(45) The fierce battles and desperate assaults into which Hector and the rest of his brothers led the Trojans did not in any way divert him from his thoughts of love, although in the most ferocious onslaughts those who happened to witness them found him performing more astonishing feats of bravery than anyone else.

Yet it was not hatred of the Greeks that led him to do this, nor was it done in the hope of delivering Troy from the pressure of the siege in which he found her – but it was for the sake of glory. He did all this to gain more favour with his lady; and if the account is true, love made him so bold and mighty in battle that the Greeks feared him like death.

(*Troiolo, becoming yet more ardent in his passion, first fears that Criseida may be in love with someone else, and then considers his own condition, and complains to Love.*)

Love had already deprived him of sleep, reduced his appetite and increased his melancholy to such an extent that the paleness of his face clearly revealed his condition – although he continually disguised this with a forced smile and a frank manner of speaking; so that those who saw him thought this was the result of his anxiety about the war.

And the true state of things is not very clear: whether Criseida because of his discretion perceived nothing of this, or whether she was pretending not to understand. But this much is clear and obvious: that she seemed to care nothing for Troiolo and the love he had for her, but remained impervious, as if untouched by love.

As a result Troiolo's sufferings grew indescribable; and he sometimes feared that Criseida might be in love with someone else and because of that would not, out of contempt, want to accept him as a servant; but after considering a thousand possibilities he did not see how in all honour he could make her aware of his fierce passion.

(50) Hence, whenever he had the opportunity, he would complain about Love, saying to himself: 'Now Troiolo, you who used to mock others are caught yourself. None of them has become so enfeebled as you have through not knowing how to protect yourself from love. Now you are

in the snare you condemned others for falling into; and you could not watch out on your own account.

'What will be said of you amongst lovers if your passion ever comes to be revealed? They will all mock you and say: "Look at this man of foresight, who used to make fun of our sighs and laments about love. Now he has come to join us, and may Love be praised for bringing him to such a state!"

'What will be said of you by noble kings and lords if this comes to be known? They may well in great disgust say: "Look at the folly of this man, embroiling himself in love during these anxious and troubled times. At the moment when he should be displaying courage in battle he keeps squandering his attentions on love."

'And granted, poor Troiolo, that you are ordained to be in love – why did you not fall for a woman who felt some small stirring of love? for you might console yourself with that. But she for whom you pine feels no more than a stone, and remains as cold as unthawed ice beneath a clear sky; whilst I melt away like snow in fire.

'And if only I had already arrived at that haven towards which my fate now draws me! That would be a relief and a great consolation to me, since by dying I should be delivered from all my pain. For if my yet unnoticed suffering should be discovered, my life would be filled with a thousand humiliations each day and I should be held in greater contempt than anyone else.

(55) 'Ah, help me, Love – and you for whom I lament in bondage greater than anyone ever knew. I beseech you to take some pity upon one who loves you much more than his life. Turn your lovely face towards him now, my lady at the behest of that god who makes me live in such torment for your sake. Thus I entreat you – ah, do not deny me this favour.

'And if you do so, my lady, I shall revive like a flower in a flourishing springtime meadow; and I shall not find it painful to wait or to encounter your disdain or haughtiness. And if this should grow troublesome to you, simply call out sharply to me, who attend upon your every wish: "Kill yourself!" For I should indeed do that, in the belief that by doing so I might please you.'[10]

Thereupon with tears and sighs he said much more, calling upon that lady's name as is usual with anyone who is very much in love. He gained no response to his laments – but they were all vain gestures lost in the wind, for none of them reached her. And thus his torment increased a hundredfold each day.

Part II

(*Here begins the second part of the* Filostrato, *in which Troiolo reveals his love to Criseida's cousin Pandaro,*[1] *who reassures him and makes this secret love known to Criseida, and through pleas and cajolery leads her to love Troiolo.*

First then, Troiolo, after various exchanges tells the young Trojan nobleman Pandaro all about his love.)

(1) While Troiolo was thus one day in his room alone with his thoughts a youthful Trojan of noble descent and great spirit unexpectedly appeared there, and when he saw him lying stretched out on his bed in tears, cried out: 'What's the matter my dear friend? Have these harsh times got the better of you already?'

'Pandaro,' said Troiolo, 'what mischance has brought you here to witness my misery? If our friendship means anything let it persuade you to go away – for I know you would find it sadder than anything to see me die; and I am not much longer for this life, so crushed and confused are my spirits.

'And do not think that the siege of Troy, the terror of battle or any kind of fear is the reason for my present distress; that, beside the others, is the least of my concerns. It is something else that makes me constantly wish for death, and hence I lament my ill fortune. Do not concern yourself about how this has happened, my friend, for I have the best of reasons for keeping silent and not saying anything to you about it.'

Pandaro's pity increased at that – as did his desire to find out the truth – and so he replied: 'If our friendship still matters to you as it used to, let me know what trouble it is that makes you so set upon death – for keeping things secret is no way for one friend to act towards another.

(5) 'If I cannot ease your affliction, I want to bear these sufferings with you, for it is right for a friend to share everything – trouble and joy. And I think you well know how I have loved you through good times and bad, and that I would do anything important on your behalf – whatever it might be, and whatever was involved.

Troiolo then heaved a great sigh and said: 'Pandaro, since you keep wanting to hear about my sufferings I will tell you briefly what it is that afflicts me – not because I have any hope that my desire can be granted fulfilment or relief through you, but only to satisfy your entreaty which I am unable to refuse.

'Love, whose opponents strive in vain and succumb all the sooner,[2] kindles my heart with so sweet a delight that for its sake I have banished all others; and this, as you can see, afflicts me so much that a thousand times I have come close to[3] taking my life.

'Let that, my dear friend, be enough for you to know about my sorrows, which have been revealed to no-one else until now. And if you have any loyalty towards our friendship, I beg you in God's name not to betray this passion of mine to others, for that could cause me a great deal of distress. You have found out what you wanted to; now go away and leave me to wrestle with my anguish here.'

'Oh –' said Pandaro, 'how could you have kept so ardent a passion as this concealed from me? For I would have given you advice or help and found some way to bring you comfort.' Troiolo said to him: 'How might I have got that from you, whom I have seen continually suffering for love, yet unable to do anything about it for yourself? How then do you expect to bring me happiness?'

(10) Pandaro said: 'Troiolo, I know you are speaking the truth, but it often happens that those who cannot protect themselves from a poison may save others through timely warning – and a squint-eyed man has indeed been known to walk where one with good sight cannot easily go. And although a man may not take good advice, he can give it when someone else is in danger.

'I have loved unhappily and still am in love, for my sins; and it turns out like this because I have not loved the other person discreetly as you have. But that will be as God wills in the end. I am still constant and shall continue so in the friendship that I have all along maintained for you – and no-one shall ever hear of what you may tell me.

'So, my friend, have faith in me, and tell me who can have led you to suffer all this affliction and distress. And never fear that I may rebuke you for loving, for wise men in the past have made it clear to us that love cannot be removed from the heart unless, after a long time, it should set itself free.

'Put aside your sorrow and sighing, and ease your affliction by talking – for in so doing your suffering will be forgotten; and furthermore the lover's fever is much abated when he finds companions with like desires. I as you know am more in love than I would wish – nor can further suffering set me free.

'Perhaps the lady for whom you are pining is one whom I may be able to influence satisfactorily on your behalf – and if I could, I would do more to fulfil your desire than I have ever done for mine. You will see as much, if only I may know for whose sake you are enduring all this. Get up – don't lie there – remember that you can talk to me as you would to yourself.'

(15) Troiolo remained uncertain for a while – then, after heaving a bitter sigh and setting his whole face aflame with a blush of shame, he replied: 'Dear friend, a very honourable reason has prevented me from making my love directly known to you – for she who has brought me to this state is a relative of yours.' And not a word more did he utter.

And he fell back again on to his bed, weeping bitterly and covering his face. Pandaro said to him: 'My faithful friend, lack of trust has planted such misgivings in your bosom. Come along – stop this wretched weeping of yours, for as I hope to live, if the woman you love were my sister and it were in my power, you should have your pleasure of her.

'Get up, tell me, say who she is – tell me, say at once, so that I can find a way to help you, for I want nothing else. Can she be a lady of my household? I beg you to tell me quickly – for if it is the one I am beginning to think of, I do not believe six days will go by before I get you out of this predicament.'

Troiolo gave no answer to this, but all the time kept hiding his face further, and only when he heard what Pandaro was promising did he somewhat take heart. He was about to speak but then held back, so ashamed was he of what he had to confess. But when Pandaro urged him on he turned towards him weeping and let slip these words:

'Dear Pandaro, I wish I were dead when I think of what love has brought me to – and if I could have concealed the matter without wronging you, I should not indeed have been driven to this pretence. But I can maintain it no longer – and, being as shrewd as you usually are, you will know that Love does not determine whom one may rightly love, once one's desire has found an object.

(20) 'Some, as you know, love their sisters, sisters their brothers, daughters sometimes their fathers, fathers-in-law their daughters-in-law – and it sometimes happens also that stepmothers love their stepsons; but it grieves me greatly that love for your cousin has me in its power – I mean love for Criseida.' And having said this, he fell weeping, face downwards, on to his bed.

When Pandaro heard her named he answered thus with a laugh: 'My friend, I beg you, for God's sake don't be dismayed. Love could not have set your desire upon a nobler object than the one that he has chosen for it. For she is truly worthy of it, if I am any judge of conduct, greatness of spirit, nobility or beauty.

'No woman was ever nobler; none more lively or eloquent; none more pleasing or gracious. None of those who ever lived was finer of spirit; and there is no affair so great that she would not undertake it as nobly as any king – nor would her heart fail her in bringing it to a fulfilment, if it were at all possible.

'My cousin, however, has one quality, apart from those I have mentioned, which is somewhat unfavourable to you. She is more honourable than other women and has greater contempt for matters of love. But if nothing else hinders us, I think that by speaking nicely to her I shall find the right way around this for you. Just be patient and keep your fierce passion firmly under control.

'You may clearly see how Love has placed you in a position worthy of your talents. Be resolute then in your noble purpose and have confidence in your success, which I think will be soon achieved if your melancholy does not make you shun it. You are worthy of her and she of you, and I shall bring all my wits to bear on the matter.

(25) 'And do not imagine, Troiolo, that I cannot well see that such passions are ill-suited to a lady's honour – and what would also happen to her and her friends if such a thing ever became common talk and she fell into disgrace because of our folly over an affair which should have been honourable since it had to do with love.

'But since your passion is thus frustrated, as all undisclosed desires are – it seems to me that the proper course for every lover like you is to persevere in his noble pursuit, provided only that he is sensible in conduct and manner and avoids bringing any shame upon those whose shame and honour are involved.

'I firmly believe that all women are at heart inclined to love and that nothing holds them back but fear of disgrace. And if a suitable remedy for this disease can decently be offered, she who does not thus cure himself is foolish and is, I think, not really troubled by the problem.[4] My cousin is a widow and has passions, and if she denied it, I would not believe her.

'Thus, since I know you to be wise and prudent, I shall be able to help her and the two of you and make things easier for you both, provided that you keep it quiet and make it seem as if nothing were going on. I should be at fault if I did not do everything I could to assist you in this – but you must be discreet then, and keep the business concealed from other people.'

Troiolo became so glad-spirited as he listened to Pandaro that he felt as if he were already freed from all his sufferings, and passion began to burn more fiercely within him. But after he had given some thought to the matter he turned to Pandaro and said to him: 'I believe what you say of her, for it is only too plain to my eyes.

(30) 'But what relief can there be for the torment of passion within me, since I have never known her to be aware of my love? She will not believe it if you tell her – and then through fear of you she will condemn it as a mad frenzy, and you will have gained nothing. And even if she was affected by it, she would not listen to you, in order to show you how honourable she is.

'Moreover, Pandaro, I do not want you to think I would desire anything dishonourable from such a lady. I want her just to let me love her, and that would be the highest favour I could entreat from her. Aim for that and I shall ask nothing more of you.' Then he hung his head rather shame-facedly.

Pandaro replied cheerfully: 'What you're talking about won't trouble us at all. Leave it to me, for I have the darts of love and speeches of that sort at the tips of my fingers, and I have already been able to bring greater affairs to fruition under unusual circumstances. The labour shall be mine entirely, but I want its sweet reward to be yours.'

Troiolo nimbly sprang from his bed to the floor and embraced and kissed him, swearing that triumph in the war against the Greeks would be nothing beside this passion which had such a hold upon him: 'Dear Pandaro, I entrust myself to you; you who are my master and friend know everything that is needed to put an end to my torment.'

(Pandaro reveals to Criseida the love that Troiolo has for her, and despite her opposition encourages her to love him.)

Then Pandaro, who was eager to help the young man he so dearly loved, left him to go where he pleased and went off to find Criseida. Seeing him coming she rose to her feet and greeted him from some way off, and Pandaro, taking her by the hand drew her aside into a loggia.

(35) Here, he spent some time over the kind of laughter, pleasantries, cheerfulness and familiar talk that relatives often indulge in – acting like someone who wants, if he can, to work round to his subject by indirect means. And he began to gaze very hard at her lovely face.

Seeing this, Criseida said with a smile: 'Cousin, is it because you have never seen me before that you are now giving me such careful scrutiny?' Pandaro replied: 'You are well aware that I have seen you and am eager to see you – but you seem much more beautiful than usual to me, and in my view have more to praise God for than any other woman of beauty.'

Criseida said: 'What does that mean? Why more so now than in the past?' And at once Pandaro answered her gladly: 'Because yours is the most fortunate face that any woman in this world has possessed. If I am not mistaken I have found it to be so extremely attractive to a certain man that in consequence he is pining away.'

Criseida when she heard what Pandaro was saying modestly blushed a little, looking like a morning rose. Then she addressed these words to Pandaro: 'Do not make fun of me, for I should rejoice at any good fortune of yours. The man who found me attractive must have had little to do – for that has not happened at any other time since I was born.'

'Let's stop bandying words,' said Pandaro then, 'and tell me – have you noticed it?' She replied: 'Not as yet[5] in one man more than another, upon my life. It's true that now and then I see, passing by, a person who always gazes at my door – but I don't know whether he is waiting to see me or looking out for someone else.'

(40) Pandaro said: 'Who is he, this man?' Criseida said to him: 'Indeed, I don't know him – nor can I tell you anything more about him.' And Pandaro, realizing that she was not talking about Troiolo but someone else, quickly went on as follows: 'The man whom you have thus stricken is not someone completely unknown.'

'Who is it then that finds such delight in seeing me?' said Criseida. And Pandaro answered: 'Young lady, I do not believe that, since he who framed the world made the first man, anyone was ever endowed with a soul more fine than belongs to him whose love for you passes expression.

'He is noble in spirit and ancestry, most honourable and eager for honour; more fully endowed with natural wisdom than anyone else; unsurpassed in knowledge; valiant, bold, bright-faced – but I cannot list all of his qualities. How fortunate indeed your beauty is if such a man prizes it more than anything else!

'The jewel will be well set in the ring – if you are as wise as you are lovely. And if you make yourself his as much as he has made himself yours, the star will be well-matched with the sun; for no young nobleman was ever so well-matched with any young lady as you will be with him if you are wise. It will be well for you if only you come to see that.

'Each living person has one chance only in this world, if he knows how to take it. If he allows it to slip by, let him mourn his misfortune for himself, and not blame others. The great beauty and charm of your appearance has gained this opportunity for you, so think about making use of it now. Leave me to mourn the evil hour in which I was born – for I have found no favour with God, the world or Fortune.'

(45) 'Are you testing me, or telling the truth?' said Criseida, 'or are you out of your mind? Who could have his full pleasure with me without first making himself my husband? But tell me, who is this man that has lost his wits on my account? – is he a foreigner of a man of this city? Tell me if you can and will, and don't cry woe for no good reason.'

Pandaro said: 'He is indeed a man of this city and not one of the lesser sort – and he is a great friend of mine. I have, perhaps through force of destiny drawn from his heart the facts I have revealed to you. He is pining away in misery and wretchedness in sorrow – so enkindled is he by the splendour of your face. And if you want to know who loves you so much – it is Troiolo who yearns for you more than anything else.'

Criseida then remained some time gazing at Pandaro in surprise, and turned the colour of the sky when it is tinted by the dawn. With difficulty she held back the tears that were ready to fall from her eyes; then, when she had recovered herself, she murmured something quietly and spoke thus with a sigh to Pandaro:

'I used to believe, Pandaro, that if I were ever to grow so foolish as to entertain any sort of desire for Troiolo, you would not only have reproved but beaten me – as any man would if he felt impelled to maintain my honour. God help me! – what will the others do, now that you are plotting to bring me under the rule of Love?

'I well know that Troiolo is noble and valiant and that any noblewoman ought to be well pleased with him. But since my husband was taken from me my thoughts have always been far removed from love. My heart is still grief-stricken because of his cruel death, and will be so long as I remain in this world, living with the memory of his loss.

(50) 'And if anyone had to have my love, then indeed I should grant it to him, so long as I could believe it would please him. But, since you must be well aware that infatuations like this one of his occur frequently, last four or six days then fade gently away as the desire finds a new object[6] – you should think again about this.

'So let me follow the course that Fortune has assigned me. He may easily find a mistress who will be as gracious and amenable as he would wish. As for me, I must remain chaste. Pandaro, I beg you, for God's sake do not take this as a rebuff, but go and console him with new pleasures and fresh pastimes.'

Pandaro, for his part, felt he had been made a fool of when he heard what the young lady was saying, and he got up as if to leave. But then he paused, turned back to her and said: 'Criseida, as I hope God may grant my prayers, I have spoken to you on behalf of a man for whom I should speak thus to my own sister, daughter of wife, if I had one, / (53) for I know that Troiolo is worthy of much greater things than your love could offer. And I saw him yesterday in such a state because of this love that I felt great pity for him. Perhaps you don't believe it, and because of that you don't care; but you would certainly be driven to feel pity for him if you knew what I do about his suffering. I beg you – take pity on him for my sake!

'I do not think there is any man in the world who is more discreet or trustworthy – and he is more constant than any other, for he desires and needs nothing apart from you. And it is you, who are still young even though you have kept yourself in mourning, that he allows himself to love. Waste no time; remember that old age or death will take away your beauty.'

(55) 'Alas!' said Criseida, 'you speak the truth, for the years do thus steal it from us little by little – and they pass more quickly as the span allotted by the light of Heaven[7] nears its end. But let us put such thoughts aside – and tell me whether I can yet find joy and pleasure in love. How did you come to notice this in Troiolo?'

Pandaro then smiled and replied: 'I'll tell you since you want to know. The other day, when things were quiet because of the truce that was then in effect, Troiolo asked me to go with him and seek amusement in the shade of the woods. There we sat down, and he began talking to me about love and then singing to himself about it.

'I was not close to him, but when I heard him murmuring I gave heed – and as I recall he was complaining in his anguish to Love and saying: "My lord, my looks and sighs have already revealed what I feel in my heart about that graceful and charming creature whose beauty holds me in her power.

"You dwell in that place where I retain the image I delight in above all else. And there you will see my soul lying grievously stricken by your lightning that holds it there continually pleading for that sweet relief which, dear lord, only this lady's fair and lovely eyes can give it.

"And so, for the love of God, if my death is unwelcome to you, make that lovely creature aware of this, and entreat her to grant that joy which so often brings your subjects repose. Ah, my lord, do not doom me to die – do this then for the love of God; you know how my troubled soul cries out day and night, so fearful is it of being destroyed by her.

(60) "Are you afraid, my lord, to kindle your flames beneath her dark garments? You could achieve no greater glory than that. Infuse her breast with that desire which dwells in mine and torments me. Come, merciful lord – do so, I beseech you – and thus through your actions her soft sighs may bring solace to my desires."

'And when he had uttered this he hung his head,·sighing heavily and saying I know not what. Then he fell silent, as made to do so by tears. Seeing this I began to have some idea of what was going on, and I decided that one day when the time was ripe I would playfully ask him what the song meant, and also what the occasion for it was.

'But an opportunity to do so did not arise until today, when I found him completely alone. When I went into his room, wondering if he were there, he was on his bed – and when he saw me he turned away. This aroused my suspicions somewhat, and when I drew closer I found that he was prostrated with grief and weeping.

'I comforted him as best I could, and by dint of extraordinary skill and various ploys I got out of him what was the matter – having first given him my pledged word not to reveal it to anyone ever. This was the concern that guided me and made me come to you,[8] and I have thus briefly told you all you wished to know.

'But what will you do? Come, tell me now – will you remain aloof and let this man who has no heed for himself suffer such a cruel death because he loves you? What a harsh fate and what ill fortune that such a man should die for love of you! At least if you were not niggardly with your sweet presence and your looks you might yet save him from a bitter end.'

(65) Criseida then said: 'By such means when you found him weeping upon his bed, you plucked out the secret from his heart even though he was clutching it close. And may God give both him and me joy and peace of mind, for pity has been aroused in me by what you have said. I am not so harsh as you think, nor so devoid of pity.'

Being by now deeply affected, she paused for a while, and then after a heavy sigh she continued: 'Come now, I can clearly see where your errand of mercy is leading you and shall accede to it, since I am bound to respect your wishes in this – and he deserves it and will be satisfied if I look in his direction. But in order to avoid shame, or worse perhaps, beg him to be prudent and do nothing that would be to my discredit or his.'

'Dear sister,' said Pandaro then, 'you have put it well, and I shall ask him to do so. Indeed, I know him to be so well-behaved and prudent that I do not think he will fail in this, unless by accident. May God prevent that – and I will make sure you get from it what you would desire. Trust in God and do your duty.'

(How Criseida, arguing with herself after Pandaro's departure, debates whether she should love Troiolo or not, and finally decides to do so.)

When Pandaro had left, the lovely Criseida went away into her room alone, pondering in her heart Pandaro's every little word and piece of news just as it had been uttered – and she dwelt upon all such matters with pleasure, sighing to herself as her thoughts focused on Troiolo much more than before:

'I am young, good-looking, attractive and happy; a widow, wealthy, noble and well-beloved; without children and at peace with the world. Why should I not be in love? If honour perhaps forbids me to do so, I shall be discreet and keep my desires so secret that I shall not be thought ever to have harboured love within my heart.

(70) 'My youth is slipping away all the time – must I surrender it so feebly? I know of no woman in the city who does not have a lover at the moment, and I am sure that many people[9] are now taking delight in love while I am squandering my time to no purpose. To do as others do is no sin, and no-one can be reproached for that.

'Who will ever want me when I am old? No-one, for sure – and to change my mind then will only increase the misery. It is pointless to regret things the day after and say tearfully: "Why did I not grant my love?" It would be right, however, to make one's preparations in advance. This man who loves you is good-looking, noble, wise, prudent, fresher than a lily, / (72) of royal blood and supremely worthy – and your cousin Pandaro speaks most highly of him. So what is the matter with you? Why not allow him the sort of place in your heart that he has given you in his? Why do you not grant him your love? – do you not hear the pitifulness of his outcry?[10] What happiness there will be for both of you if you love him as he loves you!

'And now is no time for a husband – and even if it were, to keep one's freedom is much the wiser course. Love which thus develops out of friendship always yields great pleasure to lovers, but however great one's beauty may be it soon becomes distasteful to husbands who expect something new every day.

'Water gained by stealth is a much sweeter thing than wine that can be taken freely – and so in love the pleasure that remains secret far excels that of constantly embracing a husband. So welcome this sweet love, which has surely been sent to you from God, and satisfy his burning desire.'

(75) And pausing for a moment she then veered in the opposite direction, saying: 'Wretch – what do you think you are doing? Do you not know how terrible life can be in the throes of such love – condemned to continual grief, sighing and suffering, along with jealousy, which is worse than the cruellest death?

'Moreover, this man who at the moment is in love with you is too far above your station. This passionate desire of his will fade and he will then despise you for ever, leaving you in misery, wholly dishonoured and humiliated. Take care what you do – for wisdom after the event neither was, is nor will be of any value.

'But, just supposing that such love could last any length of time – how can you be sure it could remain secret? It is vain indeed to trust in Fortune, and human judgment cannot easily foresee what may happen. And if the affair comes to light, you can bid farewell to the fine reputation you have enjoyed until now.

'Therefore leave such love to those who care for it.' Then, having said this she began to sigh deeply, and was still unable to banish the beautiful image of Troiolo from her chaste breast. Thus she fell back into her former quandary – finding fault, then approving, and delaying for a long time out of indecision.

(Pandaro informs Troiolo of what he has done, and he, having seen Criseida, gathers hope and becomes supremely happy.)

Pandaro who had gone away from Criseida well-pleased went straight back to Troiolo without going anywhere else, and even before he reached him began to say: 'Take comfort brother, for I think I have accomplished a large part of what you so desire.' And sitting down, he quickly told him without interruption how things had gone.

(80) Just as flowers that have drooped and closed because of the night frost all unfold and straighten upon their stalks when the sun shines brightly upon them – so, after his spell of weakness, did Troiolo behave then.[11] And turning to the heavens he began, like a man set free, by saying: 'Praise be, fair Venus, to your almighty power and that of your son, Love.'

Then he embraced Pandaro a thousand times and kissed him as often, and was happier than he could have been, had a thousand Troys been given him. Then he went with Pandaro and no-one else, to gaze at leisure upon Criseida's beauty – looking hard to see if he could find any change in her as a result of what she had been told by Pandaro.

She was standing at a window of her house and may have been expecting this to happen. And she did not behave cruelly or harshly towards Troiolo as he looked at her, but turning around gazed modestly at him over her right shoulder. At this Troiolo went away contented, giving thanks to Pandaro and to God.

And the fearfulness that was preventing Criseida from reaching a decision fled away as she admired his manners, his pleasing behaviour and his courtesy. And she was so rapidly overcome that she desired him more than any other kind of happiness and greatly regretted the time that had been wasted when she had not known about his love.

Troiolo sings and is supremely joyful – jousting, giving presents, and spending freely; and he often refurbishes and changes his garments, growing more passionately in love all the time. And when they agree he finds it no pain to follow and gaze discreetly upon Criseida, who no less discreetly displayed her beauty and approval to him from time to time.

(Criseida's gaze makes Troiolo yet more impassioned and he speaks about this to Pandaro, who advises him to write to her – and he does so.)

(85) But just as we always find that a fire grows as it consumes more

wood – so it happens that while hope grows passion very often still increases. Thus Troiolo felt his noble desire pricking his captive heart harder than it has done before. And hence his sighs and sufferings began to afflict him more sharply than they had to begin with.

Troiolo complained bitterly to Pandaro about this, saying: 'Wretch that I am – Criseida has so ravished my spirits with her lovely eyes that I think I am dying of this raging desire which swells my heart so greatly, burning and destroying me. Tell me, what am I to do? – for the courtesy she is showing me ought to satisfy me completely.

'She looks at me, and allows me to look respectfully at her, and that ought to content my ardent desires. But this greedy appetite looks for something more – so ill-governed are the passions that control it. And no-one who has not experienced it would believe how much this ever-increasing flame torments me.

'What am I to do then? I cannot but appeal to you, fair Criseida. You are the only one who can help me; you, my noble lady, are the only one who can quench the flame of my love – sweet light and lamp of my heart. If I might spend one winter's night with you, I would then spend a hundred and fifty in Hell.

'What shall I do, Pandaro? Have you nothing to say? Can you see me in the midst of such flames and act as if you did not notice my sighs? Look – can you not see how I burn? Help me, I implore you – tell me what I should do – give me some advice. Unless you and she can rescue me I shall fall into the toils of death.'

(90) Pandaro then said: 'I hear and understand all you are saying quite clearly, and have never hesitated and never will to help you in your troubles. I am always ready to do for you not only what I ought but anything at all, without being made or asked to do so. Just let me see plainly what your noble desire is.

'I know that in all matters you see six times more clearly than me, but nonetheless, if I were you, I should write to her about my suffering, fully and in my own hand. Furthermore, I should beg her, in God's name and in that of love and her courtesy, to think of me; and when you have written that[12] I will deliver it at once.

'And moreover I shall continue to urge her as strongly as I can to take pity upon you. We shall then be able to see how she responds – but already my thoughts clearly tell me that her reply should please you. Write then, and describe all your devotion and suffering as well as your desire. Leave out nothing that can be spoken of.'

This advice greatly pleased Troiolo, but like a fearful lover he replied: 'Alas, Pandaro, since women are known to be modest, you may find that for that reason Criseida will scornfully reject the letter you bring – and we shall have worsened our position immeasurably.'

To this Pandaro replied: 'If you want, you can do as I tell you and then leave it to me – for, as I look for love to grant me repose. I think I shall be able to bring back a reply written in her own hand. If you don't care for that, you can go on being timid and mournful about it. Go ahead then and bewail your sufferings – for as far as I am concerned nothing that could make you happy is being left untried.[13]'

(95) Troiolo then said: ' Let it be as you wish. I will go and write, and

pray Love out of courtesy to make the composition, the letter and the mission fruitful.' And he went away to his room, and in an accomplished manner[14] he quickly wrote a letter to his very dear lady in the following words.

(*Troiolo tells Criseida that his love for her and his sufferings are what make him write, and he implores her pity.*)

'How could a man who dwells in such anguish, in such deep misery, and in such a troubled state as I do because of you, my lady, offer a greeting to anyone? I do not think that should be asked of him. Hence I depart from the usual practice, and you will not receive a greeting[15] from me here – if only because I have none to give, unless you give me one.[16]

'I cannot shirk the commands of Love, who has before now emboldened worse men than I. For it is he who compels me to write the words you find – still exacting from me the obedience he is accustomed to. Therefore if I go astray here in any way give him the blame and grant me your pardon I pray, sweet source of all my hope.

'Your sublime beauty and the splendour of your lovely eyes and fine accomplishments; your precious honour, noble worthiness and supremely praiseworthy behaviour – all these have so firmly established him as lord and you as lady in my mind that no other power than death would ever be strong enough to displace you.

'And whatever I may do, your fair image continually breeds one thought in my heart which banishes all others that are concerned with anything at all but you – even though nothing else really matters to this spirit of mine; for it has become a servant to your nobility in which alone my hopes reside. And your name is always upon my lips and continually inspires my heart with fresh desire.

(100) 'From such sources, my lady, there springs a fire which night and day torments my soul and will not let me find rest anywhere. Thus my eyes weep and my heart grieves and I feel myself being consumed little by little by this flame of passion that rages within me. And hence I must rely upon your power alone if I wish to be saved.

'You alone can, if you wish, offer gentle relief for my distress and suffering. You alone, my lady, can provide true repose for my sharp afflictions. You alone through your acts of mercy can relieve me of the torment that is thus destroying me. You, who are my lady, are the only one who can bring about what my heart desires.

'Therefore if ever any man deserved reward because of pure faith, great love and the constant desire to serve well in all possible circumstances – let me be one of those, dear lady – let it be me – who can turn to you as the one who is the object of all my yearnings.

'I know well that I cannot claim what I seek by virtue of my service – but no-one save you who have wounded my heart can, if you will, make me worthy of greater things. O bliss that my heart yearns for, temper the lofty disdain of your great spirit, and be as gracious to me as you are noble in your deeds.

'Now I am sure that you are as merciful as you are lovely and that my deep anguish, transformed through our discretion into happiness and thankfulness, will not lead me, sweet lady, to die of love for you, and will moreover turn itself into sweet delight.[17] And if prayers have any power, I pray that of you – in the name of that love which is now closer to your heart.

(105) 'I may not be much of an offering, of little power and less value, but I am without doubt entirely yours. And indeed you are wise: if I do not make myself clear, you will, I know understand what I leave unsaid.[18] And likewise I hope that what then happens will be much better and finer than I deserve. May Love incline and encourage you towards that.

'There were many things that I had still to say, but in order not to vex you I shall leave them out. And in conclusion I pray my dear lord Love to make me the goal of your desire as whole-heartedly as he has made you that of my delight. Hence, whilst I am yours you may at length become mine and never be taken from me.'

Having thus written all this upon a sheet of paper he folded it properly, moistened the signet upon his tear-stained cheeks, and then sealed it and placed it in Pandaro's hands. First, however, he kissed it a thousand times and more, saying: 'What bliss it will be for you, my letter, to reach the hand of such a lady!'

(Pandaro takes Troiolo's letter to Criseida, but she before accepting it felt a little troubled.)

Pandaro, having taken this sad letter, went off to see Criseida, and she when she saw him coming left the company she was with, and as she came part of the way to meet him[19] she looked in her fear and eagerness like some pearl of the East. They greeted each other from some distance and then took each other by the hand.

Then Criseida said: 'What is it that brings you here? Do you have any further news?' Pandaro without hesitation said to her: 'Lady, for you the news I bring is fair and good, but not for others – as you will be able to see from this sad screed sent by a man whose death I expect to witness, so little do you care for him.

(110) 'Take it and read it carefully, and console him with a reply of some kind.' Criseida stood there timidly and did not take it. Then she altered her meek expression slightly, and said quietly: 'I beg you, dear Pandaro, as you wish Love to grant you peace, to have some regard for me, not just for the young man.

'Consider if what you seek is warranted now; judge that for yourself. Then you will see whether I would be right to take it and whether your request is really honourable. To help others in their suffering one should not act dishonourably oneself. I beg you, dear Pandaro, not to leave it with me. Take it back, for the love of God.'

Pandaro was somewhat put out by this and said: 'It's a remarkable thing to see how, when women very much desire something, they all seem averse from it and disturbed by it in the presence of others. I have told you a great deal about this business, so you should not at this stage start turning bashful in front of me. I beg you now not to refuse me this.'

Criseida smiled when she heard him, and took it and placed it in her bosom, and then said to him: 'When I have leisure I shall read it as carefully as I can. If I am acting less than prudently now, my reason is that

I am unable to flout your wishes. May God look down from Heaven upon this and protect my innocence!'

(Criseida reads Troiolo's letter, feels moved to be kind to him, and becomes much inclined to love him.)

Pandaro went away at once he had given it to her, and she, being very eager to know what it said, found an excuse, left her companions, went off to sit in her room, and having opened it, read and re-read it with pleasure – perceiving clearly that Troiolo was far more ardently in love than had appeared from his behaviour.

(115) This pleased her as she felt her own inmost heart had been touched, leaving her in a state of great distress – even though that was not at all evident. And having carefully noted every word that had been written, she rendered praise and thanks to Love, saying to herself: 'Now I must find a time and means to quench this flame.'

'For if I let it grow into too fierce a blaze, people might guess the truth about my secret desire because of the lack of colour in my face – and that would be no slight disgrace. But for my part I do not mean to die or cause someone else's death when I can happily avoid suffering both for myself and for him.

'I certainly do not mean to remain as I have been until now. If Pandaro returns for my reply I shall give him a pleasant and favourable one, even if it should cause me trouble – which will not be the case. And Troiolo will never again be able to call me pitiless. If only I were now held closely in his dear arms with my face next to his!'

(Pandaro returns to Criseida for her reply, which after some bandying of words she promises to give and does so.)

Pandaro, who had been constantly under pressure from Troiolo, came back to Criseida and said with a smile: 'Lady, what do you think of what my friend has written?' She immediately blushed and said no more than: 'God knows.' Pandaro asked her: 'Have you answered?' – and she mockingly replied: 'This soon?'

'If you want me ever to be able to help you,' said Pandaro, 'get it done at once.' She then said to him: 'I don't really know how to do it.' 'Come –' said Pandaro, 'think of how to please him; Love will usually give good guidance. Upon my word, I have such a great yearning to console him that you would not believe it – and only your reply can bring that about.'

(120) 'And I shall do so since you thus desire it – but God grant that it turns out well!' 'Indeed,' said Pandaro, 'it will turn out just as he deserves and will please him more than anything.' Then he went away, and she sat down in a corner of her room where no-one else usually went, and wrote in the following terms:

(Criseida replies to Troiolo, and without binding or releasing him carefully keeps him in suspense.)

'Wise and mighty friend, whom Love has much beguiled and unjustly held prisoner on my behalf – Criseida, having due concern for her honour, sends you greetings and then humbly entrusts herself to your

43

great worthiness, desiring to please you so long as my honour and chastity can be preserved.

'From him who loves you so wholeheartedly that he indeed has no kind of heed for either my honour or my reputation, I have received those pages covered with your writing on which I have read of your life of woe; and, as I hope for happiness, I was not unmoved. And although they are embellished with tears, I have nonetheless looked at them carefully.

'And giving due consideration to both your sufferings and your pleas, and weighing your faith and your hopes together – I do not altogether see how I can rightly agree to what you ask, if I wish to maintain properly and completely the state that is more desirable than any other in the world – that of living and dying in honour.

'Indeed, it would be good to grant your wish if the world were as it should be. But since we are forced to accept it the way it is, we could find ourselves in desperate trouble if we did otherwise. I must indeed own to an impulse which made me in spite of myself feel pity for you – yet you will gain little satisfaction from me.[20]

(125) 'But so great is the virtue that I feel to be in you that I am sure you will fully understand what I have to do, and will be content with the reply I give you and find some relief for your sad torment, which so offends and grieves my heart. And indeed if it did not involve dishonour I should gladly do what you desire.[21]

'My powers of expression and the skill I have shown in this letter are scanty – and I wish it could bring you more pleasure. But what is desired cannot yet be accomplished,[22] and actions must for now perhaps give place to good intentions.[23] So, if it does not seem wrong to you, allow some respite to your grief at not having had a reply to all you have said.

'The offer that you make is unnecessary[24] – for I am certain that you would do everything you say. And, as for me indeed, although I am of little account, you could have me as yours far more than a thousand times so long as the cruel flames[25] do not burn me – for I am sure you would not wish that. I say no more except to pray God to fulfil both your desire and mine.'

(Troiolo received Criseida's reply, which he examines together with Pandaro, deriving from it both hope and joy.)

And having thus written, she folded the letter, sealed it and gave it to Pandaro who at once went in search of young Troiolo, brought it to him and presented it with the greatest delight. And he took it and read with both joy and sighing what was written there – his mood altering as he followed her words.

But eventually, giving due weight to all she had written he said to himself: 'If I understand her properly love is making itself felt within her but because of her misgivings she is still keeping on her guard. But if Love gives me the strength to endure, it cannot be long before she has to adopt a very different tone.'

(130) And Pandaro to whom he told everything thought the same way about it. And as a result Troiolo draws more courage than before, laying aside his heavy melancholy and trusting that the time for him to reap the

reward for his sufferings will soon arrive. This is what he seeks and implores day and night, like one who longs for nothing else.

(Because of the growing intensity of Troiolo's passion Pandaro, eager to be of help, persuades Criseida to meet him.)

The intensity of his passion mounted day by day, and although hope helped him to sustain it his heart was still heavily afflicted by it. Hence one can imagine how often his great ardour made him write letters, to which the favourable or unfavourable replies were sometimes quick and sometimes slow in coming.

Hence he often complained about Love and Fortune, whom he saw as his foe, and often said to himself: 'Alas, if only the nettle of love which thus stings and weakens me were to prick her just a little, my desolate life would soon be brought to that happy haven which I may die before I reach.'

Pandaro, finding his friend's heart to be so ablaze with passion, lavished entreaties upon Criseida, and told her everything he knew about Troiolo's state. And she, although she was pleased to hear it, said: 'I can do nothing else. I am behaving towards him as you told me to, my dear brother.'

'That is not enough,' answered Pandaro. 'I want you to comfort him and talk to him.' Criseida however said: 'I shall never allow him that, for under no circumstances do I mean to yield him the crown of my honour. But I shall always love him most honourably like a brother because of his great goodness.'

(135) Pandaro answered: 'That crown is what priests praise when they cannot deprive the wearer of it. They all talk like saints, and then when they have lulled your suspicions they have their will of you. No-one will ever know about Troiolo, for although he is suffering a great deal he is struggling manfully to suppress it. Those who are able to do good and fail to are doing great harm – and the loss of time most displeases those who are wisest.'[26]

Criseida said: 'I know his virtue makes him hold my honour dear, and his nobility is so great that he would not ask me to do anything improper. And I swear to you, as I hope for salvation, that I am, leaving aside what you are asking, a thousand times more his than my own – so much does his courtesy please me.'

'If he pleases you, what are you looking for then? Come – have done with this churlishness. Do you mean him to die for love? Well may you prize your beauty if you kill such a man. Come, tell me when you want him to come to you, for you are dearer to him than the skies above – and say how and where. Don't try to wear out his patience to the bitter end.'

'Alas for me Pandaro, what have you brought me to, and what are you trying to make me do? You have shattered and destroyed my honour, and I dare not look you in the face. Alas for me – when may I regain it? My heart's blood runs cold when I think of what you are asking – but you behold it clearly and think nothing of it.

'I wish I had died that day when I spent so long listening to you here in the loggia; for you planted in my heart a desire that I think will never depart from it and will lead me to lose my honour and suffer endless remorse, alas. But I can hold out no longer; if it matters to you so much I am ready to do as you wish.

(140) 'But if any prayer can move you, I pray dear sweet cousin that all our words and deeds may be kept entirely secret; you are well aware of what could ensue if such an affair were to come to light. I beg you to tell him about this and make him behave prudently, and when the time is right I will do what his heart desires.'

Pandaro answered: 'Keep watch over your own tongue – for neither he, himself, nor I will ever speak of it.' 'Do you now consider me so stupid,' she said, 'when you can see how I tremble for fear of discovery? But since the honour or shame that we may reap from this affair touches you as closely as it does me, I won't pursue the matter – you deal with it as you like.'

Pandaro said: 'Have no fear, for we shall take very good care on that score. When do you want him to come and talk to you? Let's wind up this business now,[27] for since it must be done it will be much better to do it quickly; and it will be much easier to conceal your love afterwards, for by that time you will both have agreed on what you have to do.'

'You know' said Criseida, 'that there are ladies and other people in this house with me and that some of them are to attend the coming festival. I can meet him then. Do not let this delay trouble him. I shall tell you then how and where he is to come; just make sure that he is prudent and can keep his passion secret.'

Part III

(Here begins the third part of the Filostrato, *in which after the author's invocation Pandaro and Troiolo speak to each other of the need to keep quiet about the next stage in their dealings with Criseida. Troiolo then visits her in secret, takes his pleasure and converses with her, goes away and comes back, and spends his time in joy and thanksgiving. And, to begin with, the author's invocation.)*

(1) Resplendent light, whose beams, as I desired, have thus far led me through the halls of love – a double measure of your brightness will be needed now, to direct my skill and so enable me to convey a hint of the happiness of Love's sweet kingdom which Troiolo was privileged to enter.[1]

Such a kingdom will be reached by those who can faithfully, wisely and honourably endure all the pangs of love – and indeed it can rarely be reached by other means. Look upon me then, lovely lady, and grant my great desire the reward I pray for as I sing your everlasting praise.

(Troiolo is delighted with Pandaro for bringing him such a pleasing reply – and he expresses his gratitude at length.)

Although Troiolo's desire still raged he nevertheless still felt happy simply to know that he had found favour with Criseida, who seemed

46

kindly disposed in the replies she had given his letters, and even more so whenever he had seen her. For she would gaze so sweetly at him that he thought he was at the very pinnacle of his happiness.

Pandaro had, as mentioned, taken leave of the lady once they had reached agreement, and had gone off joyful at heart and in appearance to look for Troiolo, whom he had left on his departure bewildered by sweet hopes and gloomy sorrows. And he went on searching for him all around until he found him at a temple, deep in thought.

(5) And on reaching him he at once drew him aside and spoke to him as follows: 'Dear friend, I was so concerned about you when I saw you in such bitter anguish recently because of love, that my heart felt much of your suffering as its own, and I have never taken rest until I found a way of helping you.

'It is for you that I have become a go-between – for you that I have abandoned my reputation – and for you that I have corrupted my kinswoman's chaste thoughts and found your love a place within her heart. And it will not be long before you discover that, with greater delight than I can speak of, when you hold sweet Criseida in your arms.

'But as God in his omniscience knows, and as you do also, I was not induced to do this for the sake of reward. It was simply my loyalty to you as a friend that led me to plead for mercy on your behalf. So to avoid having the happiness you seek destroyed by ill luck, I beseech you to behave as a prudent man should.

'You know that her reputation is commonly held sacred and that nothing unfavourable has ever been said of her. It now lies within your power to deprive her of that if you do not behave as you should – although that could not help but bring me great dishonour, since I have been acting both as her kinsman and her go-between.

'So I beg you as earnestly as I can to maintain our secrecy in this affair. I have removed from Criseida's conscience all thoughts of shame and all scruples that stood in your way, and have so belaboured it with talk of the purity of your love that she now loves you and is ready to do whatever you may ask.

(10) 'And nothing but an opportunity is now needed to bring matters to a conclusion, and when that arises I shall leave you in her arms to take your pleasure with her. But for God's sake, dear friend, make sure that the business is discreetly handled and give none of your feelings a chance to show. And do not be annoyed if I ask you about this repeatedly, for you well know how honourable my request is.'

Who could describe all the joy that Troiolo felt in his heart as he listened to Pandaro? For the more he heard, the further his grief diminished. He gained respite from the sighs that had overwhelmed him, his desperate suffering was allayed, and his sad looks were cheered by hopes of happiness.

And just as early Spring suddenly reclothes and adorns with leaves and flowers the young trees that have stood bare during the harsh season of the year, and reclothes meadows, hills and banks everywhere with grass and lovely fresh flowers – so Troiolo's looks brightened and he suddenly became full of renewed joy.[2]

And giving a little sigh he gazed into Pandaro's face and said: 'You must

47

recall, dear friend, how I was when you once found me in tears during those bitter times that I endured for the sake of love – and likewise when your questions succeeded in discovering the cause of my suffering.

'And you know how reluctant I was to reveal it to you who are my one and only friend – yet then I faced no risk in speaking of it, even though it was an embarrassing thing to do. So ask yourself whether I could ever let other people know – for even as I speak to you about it I am trembling with fear in case anyone should find out. May God prevent any disaster of that kind.

(16) 'Nevertheless, I swear to you by the God who rules over both Heaven and earth, and as I hope not to fall into fierce Agamemnon's power – that even if my life, mortal as it is, were to last for ever, you may rest assured that I should guard this secret as closely as I could and in every way strive to protect the reputation of that lady who has pierced me to the heart.

'I fully understand and am well aware of what you have said and done on my behalf, and I could never hope to repay you for having, I may say, led me from Hell and worse into Paradise. But for our friendship's sake I beg you not to give yourself such a vile title when you have, rather, been helping a friend in need.

'Let that name be reserved for covetous wretches who are led to perform such services for gain. You, on the other hand, have done so in order to release me from my sorrowful plight and from the fierce struggle I was having with thoughts that would reject or distort every favourable sign. And that is exactly what one friend ought to do when he sees another in distress.

'And to show you how very highly I think of you, there is my sister Polyxena whose beauty is more highly praised than that of any other woman – and, as well as her, there is my sister-in-law Helen who is the loveliest of all. Let me know what you think if either of them appeals to you, and then let me get to work with whichever one you choose.

'But since you have done all this and a great deal more than I could have asked, let my desire be fulfilled when you judge the moment to be right. I depend on you and look to you alone for that supreme happiness, as well as for consolation, joy, well-being, gladness and delight – and I shall not go beyond your instructions. And if the pleasure is mine let the thanks for it be yours.'[3]

(20) Pandaro was content with what Troiolo had said, and they each attended to their own concerns. But although each day until he could hold her close to him seemed to Troiolo like a hundred, he still remained patient and with the greatest of efforts controlled his raging passions, devoting his nights to thoughts of love and his days, along with his followers, to the labours of Mars.

Meanwhile the moment both the lovers yearned for was at hand, so Criseida sent for Pandaro and told him that everything was in readiness. But Pandaro was much concerned about Troiolo, who the day before had gone some distance away with a few companions to deal with important business concerning the conduct of the war – although he would be returning very soon.

He told her of this, and she was much distressed to hear it. But nevertheless Pandaro like a diligent friend sent him a speedy messenger who, without pausing for rest, arrived within a short time in Troiolo's presence. And when Troiolo heard why he had come he joyfully set out to return.

And when he met Pandaro he heard from him all about what he was to do, and then with great impatience he waited for night, which seemed to him to be on the retreat. Then with Pandaro alone he quietly made his way towards the place where Criseida was nervously waiting for him on her own.

The night was as black and murky as Troiolo could have wished and he gave careful heed to every object in his way, for he was terrified that something might interfere with his amorous purpose and thus cause him great suffering. And through a secret entry he found his way alone into the already silent house.

(25) And, as instructed, he waited for the lady in a certain dark and secluded place; yet this delay was not irksome or painful for him, nor was his inability to see quite where he could be. But with joyful confidence he kept repeating to himself: 'This gracious lady will soon come, and I shall be happier than if I were ruler of the whole world.'

Criseida was indeed aware of his arrival, and she had coughed[4] so that from his hiding place he might hear her coming. And in order that he might not be vexed by having to remain there, she spoke all the time in a loud voice, urging everyone to go to bed as quickly as possible, and saying that she was so sleepy she could not stay up any longer.

After everyone had gone to bed and the house had become completely quiet, Criseida at once decided to go to Troiolo's hiding place. And when he heard her coming he rose with an expression of joy, and with quiet attentiveness came to meet her, eager to fulfil her every wish.

The lady was holding a lighted torch in her hand as she came down the stairs alone; and when she saw Troiolo anxiously awaiting her she greeted him, and said as clearly as she could manage: 'My lord, if I have offended you by keeping your kingly glory confined in such a place, I beg you in God's name to forgive me, sweet love.'

Troiolo replied: 'Sweet lady, my heart's sole hope and joy – the splendour and brightness of your lovely face has always been before me like a star, and this small space has assuredly been dearer to me than my palace, so there is no need to ask forgiveness about it.' Then he embraced her and they kissed each other on the lips.

(30) And before they left that spot they embraced a thousand times with sweet joy and fervent pleasure. And they kissed each other as many times and more, both burning with equal passion and showing great tenderness to each other. But when these first caresses had come to an end they went up the stairs and into a bedchamber.

It would be a long task to describe their happiness, and an impossible one to tell of the delight they shared when they were there. They undressed and entered the bed, where the lady, who still had one last garment on, asked him charmingly: 'Shall I take off everything? Newly-wed brides are shy on the first night.'

Troiolo answered: 'Light of my life, I beg you to – so that I may hold you naked in my arms as my heart desires.' And she replied: 'See how I rid

49

myself of it.' And throwing off her shift she at once enfolded herself in his arms; then clasping each other in a passionate embrace they felt love's power to the full.

What a sweet and much-desired night it was for these two happy lovers! Even if I possessed all the skills that any poet ever had, I should still be unable to describe it. Let those who have at any time advanced so far in Love's favour as these two had now think about it and they will have some notion of the lovers' joy.[5]

They did not draw apart from each other the whole night long. And although still embracing they thought they had been parted from each other – or that they were not really embracing thus but were dreaming of doing so. And they asked each other again and again: 'Am I holding you, or dreaming, or is it really you?'

(35) They gazed at each other with such passion that they never took their eyes away. And they kept asking each other: 'Tell me my love, can it be true that I am here with you?' And just as frequently would come the reply: 'Yes dear heart, thanks be to God.' And closely embracing many a time they tasted the sweetness of each other's kisses.

Troiolo repeatedly kissed Criseida's lovely, love-filled eyes, saying: 'You sent the fiery shafts of love into my heart, and set me all aflame. You caught me, though I did not seek cover in my flight, as would anyone who was afraid. Sweet eyes, you hold me, as you always will, fast in the toils of love.'

Then, whilst Criseida kissed his eyes he also kissed hers yet again, and then her whole face and her breast. And not a moment passed without their breathing a thousand sighs – not the sorrowful sort that turn faces pale, but tender ones through which the depth of the hearts affection was revealed. And these were followed by the renewal of pleasure.

Now let those wretched misers bear this in mind when they find fault with those who are in love and those who, unlike them, are not entirely devoted one way or another to the making of money.[6] And let them ask themselves if that, however dear it may be to them, has ever yielded them as much pleasure as love does in one single moment for those who find themselves blessed by it.

They may say it has but they will be lying. And, although they mock and despise love, calling it a miserable frenzy, they fail to see how a single moment will suffice to deprive them of their money and their lives, without their ever having known in this world what joy is. May God give them sorrow and give their wealth to lovers.

(40) Now that the two lovers were sure of each other they began to share their thoughts, telling each other about their past sorrows, suffering and grief. And all such exchanges were frequently interrupted by passionate kisses; and having thus overcome their earlier troubles they joyfully took their pleasure together.

There was no talk of sleeping then, for they were eager to stay wide awake so that the night should not be wasted. They could not have enough of each other, however many things they said and did that then seemed fit. And they did not let the hours pass idly by but made good use of all of them that night.

But when near day they heard the cocks crowing because the dawn was breaking, their appetite for caresses was aroused again – and they lamented the moment that would separate them and leave them in fresh torment of a sort that neither of them had known before. For they would be parted from each other, yet kindled with far greater passion than before.

And when Criseida heard them crowing she sadly said: 'My love, the time has come for you to rise if we wish to keep our passion properly concealed – but I want to caress you a little before you get up, my love, so as to feel less pain, when you leave. Come, embrace me, joy of my life.'

Troiolo almost in tears embraced her, and clasping her close to him, kissed her, cursing the day that was coming to separate them so soon. Then he began to speak to her, saying: 'This parting grieves me beyond all measure – for how am I ever to leave you, my lady, who give me all the happiness I know?

(45) 'I cannot see why it does not kill me merely to know that I have to go away thus reluctantly and indeed abandon my life, since I am thus banished with death rising up in all its power against me. And I do not know when I shall return. O Fortune, why are you driving me away from this delight which pleases me above all others? Why are you taking all my joy and comfort away?

'Ah what shall I do? – for with my very first step the urge to return comes over me so strongly that it cannot be borne. Why, merciless day, have you come to drive us apart so soon? When will you draw to a close and let us know that we can be reunited? Alas, I do not know.' He thus turned back, and kissing Criseida's fresh face / (47) he said: 'If I thought I could remain as long in your heart, sweet lady, as I shall hold you in mine, it would mean more to me than the kingdom of Troy, and I should endure this separation patiently since, reluctantly, I am facing it. And I should hope to find a time and a way to return here and slake our passions as we have done now.'

Criseida, as she held him tightly clasped in her arms, replied with a sigh: 'Light of my life, if I well remember, I heard it said some time ago that Love is a rapacious spirit, and when he seizes anything he grasps it so hard and fast with his talons that it is no use trying to find ways of releasing it.

'And because of you, my sweet joy, he has fastened on me in such a way that even if I wanted to go back to being as I was at first, do not let yourself imagine I could. You are always at the centre of my thoughts morning and evening, and if I thought I could be so with you, I should think myself happier than I could ever dream of asking.

(50) 'So you may be assured of my love which I never felt more strongly for anyone else. And if you passionately desire to return here, so do I very much more than you. And as soon as I can find a suitable opportunity you will be able to come back. Meanwhile I am in your keeping, dear heart.' And having said this, with a sigh she kissed him.

Troiolo reluctantly rose then, having kissed her a hundred times more; but when he indeed saw what had to be done he put on all his clothes, and when they had spoken a great deal more to each other he said: 'I am departing as you wish; do not let your promises fail me. I leave you in God's keeping and my soul with you.'

She could not speak to answer, so afflicted was she with the pain of parting. So Troiolo set out quickly to walk back to his palace, and keenly sensed love inflaming his desires much more than before, for his experience of Criseida had far surpassed his expecations.

(*The two lovers dwell upon what has taken place, and such thoughts make their joy in their love burn brighter.*)

When Troiolo had returned to his royal palace he quietly went to bed to see if he could sleep for a while in comfort. But sleep could not overcome him for he was made so restless by fresh thoughts, recalling the joys he had left behind and acknowledging how far Criseida's qualities excelled what he had expected.

He continued in his thought to dwell upon everything she had done and the wisdom of her words; and he recalled as well their pleasant and tender exchanges. He went on feeling much greater love for her than he could have thought possible, and such thoughts set him more fiercely ablaze with passion, but he gave no heed to that.

(55) Criseida for her part did the same as she inwardly reflected upon Troiolo, rejoicing at having such a lover and giving Love unceasing thanks for him. And indeed it seems to her like a thousand years until her lover returns to her and she may hold him in her arms and kiss him again and again as she had done the night before.[7]

(*Pandaro comes to see Troiolo, who gives both him and Love the highest praise and tells of his happy experiences.*)

When it was day Pandaro came to see Troiolo, who was already up, and greeted him. Troiolo returned his greeting and eagerly fell upon him and hugged him, saying: 'Dear Pandaro, you are truly welcome.' Then, kissing him tenderly on the forehead he said: 'My friend, you have, as I hope to live, led me out of Hell and into Paradise.

'Even if I gave my life for you a thousand times a day I could never do enough to make up a tiny part of what I fully acknowledge to be your due. For you have turned my bitter grief into joy.' And he kissed him once again and then said: 'Sweet joy of mine that brings me peace – when shall I ever be able to embrace you yet again?

'The sun that looks upon the whole world does not behold a lady who is so lovely and graceful – or who, if what I say is to be trusted, is so courteous, charming and attractive as she whose kindness truly brings more joy into my life than any other man could have. May Love be praised for making me hers – and you likewise for your good offices.

'For it is no trifling gift that you have granted me, and no trifling affair that you have involved me in. I shall be beholden to you for the rest of my life and you will always have it at your command, for you have rescued it from death.' Then he fell silent, more joyful than ever. Pandaro listened to him, paused for a moment, and then cheerfully answered him in this way:

(60) 'My dear sweet friend, if I have done something you really wanted, that is quite enough for me and makes me extremely glad. But nonetheless I must now remind you more than ever to curb your passionate impulses and be discreet – so that now your torment has been overcome

by delight and joy you may not make yourself suffer again by talking too much.'

'I shall do just as you wish in this matter' said Troiolo to his dear friend. Then with the utmost delight he told him about his happy experiences, and continued: 'Indeed, I tell you I was never so deeply embroiled in love as I am now, and the fire that I found in Criseida's eyes and face now burns me much more than any other did before.

'I am more ablaze with passion than ever, and the flames that now burn me are very different from the ones that used to. For joy wells up continually in my heart when I think of the beauty that kindled them – but my desire to return to those loving arms and kiss those delicate features is thus indeed made somewhat fiercer than before.'

The young man could not have enough of talking to Pandaro about the happiness and pleasure he had experienced, and about the ease his sufferings had found and the perfect love he had for Criseida on whom all his hopes rested, for he had become oblivious to all other concerns and desires.

(Troiolo returns to Criseida as he had done before, to converse with her and take delight in love.)

After a little while Fortune smiled on Troiolo and gave him an opportunity to fulfil his desires. So as soon as it grew dark he left his palace unaccompanied, and seeing no stars in the sky he made his way unobserved through the usual entry into the place where his delights were to be found, and remained quietly concealed in the usual place.

(65) Criseida appeared just as promptly this time as she had before, and behaved exactly as she had done then. And after they had exchanged the happy and tender greetings that suited the occasion, they took each other by the hand with great delight, went into the bedchamber together and immediately went to bed.

When Criseida had Troiolo in her arms she joyfully began to speak to him thus: 'Was there or could there ever by any woman who felt such happiness as I do now? Indeed, if there were no other course, who would hesitate for a moment to offer her life in order to share just a little of such joy?'

Then she went on:[8] 'My dear love, I cannot and could never hope to describe the joy and the fierce desire that you have kindled in my breast where I keep your image and where I should like to have all of you always. And I could ask Jupiter for nothing better than to let me hold you like this for ever.

'I do not think this passion can ever be extinguished. I thought it would once we had been together long enough, but indeed it does not seem to have been. Like a blacksmith you have sprinkled water on it to make it blaze up more than it did before – for I never loved you as much as I do now, and I yearn and hunger for you day and night.'

Troiolo said the same kind of thing to her as they lay locked in each others arms. And they murmured to each other all the endearments that often pass between lovers at the height of such pleasure – whilst they kissed each other's lips, eyes and breast, and greeted each other in a way they had not been able to in their letters.

(70) But there were clear signs of the approach of their enemy, daylight – and they angrily upbraided it, since they thought it was appearing much earlier than usual. And this indeed grieved them both, but since nothing could then be done about it they both arose without delay.

And as before they took leave of each other with frequent sighs, and they resolved for the future that they would return to those delights without delay, so that they could assuage their passionate sufferings by being together and devote the pleasant days of their youth to such joys as long as they lasted.

(The author records what Love inspired Troiolo to sing, what his life was like and what gave him pleasure.)

Troiolo was happy and spent his time singing and rejoicing. He set no store by great beauty or delightful appearance in any other woman save his Criseida, and so highly did he value and rejoice in his happiness that he thought all other men were by comparison plunged in abject poverty.

He would sometimes take Pandaro by the hand and go off into a garden with him, and having talked to him first about Criseida's nobility and graciousness, he would then in a carefree mood begin joyfully to sing to him in the form that is set down word for word here:

'Eternal light[9] whose glad brightness adorns the third sphere, from which pleasure, desire, mercy and love rain down upon us – companion of the Sun, daughter of Jupiter, gracious mistress of all noble hearts, true source of that spirit which draws sweet sighs of happiness from me – may your power be for ever praised.

(75) 'The heavens, the earth, the sea and Hell[10] all sense your power, bright light, within them. And, if I judge rightly, plants, seeds, herbs, birds, beasts and fishes, as well as men and gods, feel your everlasting influence during the season of rejoicing,[11] and no created being has strength or life without your help.

'You first made Jupiter take delight in those noble impulses from which all living things have taken their being, and make him indulgent towards those actions of us mortals that offend him – thus turning well-deserved sorrow into glad and pleasant rejoicing. And you earlier sent him down here in a thousand different shapes when you smote him with love for one woman or another.[12]

'You can as you wish make fierce Mars meek and mild,[13] and dispel all feelings of anger. You, goddess, put baseness to flight and fill those who suffer sorrows for your sake with noble pride. You make everyone worthy of such great lordship as he may desire; and you make all those who are in any way touched by your flames courteous and well-mannered.

'You, sweet goddess, keep households, cities, kingdoms, provinces and the whole world in harmony. You are the true source of friendships and of their precious fruits. You alone can see into the inmost nature of things and determine their effects in a way that strikes with wonder those who are ignorant of your power.

'You, O goddess, preserve that law by which the universe continues to exist – and no-one who is hostile to your son, and can endure to remain so, will fail to repent. For I, who before spoke seditiously about him,

54

now, as is just and proper, acknowledge myself to be more deeply in love than I could ever express.

(80) 'I little care should anyone happen to criticize me, for they do not know what they are saying. Let mighty Hercules here come to my defence, for he could not protect himself from love even though wise men all praise him to us for doing so.[14] And no-one who wished to avoid the taint of falsehood would ever say that what was right for Hercules would disgrace me.

'And thus I am in love, and of your mighty achievements this one especially pleases and delights me. I bow to it because by its means, if my soul judges rightly, all pleasures become more perfect and fulfilled than can otherwise be. All other pursuits are far less worthy than this one, which leads me to serve a lady who is lady of more virtues than anyone else.

'This now gives me cause to rejoice and will always continue to do so if I am wise. This gives me cause, O goddess, to praise your radiant and mighty beams, for whose sake I am thankful no weapons could defend me from that bright face where I saw your power displayed and your strength brilliantly apparent.

'And I bless the time – the year, the month, the day, the hour and the moment[15] when she with her modesty, beauty, grace and courtesy first met my gaze. I bless your son who through her power kindled his mighty flames within me, and makes me serve her faithfully and find my happiness in her eyes.

'And I bless those passionate sighs which once for her sake rose from my heart, and I bless the grief and suffering which have led me to win true love. And I bless the burning desires aroused by her surpassingly beautiful looks because they were what was due to one so noble and full of grace.

(85) 'But above all I give thanks to[16] God, who gave to the world such a precious lady and granted my understanding such illumination here below that I rather than anyone else had the joy of kindling a mighty passion within her. And no-one could ever fitly render the thanks that are due for such a favour.

'If I were to speak with the voices of a hundred tongues and had in my heart the wisdom of all the poets, I could never express her true qualities, her noble charms and her abundant courtesy.[17] But if anyone is able to do so I beg that he may lend me the first for a long time, and instruct me in the second.[18]

'You, O goddess, are the one who can bring that about, if only you will – and I implore you to do so. Who could then be deemed happier than I, if you order the remaining course of my life wholly according to our desires? I beg you to do this, O goddess, for I am under your control, and rejected it only when I was ignorant of your real power.

'Let those who wish to, occupy themselves with kingdoms, wealth, weapons, horses, hunting,[19] dogs and hawking[20] – with Pallas's learning and the feats of Mars. But I mean to spend my whole life gazing at my lady's lovely eyes and her true beauties – for my heart is so set upon them that they raise me higher than Jupiter whenever I behold them.

'I cannot offer you the kind of thanks that should be your due, O fair eternal radiance – and so would rather fall silent than fail to render them in full. Bright lantern, do not fail my desire. Prolong, conceal, control and guide my passion and that of the lady I serve, and let me never belong to any other.'

(90) He was always the foremost in furthering the campaign on their side with feats of arms. For he sallied forth from the city against the Greeks so courageously, powerfully and fiercely that unless the account is mistaken, they were all afraid of him. And it was Love, whose devoted servant he was, that endowed him with so much more fighting spirit than he had had before.

During the times of truce he would go hawking with falcons, gerfalcons and eagles. And sometimes he would go hunting with dogs – pursuing bears, boars and mighty lions, and spurning all lesser game. And when at the appointed times he saw Criseida he would become gentle and pleasant again like a falcon emerging from its hood.

His talk was all of love and fine conduct, and was courteous in every way. He was much in favour of honouring those who deserved it and likewise of spurning those who did not. It also pleased him to see young men endowed with noble grace of manner, and he held of no account any man who was not a lover, whatever his status might have been.

And although he was of royal blood and entitled to great respect for other reasons as well, he behaved gently to all alike, even if they were sometimes people who did not deserve it. For Love, whose power is paramount, required him to do so, in order to please another person.[21] He reserved his wrath for pride envy and covetousness, and for what each of those brings with it.

But such happiness lasts but a short while, thanks to envious Fortune who lets nothing remain constant in this world. As the result of an unforeseen accident that occurred she turned[22] a hostile gaze upon him; and turning everything upside down she deprived him of Criseida and all the pleasures he had reaped, and made the happiness of his love turn back again into bitter grief.

Part IV

(Here begins the fourth part of the Filostrato, *in which it is first shown how Criseida came to be returned to her father. Calchas asks for an exchange of prisoners and is granted Antenor. Criseida is sent for and it is decided to hand her over. Troiolo is grief-stricken to begin with, and then he and Pandaro talk about various ways of bringing him comfort. Word of her coming departure reaches Criseida; some ladies visit her, and when they have left she weeps. Pandaro arranges with her for Troiolo to go there that evening. After he has arrived she faints; Troiolo is about to kill himself and she recovers. They go to bed in grief and talk about various things. Eventually Criseida promises to return in ten days time, and Troiolo leaves.*

And to begin with, the Trojans launch an attack in which many of them are captured and killed by the Greeks.)

(1) Since the Greeks had strengthened the grip of the siege around the city, Hector, who was in charge of the whole campaign, chose some of his friends and some other Trojans, and with his picked band sallied forth valiantly on to the level plain to do battle with the Greeks as he had done with various results on many earlier occasions.

The Greeks advanced to meet him, and they spent that whole day in fierce combat. But in the end the Trojans' line failed to hold and as a result they were all forced to take flight in difficult conditions, suffering losses. Many died in anguish and misery, and many kings and great lords among them were taken prisoner.

Amongst these was the mighty Antenor,[1] with his son Polydamas, Menestheus, Xanthippus, Sarpedon and Polymestor, as well as Polites and the Trojan Ripheus and many more whom Hector's valour could not protect during the retreat. And so there was great grief and affliction in Troy, together with some apprehension of far worse trouble to come.

Priam requested a truce,[2] which he was granted, and they began that round of negotiations about the exchange of prisoners and the payment of gold as ransom for the remainder. When Calchas heard about this he came before the Greeks in a different role,[3] appealing in a feeble voice for them simply to give him a hearing.

(Calchas's speech to the Greeks in which he pleads his merits to them and then asks for a prisoner, to enable him to regain Criseida.)

(5) 'My lords,' began Calchas, 'I was as you all know a Trojan, and, if you well recall, it was I who first gave you confidence in your present mission, telling you that in the fullness of time you would succeed and gain victory in you campaign, and that at your hands Troy would be sacked and burnt.

'You know both the procedure and the tactics to adopt, since I have shown you. And in order that all your desires might be accomplished within the prophesied time I did not rely upon messengers of any kind or on private or public communications, but came to you here, as can be seen, to give you advice and help in this affair.

'Since this was what I wanted to do, I had to arrange my departure with care and great secrecy and without letting anyone know about it. And so I did:[4] as soon as the bright daylight had faded I left the city and quietly made my way here, bringing nothing with me and leaving all that I had there.

'I care little or nothing about any of it, except for a young daughter of mine whom I left behind. Alas, what a harsh, hard-hearted father I was! If only I had brought that abandoned creature to safety here! But fear and haste would not allow it; and that is what I regret most of the things I left in Troy, and that is what robs me of my happiness and joy.

'And I have not yet found any opportunity here of asking for her return; hence I kept silent. But now is the time for me to obtain her, if I may beg such a favour of you. And if that cannot be granted now, I shall never hope to see her again and will from now on let my life go as it may, not caring whether I live or die.

(10) 'With you here are noble lords and many other Trojans whom you will be exchanging with the enemy for those of you that they hold prisoner. Let me have just one out of all these, and in exchange for his release I shall be able to have my daughter again. For God's sake, my lords, bring some relief to this aged wretch who is destitute and bereft of all other comfort.

'And do not let yourselves be swayed by the desire for gold in exchange for the prisoners – for I swear to you by God that all the strength of Troy and all its wealth are indeed at your mercy. And if I am not deceived about it, the prowess of him who keeps the gates barred against the desires of all of you will soon be eclipsed, as will be shown by his violent death.'

(Antenor was granted to Calchas; and in the presence of Troiolo Criseida was asked for, and it was decided to hand her over.)

Whilst the old priest was speaking these words with a humble voice and expression he continually made his cheeks run with tears, bathing his white beard and flinty bosom with them. And his pleas did not fail to move, for when he had fallen silent the Greeks resoundingly cried out in unison: 'Let him be given Antenor.'

So this was done and Calchas was content, entrusting the business to the negotiators who conveyed his wishes to King Priam and to his sons and the nobles who were also present. They then considered the question together and briefly replied to the ambassadors that if they were to hand over those that had been requested their own people should be released.

Troiolo was present when the Greeks made their request, and when he heard them ask for Criseida he suddenly felt his heart transfixed within by such a sharp pain that he thought he would die as he sat there. But with a great effort he managed to restrain his passion and grief as he had to.

(15) And full of anguish and fierce trepidation he began to await the reply, wondering more anxiously than ever what he could do if he were so unfortunate as to find his brothers deciding between them to hand over Criseida to Calchas, and how he could effectively prevent that.

Love made him ready to face all odds and resist, but Reason on the other hand was opposed to that, casting great doubt upon such a noble impulse since it might as a result offend Criseida's modesty. So the anxious youth kept wavering this way and that, uncertain which course he should choose.

Whilst he thus remained irresolute the barons considered what events had now rendered necessary. And, as we have said, a full reply was given to those awaiting it, saying that Criseida would be handed over and had never been forcibly detained.

(Troiolo faints on hearing that Criseida is to be handed over, and then quickly leaves the council session.)

Just as the lily in the fields when sliced by the plough droops and wilts in the overpowering sun, and its lovely hue changes and fades[5] – so did Troiolo, overwhelmed by his loss and peril, collapse there stricken with grief when the Trojans announced their eventual decision to the Greeks.

Priam, Hector and his brothers raised him in their arms, overcome with dismay at what had happened. They all tried to help him and, being practical people, they attempted to bring his senses back to life first by rubbing his wrists and then by bathing his face again and again – but their efforts were of little use at first.

(20) He lay among his companions stretched out and overcome and with few signs of life yet remaining in him. His face was all pale, wan and sombre, and he looked like one more dead than alive, bearing as he did such signs of sorrow upon him that he made everyone weep. Such was the force of the bolt from on high that struck him down when he heard that Criseida was to be surrendered.

But after his sad spirit had been absent wandering for a long while it quietly returned, and then, like someone awakening all in a daze, he quickly rose to his feet and before anyone could ask what had been the matter with him he pretended he had other things to do and left them.

And he went away to his palace without listening to or looking at anyone. And in that sorrowful and pitiful state he went up to his bed-chamber, refusing all company and saying he wanted to rest. So all his friends and servants, however close they were to him, went out, having first barred the windows.[6]

(The author, who usually appeals to his lady for aid, here refuses to do so, saying that since he himself is suffering, he is thus enabled to describe the sorrows of others.)

I hardly care, sweet lady, if you have no part in what follows, for unless my feeble memory leads them astray, my own skills will suffice to convey the profound suffering that I sadly feel overcoming me as the result of your departure. And I shall need no assistance from you who have been the cause of such bitter pangs.

I have up until this point been celebrating the joys that Troiolo found in love, although these were mingled with sighs. Now I must turn from bliss to sorrow, and thus do not care if you pay me no heed, for your heart will be forced to change and inspire you with pity for my existence which is sadder than any other.

(25) But if this ever reaches your ears, I beg you for the sake of the love I bear you to have some regard for my sufferings and by returning restore the peace you took from me when you left. And if it would displease you to find me dead, return quickly, for your departure has left me with little life remaining.

(The author describes Troiolo's grief, anguish and lamentations about Criseida's coming departure.)

When Troiolo had thus been left alone in his locked and darkened room and no longer needed to pay heed to anyone or worry about being over-heard, the grief that this sudden misfortune had heaped up within his sorrowful heart began to break forth in such a way that he seemed to be not a man but a raging beast.

A bull which plunges to and fro once it has received the death-blow and shows the pain it feels by pitiful bellowing[7] acts no differently from Troiolo when, in the depths of despair, he unrestrainedly battered his head against the wall, beat his face with his hands and his wretched arms with his fists.

His sad eyes in sympathy with his heart[8] wept bitterly and looked like two fountains spouting water in torrents. His great sobs of grief made his vain words even fainter – yet these as well as his earlier wild cries went on invoking death alone as he cursed and derided the gods and himself.

But once this great fury had subsided and his lamentations had been tempered by time, Troiolo threw himself down on his bed for a while in a raging torment of grief. But he did not in any way give up weeping bitterly and sighing so deeply that his head and breast could hardly sustain the amount of distress he was causing himself.

(30) Then shortly afterwards he began plaintively to ask: 'Wretched Fortune,[9] what have I done to you to make you oppose all my desires? Have you nothing else to do but cause me suffering? Why have you so suddenly turned threatening looks upon me, when I have indeed been worshipping you more than any other god? – and that you know, cruel as you are.

'If it displeased you to see my life so joyful and pleasant, why did you not overthrow the pride of haughty Ilium? Why did you not deprive me of my father or of Hector whose valour is our only hope in these troubled times? Why did you not carry off Polyxena – ah, why not Paris, indeed, and Helen as well?

'If Criseida alone had been left me I should not have been affected or moved to complain by any other great loss. But your shafts always fly straight at what we desire most, and in order to show more fully the extent of your trickery you took away all my happiness. Ah, if only you had killed me instead!

'Alas, Love, my sweet and gentle lord – you who know what lies within my soul; what will happen to my wretched life if I lose my happiness and peace of mind? Alas, sweet Love, who used to sustain my soul – true lord, what shall I do if I lose the lady you commanded me to serve?

'I shall weep and mourn always wherever I may be as long as life lasts in this anguished frame of mine. O wretched bewildered soul – why do you not take flight from the most ill-starred body alive? Flee from my breast, sad soul, and follow Criseida. Why do you not do so – why do you not vanish?

(35) 'O mournful eyes, whose sole comfort was the sight of our own Criseida's face – what will you do? Since that is denied you, you will from now on dwell forever in bitter grief; and your powers will be destroyed, vanquished and overcome by your weeping. It will be vain for you now to look upon any other heavenly beauty, for your salvation[10] has been taken from you.

'O Criseida, sweet delight of the soul that cries out in sorrow for you – who will yet console me for my sufferings? Who will assuage my passionate longings? If you go, alas, this wretch who loves you more than himself will have to die. And I shall die, without having deserved to. Let the blame for that rest with the pitiless gods.

'If only this departure of yours could have been delayed until, through long practice, alas, I had learnt how to suffer. I do not mean that I should not have done everything in my power to prevent your going – but if I saw that it had to be, parting from you which now seems so hard would through long practice appear easy.

'And you, vicious and demented old man – what delusion or resentment made you, a Trojan, go over to the Greeks? Was any citizen or foreigner more highly honoured than you throughout our kingdom? Evil schemer with your heart full of treachery, trickery and trouble – if only I had you at my mercy in Troy!

'If only you had died the day you went away, or died at the feet of the Greeks the moment you opened your mouth to reclaim that lady who commands my love. Oh what an evil day it was for me when you came into the world! You are the cause of the grief that afflicts me so; if only the lance that Protesilaus[11] hurled could have been planted by Menelaus in your heart!

(40) 'If you were dead, I should be assured of life, for there would then be no-one seeking Criseida. If you were dead I should not be abandoned, for Criseida would not be leaving me. If you were dead I know very well I should no longer be suffering the pain I now feel. Thus your life is the miserable cause of my death and my sad fate.'

(Troiolo falls asleep; then he has Pandaro called, and they commiserate with one another, considering a number of ways of assisting Troiolo.)

A thousand sighs, fiercer than fire, flowed without ceasing from his passionate breast. And such lamentations so exhausted him that the young man could do nothing other than fall asleep, but he had slept hardly any time before he awoke again.

And sighing he rose to his feet, went to the door he had locked, opened it and said to a manservant of his: 'Make no delay but quickly call Pandaro and get him to come to me.' Then he sorrowfully withdrew into the darkness of his room, full of sad thoughts and heavy with sleep.

Pandaro arrived; he had already found out what the Greek envoys sought and furthermore how those in authority had decided to hand over Criseida. Thus with a look of utter dismay and his mind upon Troiolo's troubles, he entered the dark and silent room, not knowing whether to speak sadly or cheerfully.

As soon as he saw him, Troiolo ran and threw his arms about his neck, weeping so bitterly that no-one could fully describe it. Pandaro, already sorrowful, was so moved with pity for him that seeing this he began to weep. And this was how they remained for a time, doing nothing but weep bitterly with neither of them speaking a word.

(45) But when Troiolo had drawn breath he spoke first, saying: 'O Pandaro, I am dying. Alas – my happiness, my sweet solace, has been exchanged for grief. Treacherous Fortune has borne it away, together with all my pleasure and delight. Have you yet heard how my Criseida is to be taken from me by the Greeks?'

Weeping no less bitterly Pandaro replied: 'Yes – if only it were not true! Alas for me, I never thought that such a sweet, untroubled[12] time as this could end so soon – nor could I see what, apart from discovery, could have stopped you being entirely happy. Now I see our judgment was wholly at fault.

'But why are you making yourself so miserable? – why all this grief and affliction? You have had what you sought and should content yourself with that alone. Leave such laments to me, along with others – for I have loved constantly and never received a glance from the lady who is destroying me and who alone can bring me peace.

'And moreover this city appears to be full of lovely and graceful women, and, if my goodwill towards you can be trusted, there is none of them – even the sweetest you could wish for – who would not be happy to have pity upon you if you started suffering pangs of passion for her sake. So if we lose this one we shall find plenty more.

'And, as I have often heard tell, a new passion always drives out the old,[13] and new delights will chase away your present sufferings if you do as I say. So do not think of dying for her and do not think of doing yourself harm. Do you think that by weeping you can get her back, perhaps, or prevent her going away?'

(50) When he heard Pandaro, Troiolo began to weep more bitterly, saying then: 'I pray God may send me death before I commit any such outrage. Although, I grant you, other women may be lovely, graceful and wise, none of them at all resembles the one I so devotedly belong to.

'From her lovely eyes issued the sparks that set the fire of passion ablaze within me. These, passing in their thousands through my eyes, gently ushered Love into my heart, where he placed them according to his will. And there they kindled for the first time that fire whose mighty power has been the source of all my noble deeds.

'And even if I wanted to – as I do not – I could never put that out, for it is too strong. And if it were yet stronger I should still not complain, so long as Criseida remained with us – for it is her departure, not love, that inflicts such piercing grief upon my loving heart. And, without meaning to offend the others, there is no other woman who can match her in any way.

'So how could Love or words of comfort from anyone ever turn my desires towards another woman? My heart has much anguish to bear, but suffering would have to have made me desperate before I would set my heart upon anyone else. May Love, God and the whole world prevent that.

'And death and the grave alone can make me part with this constant love, whatever I may have to endure. They will make my soul accompany it[14] down to their final torments in Hell. Together there they will weep for Criseida whom I shall always belong to wherever I am, so long as love is not forgotten in death.[15]

(55) 'Therefore in God's name, Pandaro, cease this talk of another woman entering my heart. There Criseida with her virtuous demeanour[16] remains as the true object of my delight, however much her departure, which we have spoken of, may affect a heart that is so quick to suffer – for we cannot begin to think of her going.

'Yet you speak of it in rational terms[17] as if it were less painful to lose than never to have possessed at all. And that is plain foolishness, Pandaro; you should remember that the kind of suffering ill fortune inflicts on those who have once been happy exceeds all others[18] – and those who say otherwise are mistaken.

'But if you are so anxious about my love and think it so easy to change lovers as you have just said – tell me, why have you not altered course, since your frustrated passion brings you so much pain? Why did you not go after some woman who could have made your life happy?

'If you who have been used to suffering for love have been unable to turn elsewhere – how should I, having gained happiness and joy from it, be able to dismiss it as you advise, just because I now find myself suddenly faced with pain? I am more deeply affected than you could ever imagine.

'Believe me, Pandaro, that once Love has taken hold[19] and given the utmost pleasure to one's soul it can never be driven out, although it may well fall away in the course of time through sorrow, death, poverty or the lover's absence – as has indeed been the case for many people.

(60) 'What then shall I do, luckless wretch that I am, if I thus lose[20] Criseida? For Antenor has now been exchanged for her. Alas, I would rather have died or never been born. What shall I do, pray? My soul despairs, and I beg you, Death, to come now I call for you. Come, I beg, and do not let me pine away for love.

'You will be as pleasant to me, Death, as life is to one who lives in happiness. Your terrible countenance no longer makes me afraid – so come and put an end to my suffering. I beg you not to delay, for this fiery torment has so inflamed all my blood that your stroke will come to cool my fever. Come, I beg, now that my heart yearns for you alone.

'Kill me in God's name; do not let me live in this world long enough to see the heart departing from my body. Come, Death – do so, I beg you for God's sake, for that would grieve me far more than dying; grant that much of my desire. Indeed, you slay so many others against their will that you could well do me this favour.'

Thus Troiolo lamented as he wept; and Pandaro wept too – often trying nonetheless to console him as sympathetically as he could. But such consolation had no effect. Instead his sorrowful lamentations and his suffering increased, so desperate had he now become.

Pandaro said to him: 'Dear friend, if my arguments fail to interest you, and if this coming separation from her is as bitter for you as it appears, why do you not take the remedy for the situation into your own hands and carry her off? Paris went to Greece and brought away Helen, the flower of all women, / (65) and do you not dare in Troy to carry off the woman you desire? If you have faith in me you will do so. Have done with your grief – have done, and banish your sorrows and your woeful laments. Wipe away the sad tears from your face and show what a noble soul you have by taking steps to make Criseida ours.'

Troiolo then answered Pandaro: 'I see well, my friend, that you are trying with all your skill to ease my desperate sufferings. I have thought about what you say and have also been considering many other possibilities, even though I have been weeping and giving way to this grief which has come as such a shock and overwhelmed all my powers.

'Yet in spite of my desperate passion it[21] has not completely robbed me of my judgment. And having thus considered, I have realized that the moment is not right for such extreme measures. If all our people, including Antenor, were back in this very place, I should not be concerned about breaking faith – but, come what may, I would do it.

'I am also afraid that I may cast a slur upon her honour and reputation by abducting her; and I am not sure whether she would be happy about it, even though I know she loves me so much. And so my heart is unable to decide – being driven by desire on the one hand, and on the other fearing to offend. For I should not wish to keep her without her consent.

'I had also thought of asking my father for her to be bestowed on me as a favour. But then I thought that this would be tantamount to accusing her and making what we have done public knowledge. Nor do I even have any hope that he would be able to let me have her – both because he would not want to break the terms of the agreement and because he would say that she is not a proper match for me, since he wishes me to wed a lady of royal birth.

(70) 'Thus, alas, love keeps me in a state of miserable uncertainty, and I know not what to do. For whilst the strength of passion alone increases in me, I find my own strength failing, hope taking flight in all directions and the sources of pain multiplying. I wish I had died the day such desire was first kindled within me.'

Pandaro then said: 'You will do as you please, but if I were in such a blaze of passion as you appear to be, and although it would be a grave responsibility – given the power you have and provided she was not withheld from me by force – I should do my utmost to get her away regardless of anyone it might offend.

'When a passionate soul is well and truly aflame Love does not make such fine distinctions as you appear to do. And if Love is attacking you as fiercely as you say, bow to his will and face this cruel affliction manfully, choosing rather to risk some reproach than suffer and die in woe.

'You will not be carrying off a woman whose wishes are far from your own but one who is prepared to approve whatever you do. And if you encounter a great deal of trouble or reproach because of this, there is a speedy way to deal with it – in other words by giving her back. Fortune favours the bold and spurns the fearful.

'And even if this action gave offence, you would soon be reconciled with her about it – although I think that she appreciates your love for her so well that she would not let it bother her. As for losing her reputation – that, to tell you the truth, is less of a problem or disgrace. Let her do without it, as Helen does, so long as she does everything you wish.

(75) 'So take courage and be brave – for love heeds neither promise nor pledge. Show some spirit at this stage, and look to your own interests. I shall give you support at any dangerous moments as far as I am able to. If only you are bold enough to act, it will then be up to the gods to lend us their aid.'

Troiolo listened very closely to what Pandaro was saying and replied: 'I agree – but even if the flames of my passion were a thousand times fiercer and my suffering greater than it is, I would sooner die than cause the slightest trouble to that gracious lady by seeking my own satisfaction. So I want to hear about this first from her.'

'Then let us rise up and make no more delay. Wash your face, and let us go back to court hiding our sorrow behind a smile. People have discovered nothing yet, but if we stay here anyone who finds out about it will be led to wonder. Take care then to keep things well concealed, and I will arrange for you to speak to Criseida this evening.'

(*The news of her departure reaches Criseida, and a number of women visit her, and cause her no little distress.*)

Rumour, the speediest of creatures,[22] who brings false and true reports alike, had flown all through Troy on the swiftest of wings, and described most precisely what the purpose of the Greek mission had been and that Criseida had been given to the Greeks by the king in exchange for Antenor.

As soon as she heard this news Criseida, who indeed no longer cared for her father, said to herself: 'Alas, my poor heart!' And this gave her great distress, for she had given her heart to Troiolo whom she loved beyond all others. And she did not dare to ask about what she had heard for fear that it was true.

(80) But just as it is usual for one woman who is fond of another to call on her when her circumstances change – thus a number of them came, all overcome with both sadness and joy, to be with Criseida during the day – and they began to tell her step by step what had taken place, how she had been given up, and what the terms were.

One of them would say: 'I'm really very pleased that you'll be going back to be with your father.' Another would say: 'Me too – but I'm sorry to see her leaving us.' Another would say: 'With him she'll be able to make peace for us – and he, you know, as we have heard, can make the others do anything he wants.'

She listened to this and much more women's talk as if she were not there, and gave no reply since she held it of little account. But her lovely face could not conceal the deep and noble concerns about love that had been prompted by the news she had heard. Her body was there and her soul elsewhere searching for Troiolo, it knew not where.

In her own thoughts she was much vexed by these women who thought they were bringing her comfort by being there – and, for her own part, her soul was stirred by passions far different from the ones those present imputed to her. And again and again she would politely take leave of them, so strong was her desire to be rid of them.

But she could not keep back a sigh or two, and occasionally a small tear gave, as it dropped, a hint of the suffering that oppressed her soul. But those foolish women gathered about her thought the young woman was behaving thus because she was going to be deprived of their accustomed companionship.

(85) And they each sought to give her comfort about the very things that gave her no pain. They spent a great many words consoling her for having to leave them – and that was just like scratching her on the heels when her head itched, for she cared nothing about them but only about leaving Troiolo.

(*When the women have left Criseida weeps and bewails her coming separation from Troiolo.*)

But after a great deal of the pointless chatter women usually indulge in, they took their leave and went away; and then, suddenly overwhelmed and impelled by bitter grief, she went weeping softly into her chamber, and without restraining her great distress in any way she wept as no-one has ever done before.

The grief-stricken woman had flung herself down upon her bed, weeping more bitterly than could be described – beating her white breast again and again – calling upon Death to slay her, since she was cruelly destined to abandon all her joys – pulling and tearing her golden hair, and continually praying for death a thousand times each hour.

She said: 'Alas for me, luckless and wretched woman – where am I to turn in my misery? Woe is me – what an evil hour it was when I was born! Where am I leaving you, my sweet love? If only I had been smothered at birth or never seen you, sweet desire of mine – since such a cruel fate is robbing me of you and you of me.

'What shall I do, my poor soul, when I can no longer see you? What shall I do, Troiolo, when I am parted from you? I know for certain I shall never eat or drink – and if my desperate spirit does not leave my body of its own accord, I shall do my utmost to drive it out through hunger, for I can see that from now on my fortunes will continue to go from bad to worse.

(90) 'Now I shall indeed be a widow, since I must be deprived of you, dear heart of mine, and black clothing will bear true witness to my suffering. Alas for me, what terrible thoughts does parting raise in me! Alas, Troiolo, how can I bear to see myself separated from you?

'How shall I be able to live without a soul? Surely it will stay here together with our love and you to bewail the sad parting which has been brought upon us as the reward for such true love. Alas, dear Troiolo, can you bear now to see me go? Why do you not do all you can to hold me back by tenderness or force?

'I shall depart not knowing whether I shall every be able to see you again, my sweet love. But if you love me so much what will you do? Will you, alas, be able to bear the pain? I indeed shall not do so, for I am sure that overwhelming grief will break my heart. Ah, if only that would happen soon, then I should be released from this deep anguish.

'O father, how unjust and disloyal you have been towards your native land – and may the moment be accursed when that evil impulse to join the Greeks and leave the Trojans entered your breast! God grant you may go down to the pit of Hell when you die, you evil old man who have acted so treacherously in your last years!

'Alas for me, I in my grief and woe am made to do penance for your sin! My own faults did not make me deserve such a miserable fate. O heavenly justice, light of mercy – how can you let it be decreed that one should commit the sin and the other weep for it as I am doing? For I did no wrong and yet am consumed with grief.'

(*Pandaro finds Criseida weeping, talks to her for a while and then arranges for Troiolo to come.*)

(95) Who could ever recount all that Criseida said in her grief? Not I certainly, for her distress was so cruel and fierce that words fail to describe it. But while such laments are being uttered Pandaro, to whom the door was never barred, arrived and went into the chamber where she was weeping so miserably.

He found her upon the bed overwhelmed with sobs and sighs of grief – her whole face and bosom bathed in tears, her eyes two wells of weeping[23] and her dishevelled appearance truly reflecting her bitter sufferings. And when she saw him she buried her face in her arms for shame.

'It was a sad moment' began Pandaro, 'when I left my bed, for wherever I go today I find sorrow, suffering, tears, anguish and loud laments; and sighs, distress and bitter despair seem to be everywhere. O Jupiter, what are you about to do? I think you disapprove so much of what we have done that you are raining down tears from Heaven.

'And you, my unhappy sister, what do you think you are doing? Do you think you can fly in the face of Fate? Why are you ruining your beautiful appearance with such bitter and excessive grief? Get up, turn this way and speak to me. Lift up your face, dry your mournful eyes a moment and listen to what I am saying, for it is your dear friend who has sent me.'

Criseida then turned around and with an outburst of weeping that could not be described she gazed at Pandaro and said: 'Woe is me – what does he want, my own soul whom I am destined to yield up in tears, not knowing if I will ever be able to see him again? Does he want sighs or tears? – or what does he require? I have plenty of them, if they are what he is sending for.'

(100) To look at her appearance was like looking at a woman being borne to the grave, and her face that had been moulded in Heaven appeared completely changed. Her charm and pleasing smile had fled and abandoned her,[24] and around her eyes a purple ring bore witness to her suffering.[25]

Pandaro who had been weeping with Troiolo much of the day could not restrain his tears when he saw this, but started to do the same, forgetting what he had meant to say and joining her in her bitter weeping. But when they had both continued thus for a while Pandaro was the first to check his tears.

And he said: 'My lady, I think – indeed I am sure – you have heard how you have been asked for by your father, and that it has been decided by the king to give you up; so that, if what I hear is true, you will have to go within the week. And I can hardly say how painful this is to Troiolo who is thus overcome by grief and seeking to die.

'And he and I have shed so many tears to-day that I cannot think where they have come from; but now at last, on my advice, he has restrained his weeping for a while and seems to want to be with you. Hence, as he wished, I have come to let you know, so that you may unburden your hearts to each other for a while before you part.'

'My grief is great,' said Criseida, 'as befits one who loves him more than herself. But his is much greater than mine since, as I hear, it is because of me that he longs for death. Now if hearts can be broken by bitter grief, mine will be. Now I recognize Fortune's sly treachery, for she is taking her fill of my sufferings.

(105) 'God knows this parting is hard enough for me to bear, but I swear I find the sight of Troiolo's sufferings so unbearable that it will make me die at once. And I seek death without hope of being spared, since I know that my Troiolo is thus stricken. Tell him to come when he will, for that would give the greatest possible relief to my anguish.'

And having said this she flung herself down once more and began to weep again with her head buried in her arms. Pandaro said to her: 'Alas, poor wretch, what are you going to do now? Does it give you no comfort to know that you will very soon be embracing the man you love so much? Get

67

up – pull yourself together, and don't let him find you in such a desperate state.

'If he knew that this is what you were doing, he would kill himself and no-one would be able to stop him. And if I thought you were going to remain this way, he would not set foot here while I could do anything about it – for I know it would be at the risk of his life. So get up and start setting yourself to rights, so that you can relieve his suffering, not increase it.'

'Go, dear Pandaro,' said Criseida, 'I promise you I will do my best. When you have left I will get up from bed at once and keep my troubles and the thought of my lost joys securely locked within my heart. Just let him come exactly as he has done before; he will find the door ajar as usual.'

(Pandaro comforts Troiolo once again, telling him that he is to go to Criseida the next evening – and so he does.)

Returning to Troiolo, Pandaro found him in such a sad state and looking so utterly dejected that he was seized with pity and sorrow, saying to him: 'Are you then as discouraged as you look, my brave young fellow? Your loved one[26] has not yet left you, so why are you now so desolate that the very eyes in your face look dead?

(110) 'You lived for a long time without her; can you not find the courage to go on living still? Did you come into the world for her sake alone? Show some manliness; take heart again and rid yourself of these sorrows and lamentations to some degree at least. I have not stopped anywhere, save here with you, since speaking to her and spending a great deal of time with her.

'And from what I saw, you do not feel half the distress that she does, for there is such passion behind her sighs because of her unhappiness at this parting that each of them is twenty times greater than yours. So give yourself some consolation; for in this sad state of affairs you can at least be sure how dear you are to her.

'I have just arranged with her for you to go there and be with her tonight. And then you can present her with what you have just decided in the most attractive way possible. You will very soon see how to gain her complete approval, and perhaps you will also find ways of achieving considerable relief from your sufferings.'

With a sigh Troiolo answered him: 'Your advice is good, and I mean to follow it.' And he said a great deal more, but when he thought it time for him to go, he went away leaving Pandaro to think about it. And it seemed to him like a thousand years before he could be in the arms of his dear delight, whom Fortune afterwards unjustly took from him.

(Criseida faints in Troiolo's arms and he, thinking her to be dead, draws his sword with the intention of killing himself.)

Criseida at the accustomed hour and moment came to meet him with a lighted torch,[27] welcoming him with an embrace; and he did the same, overwhelmed as he was with deep sorrow. And, though silent, neither of them could conceal the pain they each felt in their hearts; but having embraced without exchanging a word, they began to weep long and bitterly.

(115) And in floods of weeping they held each other close, and although they wanted to speak they could not, for they were so overcome by anguished tears, sobs and sighs. But nonetheless they kissed again and again, and drank each other's tears as they fell, not caring how much more bitter than usual they were.

But once their distress had been sufficiently eased to let the spirits disturbed by their anguished tears and sighs return to their dwellings,[28] Criseida raised her eyes that were full of sorrow and fierce yearning to Troiolo, and asked in broken tones: 'O my lord, who is it that is parting me from you, and whither am I going?'

Then her heart was wrung with such grief that her strength failed her and she fell fainting with her face upon his bosom, and her soul struggled to take flight. And Troiolo as he gazed into her face, calling her yet not making himself heard, was convinced by the way she had closed her eyes and collapsed that she was dead.

When he saw this he was stricken with redoubled grief and laid her down, kissing her tear-stained face again and again – looking to see if he could find any sign of life in her. He sadly examined her and sorrowfully concluded that as far as he could judge she had departed from a life that had become so comfortless.

She was cold and completely unresponsive as far as he could see, and he thought this was clear proof that she had come to the end of her days. And so, after much lamentation and before going on to do anything else, he dried her face and arranged her body in the way people usually do with those that are dead.

(120) And when he had done that he resolutely drew his own sword out of its scabbard – fully resolved to seek death, in order that his spirit might follow the same sad fate as his lady's and dwell with her in Hell, since harsh Fortune and cruel Love had banished it[29] from this life.

But first, burning with noble indignation, he said: 'See now, cruel Jupiter and you, evil-minded Fortune, how I have been brought to the point you desired. You have bereft me of my Criseida, whom I thought you would take from me in a different way;[30] and where she is now, I do not know; but here I see her body most unjustly struck down by you.

'And since that is what you want, I shall also leave this life and follow her as a spirit. Perhaps in the beyond I shall have better fortune and be able to assuage my desires with her – if they continue to love there as I have sometimes heard they do.[31] So, if you do not wish me to remain alive, at least let my soul follow hers.

'And you, my city that I leave in the throes of war, and you Priam, and you my dear brothers – I bid you God-speed, for I am going down to the underworld to follow Criseida's lovely eyes. And you, Criseida, who are making me endure such grief and are plucking the soul from my body – receive me.' This is what he was in the midst of saying, with his sword already placed against his breast in readiness for death – / (124) when she, recovering herself, heaved a great sigh and called for Troiolo. And he said to her: 'My sweet love, are you still alive, then?' And weeping he took her in his arms again and soothed her suffering as best he could with words of comfort, and her wandering soul returned to the bosom from which it had fled.

(*The two lovers go to bed and there they sigh and weep and talk about many different things, and then in the morning they rise.*)

(125) Being utterly dazed for a while, she remained silent. But then, seeing the sword she began to ask: 'Why has that been drawn from its scabbard?' And Troiolo then weeping told her of the state he had been in. At that she said: 'Can what I hear be true? If I had then stayed thus a little longer, would you have killed yourself here?

'Alas, woe is me – what have you told me? I would never have remained alive after you, but would have plunged the sword into my own sorrowful heart. So now we have much to thank God for. Let us for the time being go to bed,[32] and there talk over our troubles. From the amount that the torch has burnt down, I think a great deal of the night has already gone by.'

Their embraces were just as passionate on this occasion as they had been on others, but they were now rendered more bitter by tears than they had ever been sweetened by pleasure. They started their sorrowful conversation straight away. And Criseida began by saying: 'Dear friend, listen very closely to what I say.

'After I had heard the sad news about that wicked traitor, my father, I then – as I hope God may preserve your lovely face for me – felt such pain as I have never felt before. For I am not one to care for gold, cities or palaces – all I want is for me to be happy and contented with you and you with me.

'And I was on the way to utter despair, since I thought I should never see you again. But since you saw my spirit go wandering and then come back once again, I have found some ideas which may be useful entering my mind, and I want to explain these to you before we make ourselves yet more unhappy – for we may yet perhaps have good grounds for hope.

(130) 'You know that my father is asking for me, but I should not consent to go back to him were I not compelled to do so by the king – and his word, as you must know, has to be kept. So when Diomedes, who has helped bring about this wicked agreement, comes back, I shall have to go away with him. God grant that neither he nor such an evil moment may ever arrive!

'And you know that all my relations apart from my father are in this place and that all my belongings remain here. And, if I remember rightly there have been continual talks between yourselves and the Greeks about concluding this perilous struggle with a settlement. And, if Menelaus's wife is given back to him, I think you will get it, for I already believe you are very close to doing so.

'And if you achieve that, I shall come back here, for I have nowhere else to go; and if by chance you should fail to do so, I shall find opportunities to come here during times of truce, for you know that permission to make such visits is seldom denied to women. And my relatives will be very eager to see me and invite me here.

'And then we may rejoice somewhat, even though the delay will cause us great distress. But one must be ready to bear the burden if one wishes afterwards to taste the joy with keener pleasure. I know that even while in

Troy we sometimes have to spend many days in terrible torment, not being able to see each other.

'And, peace or no peace, yet more hope of returning here now stirs within me. My father is affected by this longing at the moment, perhaps believing that as a result of his crime I cannot remain here without the risk of being subjected to violence or abuse. When he finds out how respected I am here, he will not worry about my coming back.

(135) 'And what purpose would he have for keeping me among the Greeks, who, as you know are always in readiness for war? If he does not keep me there, I do not see that he can send me elsewhere – and even if he could do so, I do not think he would, for he would be unwilling to entrust me to the Greeks. It will be best for him, then, to send me back here, and I do not foresee anything to prevent that.

'He is, as you know, old and miserly, and has affairs that need to be dealt with or discussed here. And for that reason I shall tell him that if they matter to him, he had better let me come back here – showing him that I can protect his interests against all dangers that may arise. And his greed will make him glad to let me return.'

Troiolo listened to his lady closely, and what she said affected him. It seemed to him that what she declared certain would be quite likely – but since he loved her so dearly, he gave credence to it only slowly. But in the end, although he was much inclined to seek further evidence, he brought himself to believe her.

Thus part of their deep sorrow disappeared and hope returned; and having become less gloomy in their thoughts, they entered once more upon the familiar delights of love. And just as a bird, hopping from leaf to leaf in the springtime, takes delight in its song, so did they in talking together about a number of things.

But Troiolo could not rid his heart of the knowledge that his lady would have to leave him, and so he began to speak to her in this way: 'O Criseida, my love – you are dearer to me than any goddess, and command more devotion, for I was about to kill myself when I thought you were dead. What sort of life do you think will be left me if you do not return quickly?

(140) 'You may be as sure as death that I will kill myself if you delay coming back here at all long. I do not yet know how I am to survive without painful and bitter affliction when I know that you are somewhere else; and fresh doubts are springing up in me that Calchas may perhaps keep you back, and that what you are speaking of may not happen.

'I do not know whether peace between us will ever be achieved, but peace or no peace, I think Calchas is far from wanting to return here at any time; for – let us not deceive ourselves – he could not imagine[33] he would be able to live here free from the stigma of his crime, grave as it was. And as he is asking for you so insistently, I can hardly believe he will send you back.

'He will choose a husband for you from among the Greeks, and will claim that for you to remain amongst those beseiged[34] would make you risk falling into trouble. He will flatter you and make the Greeks honour you, for he is, as I hear, highly respected there and his powers much valued. And so it gives me no little distress to think that you will never return to Troy.

'And that is a thought that oppresses me more than I can tell you, sweet soul. For you alone hold the keys of life and death for me, and I know that you can make my existence wretched or happy for me as you wish, bright star that shows me the way to a haven of bliss. But if you leave me, remember I shall die.

'So in God's name let us see if any means or reason can be found to prevent you from going. Let us go away to another country and not worry about the King's promises being unfulfilled, so long as we can avoid his vengeance. Far from here there are people who would willingly welcome us and furthermore continue to treat us according to our high rank.

(145) 'Let us then secretly elope and go there, you and I together – and let us then, my own heart, spend what remains of our life in this world happily together. This is what I wish and desire if you will agree to it – and this is the safest plan, for I find all other alternatives too difficult.'

Criseida answered him with a sigh: 'Dear happiness and joy of my heart – all of these things and more could happen in the way you have said. But I swear to you by the shafts of passion that pierced my breast because of you that neither commands, flattery nor the prospect of a husband will ever turn my desires away from you.

'But what you have said about going away does not seem to me to be a wise plan. We must bear in mind that these are difficult times and you must show concern for yourself and your friends. If we were to go away as you say, you would find that three unfortunate consequences would ensue. One would be the effect of breaking a pledge which causes more trouble than most people think.

'And it would be dangerous for your friends, for finding themselves left without aid or advice because of a woman, they would affect others with fear of further troubles. And, if I read the situation aright, you would thus attract a great deal of blame, and those who saw only what had happened would never believe the real truth of the matter.

'And if ever there was a moment for trust and loyalty it would seem to be during times of war – for then no-one is able to act effectively for himself alone. Many then join together trusting that the faith they pledge to others will be reciprocated – for they have themselves laid their lives and property at stake and proceed upon that understanding.

(150) 'On the other hand, what do you think people would say if you left? They would not say that it was the fiery darts of Love that made you decide to do such a thing, but fear and cowardice. So put such ideas out of your mind, if they ever entered it and if you care at all about your reputation for bravery which is now so loudly proclaimed.

'Then consider what a slur would be cast upon my honour and chastity, which are so highly regarded. They would indeed be totally ruined and lost as far as I was concerned, and could never be restored by any excuses that might be made or by any good deeds I might do, even if I went on living for a hundred thousand years.

'And I also want you to bear in mind what nearly always happens in such cases. If you consider carefully, there is nothing so worthless that it cannot provoke ardent longing. And the more you burn to possess it the quicker will your heart turn away from it if you are allowed to see and possess it at will.[35]

'The reason why our love is such a delight to you is that you are able to attain this paradise[36] only rarely and by means of stealth. But if you were able to possess me without difficulty, the torch of passion which now makes you burn would quickly be put out, and the same would happen with me. Thus if we want our love to last, we must always enjoy it secretly as we are doing now.

'So take heart, for you can exhaust and defeat Fortune by turning your back upon her; no person of upright spirit can ever be overcome by her. Let us follow her direction, and during this time of waiting make up an excuse for going on a journey and forget your troubles meanwhile, for I shall be back here without fail in ten days' time.'

(155) 'If' said Troiolo, 'you are here in ten days, I shall be happy. But in the meantime who will there be to bring my woeful laments any kind of comfort? I cannot now, as you know, endure a single hour of being unable to see you, without great suffering. How shall I be able to last the ten days till you return?

'Ah, in God's name find some way to stay – do not, I beg you, go if you can think of any other plan. I know you are perceptive if I judge rightly from what I have heard you say – and if you love me you will well understand that simply to think about your going away makes me desperate. You can well imagine what my life will be like then if you do go away.'

'Alas', said Criseida, 'you are killing me with grief and making me unhappier than you know when I see that you cannot, as I hoped, take me at my word. Tell me, sweet joy of my heart, why are you so mistrustful? Why have you thus lost control over yourself? Who would have thought that a mighty warrior could not stand a delay of ten days?

'I think it would be better by far to follow the plan I have described. Be content with that, my sweet lord, and rest assured in your heart that at the thought of being parted from you my very soul grieves more deeply than you can perhaps imagine or understand – and I feel that keenly with all my senses.

'Sometimes, dear heart, it is worth spending time in order to save time. I am not, as you think, lost to you just because I have been surrendered to my father. And do not let yourself be convinced that I am so stupid as to be unable to find ways and means of coming back to you, whom I desire as strongly as life – for I love you far too much.

(160) 'And so, if my pleas are of any use, I beg you for the sake of your great love for me, and that which I likewise have for you, to console yourself about this parting. For if you knew how much it hurts me to see you weeping so much and sighing so heavily, you would be sorry and regret having done that.

'I shall hope to remain in joyful anticipation, and return quickly, and find a way of accomplishing what you and I desire. Try to let me see you in a like frame of mind before I have to leave you, so that I do not have more pain than over-ardent love has already made my heart endure. Do so, I beg you, my sweet delight.

'And I beg you while I am away not to let yourself be attracted to any other woman or by the charms of someone new. For if I came to hear of that, you may be sure that, like a madwoman, I would kill myself out of grief for you, since you had failed in your duty and abandoned me for another whilst knowing that I loved you more than any woman ever loved a man.'

To these last words Troiolo replied with a sigh: 'Even if I wanted to do what you have just now suspiciously implied, Love holds me so fast in the grip of passion for you that I do not see how I ever could. Nor do I see how my love for you can ever cease as long as I live, and I will tell you in short why that is.

'It was not beauty that led me to love you, although it very often ensnares others. Nor was it breeding that drew me to you, although that often attracts men of rank. Nor was it adornments or wealth that inspired my heart with passion for you – although you are richer in all of these than any desirable woman ever was.

(165) 'But your noble, queenly actions, your worthiness and courteous speech; your manners that are nobler than anyone's and your charming womanly pride which makes each common desire and deed seem worthless in your eyes – these, my sovereign lady, have given you the place of love within my heart.

'And the shifting fortunes of the years cannot affect these qualities, and that is why, in the midst of deep anguish and great grief, I long in my heart to possess you always. Alas for me, what comfort can there be for my sufferings if you leave me, my sweet love? None now but death – for that alone will put an end to my woes.'

Having spoken and wept a great deal together, they ceased to do so because dawn was approaching and held each other in a fervent embrace. But when the cocks had crowed many times and after more than a thousand kisses they both arose and bade each other farewell, and parted thus in tears.

Part V

(*Here begins the fifth part of the* Filostrato *in which Criseida is given up. Troiolo accompanies her and returns to Troy lamenting by himself and then with Pandaro, at whose suggestion they go to stay several days with Sarpedon. They return to Troy, where every place reminds Troiolo of Criseida; and in order to relieve his sufferings he puts them into song whilst he waits for the tenth day to pass.*

First then, Criseida is handed over to Diomedes, with Troiolo keeping her company until she is out of the city; and after he has left her she is joyfully welcomed by her father.)

(1) That very day Diomedes[1] was there in order to give the Trojans Antenor, in exchange for whom Priam gave him Criseida who is so overwhelmed with sighs laments and suffering that whoever looks at her feels pity. On the other side stood her lover, so grief-stricken that no-one ever saw a man in such a state.

Indeed it was with much effort that he managed so wonderfully well to keep locked in his sorrowful heart the struggle he was waging with sighs and lamentations. And little or nothing of that yet showed in his face, although he was waiting until he was alone so that he could there weep and lament and give vent to his feelings quite freely.

What thoughts thronged into his noble mind there as he watched Criseida being delivered to her father! Trembling all over with mingled rage and distress he chafed inwardly and said softly: 'Sad wretch that I am, what am I waiting for? Is it not better to die at once than to live in constant grief and pining?

'Why do I not use force to break this agreement? Why do I not kill Diomedes here? Why do I not strike down the old man who has brought this about? Why do I not defy all my brothers? – if only they had all been destroyed! Why do I not make Troy resound with cries and weeping? Why do I not now seek my own remedy and snatch Criseida away?

(5) 'Who will stand in my way if I really mean to do that? Or why do I not approach the Greeks, to see if they would give me Criseida? Ah, why am I hesitating, instead of rushing over to them at once and making them yield her to me?' But fear that in the struggle Criseida might be killed made him abandon this bold and spirited plan.

When Criseida saw that, however unhappy it made her she would have to go, she mounted her horse along with those who were to accompany her and began to exclaim to herself indignantly: 'Alas, cruel Jupiter and baleful Fortune, where are you making me go? Why do you take such delight in making me suffer?

'You are harshly and ruthlessly taking away the joy that was closest to my heart, and you expect, perhaps, to be appeased by some kind of sacrifice or worship from me. But you are mistaken; I shall continue to revile and despise you in my grief until I can return to look upon Troiolo's fair face again.'

Thereupon she turned disdainfully towards Diomedes and said: 'Let us leave now; we have paraded ourselves enough before these people, who may now expect a happy end to their troubles if they look closely enough at this noble bargain you have struck in giving up such a great, and much-feared king in return for a woman.'

And having said this she spurred forward her horse without saying anything more than farewell to her friends; The king and his nobles grew well aware of the lady's contempt. Then she left without listening to any farewells or speeches or glancing at anyone, and departed from Troy, never to return there or be with Troiolo again.[2]

(10) In order to show courtesy Troiolo mounted his horse with his hawk on his wrist, and together with some companions escorted her beyond all the fortifications. He would willingly have accompanied her all the way to where she was to stay, but this would have been too open and would also have seemed ill-judged.

And Antenor had already joined them, having been handed over by the Greeks – and the young Trojans welcomed him with great joy and honour. And although his return gave Troiolo much inward grief because Criseida had been given up, he still welcomed him with a cheerful expression and made him ride ahead of him with Pandaro.

And as it was now time to take leave he and Criseida halted for a moment and gazed into each other's eyes – at which the woman was unable to restrain her tears. After that they took each other by the right hand and Troiolo then, drawing close enough for her to hear him speaking softly, said: 'Come back again; do not let me die.'

And with no more ado he turned his horse about with the colour rising to his face and not saying anything at all to Diomedes. And through such behaviour Diomedes came to recognize what love there was between the two of them, confirming his opinion through a number of signs. And while he murmurs to himself about this he becomes secretly attracted to her.

Her father welcomed her most joyfully, although such affection was irksome to her. She remained silent and withdrawn and led a wretched life, pining away in torment and keeping her heart wholly constant to Troiolo – although she was soon to change completely and abandon him for a new lover.[3]

(*Troiolo, returning to Troy, sighs and grieves and recalls with lamentations the delights Criseida has given him.*)

(15) Troiolo in a sadder and more anguished state than anyone ever was before, and wearing a grim and wrathful expression, went back to Troy, not pausing until he had reached his palace. Dismounting there in a much gloomier mood than he had ever yet experienced, he would not listen to a word from anyone but went off alone into his room.

Here he gave free rein to the grief he had been restraining, calling for death and bewailing the happiness he thought he had lost. And his cries were so loud that he might even have been heard by those who were going about in the courtyard. And in such misery he remained the whole day, with neither servants nor friends setting eyes upon him.

If the day had been spent in sorrow, the night that now fell did nothing to relieve it – but he was such a prey to sorrow that his weeping and woe were redoubled. He cursed the day he had been born and the gods and goddesses and Nature,[4] and his father and whoever had given their consent for Criseida to be handed over.

He cursed himself for thus having let her go – for not acting on his earlier decision to try to elope with her (and that he bitterly and most desperately regretted) – and for not at least asking for her, since she might perhaps have been granted to him.

And turning this way and that, finding no place to rest in his bed, he then said to himself sorrowfully: 'What a night this is compared to the one gone by, when I think what time it is now! At such a time I was kissing my lady's white breast, her mouth, her eyes and lovely face, and holding her close to me.

(20) 'She was kissing me and we were gladly and joyfully talking together. Now I find myself alone – wretched, sorrowful and doubtful whether such a happy night can ever be experienced again. Now I find myself embracing my pillow, feeling my passion's flame increasing and hope diminishing as grief overwhelms it.

'What am I to do then in my misery? I shall be patient as long as I can, but if my spirit is so grief-stricken by her departure, how can I expect to continue thus? Those who are truly in love do not know what it means to rest.' And he continued in this manner all that night as he had during the day that had gone before.

(Troiolo sorrowfully describes to Pandaro what he has endured that night; and he rebukes him and urges him to go visiting.)

Neither Pandaro nor anyone else had been able to reach him that day, and so when morning came Troiolo quickly sent for him so that by talking to him about Criseida he might ease his heart's misery for a while. Pandaro arrived, with a very shrewd notion of what he had been doing that night and what it was he wanted now.

'O Pandaro my friend,' said Troiolo in a voice weak with groaning and much weeping, 'what can I do now that the flames of passion have taken such a hold upon me that I can gain no rest of any kind? What am I to do in this sad pass, now that Fortune has turned against me and made me lose my sweet friend?

'I do not expect to see her ever again – so I wish I had fallen down dead the moment I let her leave me yesterday! Sweet happiness, delight of my heart, fair lady whom I serve – sweet soul of mine, sole solace of these eyes that have now turned to wells of grief – ah, can you not see I am dying? Why do you not help me?

(25) 'Who is looking at you now, sweet lovely creature? Who is sitting with you, dear heart of mine? Who is listening and speaking to you now? Alas not I – sadder as I am than anyone else! Ah, what are you doing now? Is your heart still tender towards me or have you thrust me from your thoughts in favour of your old father who has you with him now, whilst I remain in such dire torment.

'I have been saying what you now hear, Pandaro, the whole night long, and this lovesickness of mine has given me no rest. And even if my sufferings do give place at all to sleep, that does me no good – For while I sleep I dream of being pursued or being alone in fearful places or in the hands of fierce adversaries.

'And this so distresses me and strikes such terror into my soul that I had rather suffer while awake. And often I am shaken and aroused by feeling a shock which makes me think I am falling from a height. And when I wake I call out loudly both to Love and Criseida, sometimes appealing for pity and sometimes for death.

'I have thus wretchedly been reduced to the condition that I have told you about, and I grieve both for myself and because of this separation more than I would have thought possible. Oh, I will admit I ought to hope for relief, and that my sweet lady will yet bring it when she returns, but my love-lorn heart will not let me rest in that belief and keeps on calling for her.'

When he had said a great deal more of this kind of thing, Pandaro, who was saddened to see such deep distressing affliction in him, said: 'Come Troiolo, as you hope this sorrow may come to an end – do you think no one but you ever suffered the blows of love or had to be party to a parting?[5]

(30) 'I swear by Pallas, there are others for sure who are just as much in love as you are – and I am certain that there are also some who have had even worse luck. Yet they do not resign themselves to a life of misery as

you are doing – but when their sorrow grows too much for them they find ways of easing it through hope.

'And you should do the same. You say she has given you her word to come back here within ten days. That is not such a long time to wait, and you should be able to put up with it without getting gloomy and mooning about. How would you manage to stand the strain if she had to go away for a year?

'Have done with dreams and throw them to the winds for that is all they are worth. They are the effect of melancholy and will show you only things that scare you. Only God knows for sure what will happen, and the dreams and portents that fools believe in are not worth a straw[6] and are no use at all for foretelling the future.

'So for God's sake have pity on yourself and give this bitter grief of yours a rest. Do me a favour and reward me by getting up and being more cheerful. Tell me about the joys you have had and prepare your noble heart for those that are to come, for they will soon return. So look for the best and take heart.

'Our city is large and full of delights, and is now, as you know, at peace.[7] Let us go to some pleasant place far away from here, where you can stay with one of the princes and with him while away the tedious hours until the date fixed by the fair tormentor of your heart comes round.

(35) 'Come, I beg you – get up and do that. It shows no spirit to remain prostrated by grief in this way, and if the news got out that you were acting so foolishly and wildly you would be embarrassed, and people would say you were lamenting like a coward for our present troubles, not for love – or that you were feigning illness.'

'Alas, he whose loss is great must greatly grieve – and those who have not endured that cannot understand what kind of joy it was that I have parted with. So I ought not to be blamed if I did nothing at all but lament. But since you, my friends, have begged me to do so, I shall do my best to be cheerful for your sake and to make you happy.

'May God send the tenth day soon, so that I can once again be as happy as I was at the time they agreed to give her up. For no rose ever returned to bloom in the sweet springtime as readily as I should do on seeing in Troy again the clear countenance of that lady who is the source of both my torment and my joy.[8]

'But where could we go to amuse ourselves as you suggest? Should we go to Sarpedon's? And how can I stay there? I shall always be wondering whether she might for some reason return before the appointed day – and I should not want to miss being here when she came for anything the world could offer in the way of happiness.'

'Come,' replied Pandaro, 'I shall arrange that if she returns someone will seek me out without delay. I shall leave a man here for that purpose alone – so it will be easy for us to find out about it. If only it were now! – no-one could desire that more than I do. So you certainly must not fail to go on that account; let us go then to the place you spoke of.'

(Troiolo and Pandaro go to Sarpedon's together, but Troiolo can hardly bear to stay five days there.)

(40) The two companions set off, and after about four miles they came to

where Sarpedon lived; and when he heard about it he joyfully came out to meet Troiolo and made much of him. And they, although worn out with all their grief, still cheerfully made merry with that noble prince.[9]

He, who in nobility of heart surpassed all others in every way, entertained them both superbly well – sometimes with hunting and sometimes with feasts graced by lovely ladies of high nobility – with songs and music, and always with such style and scale of banqueting that nothing like it had ever been provided in Troy before.

But what good was all this feasting to poor Troiolo who had no heart for it? He was where his heart's desire[10] would often lead him – with his mind's eye fixed all the time upon Criseida as his only God, calling to mind one thing after another about her, and sighing passionately again and again.

He found it irksome to look at any other woman, however noble and lovely she might be. All pleasures and all sweet songs were repugnant to him when he could not see the lady whom Love had given control[11] over his wretched existence; and the only happiness he had was when he could abandon all other pursuits to think of her.

And not an evening or morning went by when he did not appeal to her with sighs as 'fair light' and 'morning star'.[12] Then, as if she were there listening to him, he would call her a rose among thorns more than a thousand times, so that he would always have her greet him before he would cease – but his greetings would end in sighs.

(45) Not an hour of the day went by without him calling out to her a thousand times. Her name was always on his lips, and her lovely face and eloquent words were engraved upon his heart and mind; and every day he read again the letters she had sent him over more than a hundred times – such delight did he take in looking at them again.

They had not been there three days when Troiolo began to ask Pandaro: 'What more is there for us to do here? Do we have to spend the rest of our lives here, or are we waiting to be told to go? To tell you the truth, I should like to go. Come, let us leave for God's sake; we have spent long enough with Sarpedon and had a warm welcome.'

Pandaro answered: 'Did we come here just to fetch a light,[13] or has the tenth day arrived? Come now, restrain yourself a little longer; it would look rude if we left now. Where would you go now and where would you find a pleasanter place to stay? Come, let us stay another couple of days and then we will leave and go back home if you like.'

Although Troiolo did not wish to do so he stayed nevertheless, keeping his thoughts fixed upon their usual object and remaining unaffected by what Pandaro kept telling him. But however reluctant Sarpedon was to see them go, they took their leave on the fifth day and returned home, with Troiolo saying as they went: 'O God, shall I find that my love has returned?'

But Pandaro, fully realizing Calchas's intentions, had other opinions and said quietly to himself: 'If I am not deceived by what I have heard since she left, this fierce and ardent desire of yours may well cool, and I think the tenth day, month and year will pass before you see her again.'

(*Having returned to Troy Troiolo goes to see Criseida's house and finds that every place in which he has seen her before reminds him of her.*)

(50) When they had arrived home they went into a room together and sitting down they talked a great deal about Criseida, while Troiolo sighed ardently without ceasing. But after a while they rose and Troiolo said: 'Let us go now and at least look at her house, since there is nothing else we can do.'

When he had said that he took his friend Pandaro by the hand, and putting on an expression of cheerfulness he left the palace, providing various excuses in order to keep his companions ignorant of the wounds love had inflicted upon him. But when he set eyes upon Criseida's house, all shut up, he was once again seized with dismay.

And he felt his heart would break when he saw the door and windows barred, and this fresh access of passion made him so distressed that he did not know whether he was moving or standing still. And the utter transformation that came over his face would have clearly revealed as much to anyone who saw him at that time.

Then, as best he could while suffering from this fresh affliction, he began to speak to Pandaro, and then said: 'Alas, what a bright and pleasant place you were when you held that beauty whose eyes are my sole source of comfort.[14] Now you have been left without her, in darkness, and I do not know if you will ever receive her again.'

As he rode by himself through Troy he would speak to himself about each of the places that stirred his memory: 'There I saw her laughing joyfully. There I saw her gazing at me. There she greeted me with kindness. There I found her happy, and there sad – and there she showed her pity for my suffering.

(55) 'There she stood when her lovely, charming eyes captured my love. There she stood when she set my heart aflame with a sigh of greater power. There she stood when like a noble lady she responded graciously to my desires. There I found her disdainful; and there my noble lady displayed her courtesy to me.

Then, pondering this, he went on to say: 'O Love, you have made a lengthy example of me,[15] if I do not try to deceive myself and if my memory duly recalls the truth. In every place I pass through or linger in I can find, if I look closely, over a thousand reminders of the victory you triumphantly gained at my expense after I have mocked all those who were in love.

'You have properly avenged the wrong you have suffered, my mighty and most fearful lord. But since my soul as you can clearly see, is wholly devoted to your service, do not let it perish in despair. Restore it to its former happiness by exerting your power over Criseida as you do over me and making her return to put an end to my woes.'

He would sometimes go off towards the gate through which his lady had left the town: 'Out of here went the lady who brings me solace; out of here went all the sweetness of my life. I went with her as far as that spot, and there I took leave of her, and there, alas, I held her hand.' So he would say as he followed step by step.

'That was the way you went, my own dear heart; when, my dear joy and sweet desire, will you ever return from there? Indeed, I do not know, but these ten days are turning into a thousand years! When shall I ever see you return as you have promised, to delight me with your graceful ways? Ah, will it ever happen? If only it could do now!'

(Troiolo, having considered his position, describes his state of mind in verse.)

(60) He thought he had less colour than usual in his face and for that reason believed that people would keep pointing him out, as if, in drawing attention to him, they were saying: 'Why has Troiolo become so feeble and confused?' That was not what they did, but only those who are sure of the truth are never unburdened by suspicions.[16]

He thus chose to reveal in verse who had been the cause of this, and during those difficult days of waiting he would, when he was worn out with lamentations allow his grief some kind of respite. And in a low voice he would recite verses of this kind in order to console a spirit that had been overwhelmed by the intensity of passion.[17]

'The sweet sight and lovely gentle gaze of the fairest eyes ever to be seen make my life, now I have lost them, seem so hard that I go about wailing with grief.[18] And that has already brought me to such a pass that instead of heaving sweet and joyful sighs as I used to do, I long for the haven of death – so sharp is my pain at this parting.

'Ah Love, why did you not give me my death-blow at the outset? Why, alas, did you not release from me the afflicted spirit I now bear, finding myself down in the depths, when I had been raised high? There is, Love, no solace for my grief but death, since I find myself robbed of those fair eyes in which I once beheld you.

'When in reply to some courteous greeting I turn my eyes awhile towards some lovely woman, my strength is so completely overpowered that I cannot restrain the tears within me. Such are the wounds of love I endure when I recall my lady from whose sight I am, alas, so far removed that if Love would grant it, I should wish to die.

(65) 'Since my fate is so harsh that whatever meets my eyes increases my grief – then in God's name, Love, let your hands close them since I have lost the object of my passionate gaze. Abandon this wasted body,[19] O Love, for when life is gained by death it should be a joy to die. And you well know where my soul will go from here.

'It will go to find those fair arms from which evil fortune tore this body. Do you not already see from my face, Love, that I am marked with the colour of death? You can see the agony with which my soul is being forced from me; take it from me yourself and bear it to her bosom which it loves above all, and on which it seeks its repose – for already it find no joy in anything else.'

When he had thus recited his verses he returned to his former grief. While he went about during the day and as he lay in bed at night his thoughts were always of his Criseida, and he took delight in almost nothing else. And he would often count the days that had passed, thinking that the tenth, when she was to return to him from the Greeks, would never be reached.

The days seemed longer than usual to him and the nights yet longer. He measured the time from the first signs of dawn until the stars came out, and declared that the sun had started to go astray and its horses were not keeping to the same course as before. He said the same thing about the nights and claimed that each of them had become two.

The old moon's horns had already appeared at the time Criseida went away, and he had seen them when he left her that morning. And so he would often say to himself: 'As soon as it has grown new horns like those it had when my lady went away, then that soul of mine will return here.'

(70) He gazed towards the Greeks encamped before Troy, and whereas it once used to infuriate him to see them, he now looked upon them with delight. He came to think that the breezes he felt upon his face were in fact sighs coming from Criseida and he would often say to himself: 'In one or other of those places is that sweet lady of mine.'[20]

In this and many other ways he spent his time yearning. And Pandaro was always there to console him as he did so – and would try his utmost to make him talk about pleasant and cheerful subjects, all the time strengthening his hopes about the sweet and worthy lady that he loved.

Part VI

(Here begins the sixth part of the Filostrato, *in which first of all Criseida, now with her father, laments her separation from Troiolo. Diomedes visits and talks to her, disparaging Troy and the Trojans, and then confesses his love for her. Her answer leaves him in doubt about whether she finds him attractive or not; but having in other ways become cooler towards Troiolo she begins to forget him.*

And to begin with, Criseida laments her separation from Troiolo.)

(1) On the other side, by the seashore, Criseida remained with a few of her ladies amongst the armed men, and spent her nights in bitter weeping, since during the daytime she had to restrain herself completely from doing so. Thus, because of her absence from her heart's desire, her tender and exquisite cheeks grew thin and pale.

She wept as she remembered[1] the joy she had found with Troiolo before, picturing to herself all they had done together and recalling all they had said whenever she had time and opportunity to do so. And finding herself thus far away from him she let her eyes become one well of bitterness.

And no-one could have been hard-hearted enough to forbear weeping with her, after hearing her woeful lamentations. Given the slightest chance she would weep more bitterly than could fully be described, and what made it worse for her was that she had no-one with whom to share her grief.

She would gaze at the walls of Troy, its palaces, towers and fortifications, saying to herself: 'Alas, how great was the happiness, pleasure and delight I once found there – and now my precious beauty is being consumed by grief and pain. Alas, dear Troiolo, what are you doing now? Do you still think of me at all?

(5) 'Alas for me! if only I had trusted you and we had gone away together to any country you wished! Then I should not have had to endure these sufferings, and so much good time would not have been wasted! We would then have returned at some time, and who would ever have spoken ill of me for going away with such a man as you?

'Alas for me! I found that out too late, and now my wisdom turns against me. In fleeing from what was bad I sought something worse, and thus my heart is bereft of joy. I cry out in vain for death to ease my suffering now that I cannot see you, my sweet love – and I fear I may never see you again. Let the Greeks, then, be defeated soon!

'But if I am not allowed to leave in any other way, I shall do all I can to escape from here and return to you as I promised. Let the smoke blow where it will, and let me face whatever consequences there may be. For rather than die of grief I would sooner let them talk and bay at me as they please.'

But from such a high and noble purpose a new lover soon diverted her. Now Diomedes tries[2] every trick he knows to win her heart; and his strategy did not fail to find an opening, for in a short time he had driven Troy and Troiolo out of it, along with all other thoughts she had of him, false or true.

(How Diomedes talks to Criseida about a variety of things, and eventually confesses his love for her.)

She had not been there more than four days after that bitter parting when Diomedes found a respectable excuse for visiting her.[3] He found her alone, grieving and almost completely transformed since the day when they had first ridden together, bringing her back from Troy – and he thought that was most strange.

(10) And at first glance he said to himself: 'I think this will be a fool's errand; I can see that the lady is deep in sorrow, grief and mourning for the sake of someone else. Anyone who wanted to banish and supplant a former lover there would have to be an extremely skilful operator.[4] Alas, what a luckless journey to Troy it was for me when I went to bring her here!

But, being a man of great boldness and courage, he made up his mind that if he was not to face certain death he must, having come this far, make her aware of the sharp pangs that Love was making him endure because of her – and how his passion for her had first been kindled. And having sat down, he began to talk of things that were quite distant from his purpose.[5]

And he began to converse with her first about the fierce conflict between themselves and the Trojans – asking her what she thought of it, and whether she thought their cause was foolish or hopeless. Then he began to ask whether the ways of the Greeks seemed strange to her – and he did not leave it much longer before asking why Calchas had not yet found her a husband.

Criseida, whose heart was still set upon her dear lover in Troy, did not recognize his cunning but answered him as her master, Love, would have wished – frequently piercing his heart with sharp sorrow, yet sometimes gladdening him with hopes of what he sought.

And he, having put her at ease, began in the course of conversation to say to her: 'My lady, youthful as you are – when I look closely at your angelic face – which is more to be prized than any I have ever seen – I think it has been much wrought upon by pain and distress since that day when we left Troy and, as you recall, came back here.

(15) 'I do not know whether love can be the cause, but if it is, you will, if you are wise, have done with it when you hear the reasons I shall give you for doing so. The Trojans are, it may be said, held captive by us – as you can see; and we are resolved not to turn back until we have destroyed the whole city with fire and sword.[6]

'And do not think that anyone in Troy will ever again find pity in us. And no-one who ever committed such an outrage – or does so again, even if the world lasts for ever – will fail to find, either here among the living or among the dead in Hell, a very clear example in the punishment that we shall, if possible, inflict on Paris for the crime he has committed.

'And even if there were more than a dozen Hectors, instead of just this one, and six times as many brothers – we should, unless Calchas is leading us on with cunning and trickery, soon gain the victory we long for, however strong they might be. And their destruction, which will shortly follow, will make clear that our hopes are not in vain.

'And do not think that Calchas would have asked for you so insistently, had he not foreseen what I am talking about. Before he did so I discussed the question thoroughly with him, and considered all the circumstances. And as a result he made up his mind to ask to have you back here, in order to rescue you from such dangers.

'And I encouraged him to do so, as I had heard of your marvellous gifts and noble qualities. And when I heard that Antenor had been given him to exchange for you I offered to act on his behalf, and he trusted me to do so, for he recognized my good faith. And it was no hardship to me to travel there and back if by doing so I could see you, speak to you, listen to you and come to know you.

(20) 'What am I trying to say then, dear sweet lady? Leave behind you the false love of Trojans – banish these tormenting hopes which now make you sigh in vain – and call back the freshness of your beauty, which gives more joy than any other to the beholder. For Troy is now in such a state that all hopes pinned upon her are lost.

'And even if she were to stand for ever, the king, his sons and the citizens are barbarous, ill-bred and worthless by comparison with the Greeks, whose noble manners and fine appearance give them the advantage over all other nations.[7] You are now with men of breeding, whereas before you were with ignorant brutes.

'And do not imagine that with the Greeks love is not a nobler and more refined thing than it is for the Trojans. Your great nobility and beauty and your heavenly looks will here gain you a lover who is indeed worthy of you, should you care to choose one. And if it did not displease you, I should more willingly be he than kings of the Greeks for ever.'

And as he said this his face turned flaming scarlet, while his voice trembled a little and he lowered his gaze, turning his eyes away from her for a moment. But he soon regained his composure, becoming more confident than he had been before, and continued smoothly: 'Do not be offended; I am as noble as any man in Troy.

'If my father Tydeus, who died in battle at Thebes, had lived, I should have been King of Calydon and Argos – as I still mean to be. And I came to one of those kingdoms not as a stranger but as a man of renown, ancient lineage, great honour and, if it can be believed, divine descent. So I am of no small importance here among the Greeks.[8]

(25) 'And so if my prayers can move you at all, I beg you to banish all this gloom and accept me as your servant if I am fit to be commanded by you. I shall behave as befits your reputation and the grace that I know abounds in you more than any other woman – so that you will continue to cherish Diomedes.'

(Criseida, surprised by his boldness, replies to what he has said.)

Criseida listened, and with a few hesitant words gave a modest and fitting reply to what he had said. But on hearing his final words she thought him extremely bold and haughtily looked askance at him – for Troiolo still had that much influence over her – and quietly spoke as follows:

'Diomedes, I love that city where I was raised and nurtured. The war she endures gives me the greatest possible distress, and I would willingly see her released from it. And the fact that a cruel destiny has barred me from her[9] naturally afflicts me deeply. But I pray that you may be duly rewarded for all the pains you have taken on my behalf.[10]

'I am sure that the Greeks are, as you say, of great nobility and breeding – but the Trojans' noble endowments are hardly inferior and they have demonstrated their qualities under Hector's leadership.[11] And I do not think it wise to belittle others through enmity or for any other cause, and then set oneself up above all of them.

'I have not known love since the death of the man I served devotedly as my lord and husband. I have never looked upon either Greek or Trojan with that in mind; I am not interested in any of them, nor will I ever be. I do indeed believe you to be of royal blood, and have given that due consideration.

(30) 'And it astonishes me greatly that you could set your heart upon such a lowly and insignificant woman as I. Fair Helen would be more suitable for you; whereas I am burdened with troubles and unfit for such a venture. But I certainly do not mean that I regret being loved by you.

'These are difficult times, and you are in the midst of a war. Wait until the victory you expect has been achieved, and then I shall have a much better idea of what I should do. Perhaps such pleasures will tempt me more strongly than they do now, and you will be able to speak to me again. Perhaps I shall then find your arguments more attractive than they now are. You have to choose your time and moment carefully if you want to lay hold on someone's affections.'

These last words gave Diomedes great pleasure and he thought he could surely hope for further reward of the kind he was later to enjoy, and he answered her: 'My lady, I swear to you as solemnly as I can that I am and always will be ready to obey your wishes.' And having talked further he then went away.

He was tall and handsome in appearance, and was a young man full of vigour and charm – strong and bold, as we have said, as eloquent as any Greek had ever been, and naturally inclined to be passionate in love. And when he had gone Criseida, in the midst of her grief began to consider these qualities – uncertain whether to draw closer to him or flee.

For these were what cooled her still ardent determination to return. They breached the integrity of her devotion to Troiolo; her desires turned in a different direction, and a new kind of hope slightly eased her fierce torment. And thus it was that, yielding to such pressures, she failed to keep her promise to Troiolo.

Part VII

(Here begins the seventh parth of the Filostrato, *in which, to begin with, Troiolo waits for Criseida at the gate on the tenth day. When she fails to appear he makes excuses for her – going back there on the eleventh day and many others; and as she still does not arrive he returns to his grief. Troiolo begins to pine and Priam asks him the reason, but he refuses to say. He dreams that Criseida is being taken from him, tells Pandaro about it and tries to kill himself. Pandaro restrains him and persuades him not to do so, and he writes to Criseida. Deiphebus becomes aware of his suffering, and some ladies visit him as he lies sick. Cassandra rebukes him and he rebukes her.*

And to begin with, now the tenth day has come, Troiolo and Pandaro await Criseida above the gate.)

(1) Troiolo, as we have already said, spent the time looking forward to the appointed day, which arrived only after it had long been awaited. And thus, pretending he had other things to do, he went off without followers towards the gate, talking constantly to Pandaro about what was to come. And they began to look across the plain to see if they could glimpse anyone coming towards Troy.

And each person they both saw coming towards them – whether alone or in company – was thought to be Criseida, until close enough to be clearly identified. And thus they remained for more than half the day, continually deluded by their hopes, as subsequent experience was to show.

Troiolo said: 'I cannot believe now that she will come before she has dined. I think she must be having much more difficulty than she would have wished in getting away from her old father. But I still think she would have come if she could, and if she had not stayed to eat with him.'

Pandaro replied: 'I think you are right – so let us go away and then come back later.' Troiolo agreed at length, and they did so. They stayed away a very short time before returning, but it became clear that their hopes were deceiving them and were, as they found, groundless. For that noble lady still did not appear, and already the sun above was entering its ninth hour.

(5) Troiolo said: 'Perhaps her father will have been delaying her and asking her to stay until vespers,[1] and that is why she is now leaving it so late to return. Let us go and stand outside so that she may be let in more

quickly, for the gatekeepers here often tend to keep people talking when they arrive, without properly considering who they may be.

The hour of vespers came and then came evening, and many figures had misled Troiolo, who had constantly been scanning the plain and gazing at all those coming towards Troy from that part of the countryside.[2] He asked some of them for news, but found out nothing of what he wanted to know.

And so he turned to Pandaro and said: 'My lady, if I rightly understand her behaviour, is acting thus out of discretion. She is waiting for nightfall so that she can arrive without being seen – and I approve of that. She will not want to make people wonder or say: "This woman who was asked for in exchange for Antenor – why has she come back so soon?"'

'So I beg you in God's name, dear Pandaro, not to begrudge the waiting. We have nothing else to do at the moment, so do not let it distress you to do as I wish. And if I am not mistaken, I think I see her. Look, look down there – do you not see what I do? 'No,' said Pandaro, 'if I open my eyes properly I think what you are showing me is a cart.'

'Alas, you are right!' said Troiolo. 'That is what comes of letting myself be carried away by thoughts of what I should like to happen now!' The sun's rays had already faded and a few stars appeared to have come out in the sky when Troiolo said: 'Some sweet kind of hope still comforts my desire; you may be sure she will come now.'

(10) Pandaro laughed to himself, but quietly, at what Troiolo said, fully understanding what had led him to speak like that. And in order not to make him more wretched than he was, he gave the appearance of believing him, whilst saying: 'The poor young fellow is waiting for a breeze from Etna!'[3]

The wait was of no avail, and the sentries began to make a great clamour above the gate – calling in all the citizens and strangers who did not wish to stay outside – as well as all the countryfolk and their animals. But Troiolo made them delay more than two hours, and then, when the sky was all full of stars, he went back with Pandaro inside.

And although that day he had frequently deluded himself with one sort of hope or another, Love still meant him to trust in one of the least foolish of all these. So once again he turned and spoke to Pandaro, saying: 'We are fools to have waited for her here to-day.'

'She told me she would stay ten days with her father, and delay not a moment longer but come back again to Troy after that. The end of that period falls on this very day – so if we reckon rightly, she must be coming tomorrow. And our eagerness has made us so forgetful that we have been standing about here all day!'

'We shall have to come back here tomorrow morning early, Pandaro.' And so they did. But it did little good for them to gaze up and down, for she had already set her heart on someone else. As a result they both, after watching as carefully as they had on the first day, went back inside again at nightfall – and that was a supremely bitter blow for Troiolo.

(15) And the fair hopes that he had entertained now had almost nothing left to rest upon; and he thus grew very despondent and began to complain bitterly about both her and Love – seeing no reason for her to put off her return so long, since she had given him her pledged word that she would come back.

But now the tenth day had gone by Troiolo anxiously awaited the third, fourth, fifth and sixth days that followed, full of hopes and doubts about whether she would come back. After that hope urged him to spend yet longer waiting – and all to no avail. She still did not return, and hence Troiolo's courage began to fail.

The tears and sighs that had been held in check by Pandaro's reassurances came back uncalled for, prompted by his ardent desires. And those that had been restrained by hope now issued forth redoubled by his sufferings which as a result of his delusions had become twenty times fiercer than they had been before.

All his former longings came over him once again, accompanied by a sense of betrayal and by the grim effects of jealousy, which gives one no rest and is worse than any other affliction, as those who have experienced it will know.[4] Thus day and night he gave up his eyes and himself to as much weeping as they could bear.

He hardly ate or drank, so full of anguish was his sorrowful heart; moreover, he was unable to sleep except when exhausted by sighs. He held his life and himself in utter disdain, fled from pleasure as from fire, and likewise shunned all festivities and gatherings as often as he could.

(20) And his face had become so changed that he looked more like a wild creature than a man, and his looks were so pale and distracted that no-one would have recognized him. All the spirit had left his body and his limbs had scarcely enough strength left to support him, nor would he accept any comfort that anyone might offer.

(Priam and his sons are astonished to see Troiolo thus transformed, but are unable to find out from him what the matter is.)

Seeing him thus distracted Priam on occasion would call him into his presence, saying: 'What has happened to you, my son? What can it be that troubles you so much? You have lost so much colour that you no longer look the same; what is making your life so wretched? Tell me, my son – you can hardly stand and, if I judge rightly, you are near to giving way completely.'

Hector, Paris and his other brothers all said the same, asking him how such great distress had come upon him, and what evil tidings had been the cause of it. He told them all that his heart was full of troubles, but no-one was able to question him closely enough to find out more about them.

(In a dream Troiolo sees Criseida being taken from him. He complains about her to Pandaro and tries to kill himself, but Pandaro, with great difficulty restrains him.)

Troiolo had one day fallen asleep in deepest grief because of the pledge that had been broken and in a dream he perceived the dire treachery of the woman who was making him pine.[5] For he thought he heard a loud and ugly noise resounding through a shadowy wood, and raising his head at that, he thought he saw a great boar charging forward.

And then he thought he saw Criseida under its feet, and it was tearing her heart out with its tusks. And Criseida did not, he thought, seem to care about that great injury, but took a kind of pleasure in what the animal was doing – and that provoked such indignation in him that it broke into his shallow slumber.

(25) When he was awake he began to think about what he had seen in his dream, and he thought it an easy thing to interpret the meaning of what he had been shown. He quickly summoned Pandaro, and when he came he began tearfully to tell him: 'Dear Pandaro, God no longer wishes me to live.

'Your Criseida, in whom I trusted more than any other woman, has betrayed me. She has granted her love to someone else, and that grieves me more than death itself. The gods have shown as much in a dream.' And thereupon he described the whole dream to him. Then he began to explain what such a dream might mean, telling him as follows:

'The boar that I have seen is Diomedes – for, if our forefathers can be believed, his grandfather killed the Calydonian boar, and his descendants have ever after, as we know, borne the pig as their emblem.[6] Alas, what a bitterly truthful vision! He must have drawn out her heart – in other words her love – by means of his speech.

'It is he who is keeping her back and making my life miserable, and he alone is standing in the way of her return. If it had not been for that she would have found it very easy to come back, and neither her old father nor any other concern would have prevented her. So in trusting her I have been deceived, and have been beguiled into waiting for her in vain.

'Alas, Criseida – what subtle approaches, what fresh pleasure or pleasing looks – what anger or just indignation against me – what fault of mine or what cruel perversity have managed to turn your noble heart elsewhere? Alas, constancy that was sworn to me – alas, trust and fidelity – who has banished you from the lady I love?

(30) 'Alas, why did I ever let you go? Why did I heed your ill-fated advice? Why, alas, did I not take you away as I had a mind to do? Why did I not overturn the agreement that had been made, as I felt urged to do when I saw you being handed over? You would not then have become unfaithful and false, and I should not now be in misery.

'I trusted you, and firmly believed your pledge to be sacred and your words more constant and clear than the light of the sun is to men. Yet you were speaking deceitfully and insincerely as your falsehoods now seem to show – for you have not only failed to return to me but have given your love to another man.

'What am I to do, Pandaro? I feel within my heart a great, newly-kindled flame that will not let me live at peace with my thoughts. I shall seek death at my own hands then, for it can be no pleasure to continue with a life of this sort[7] For Fortune has brought me to such a grim pass that dying will be a pleasure and life a torment and affliction.'

Thus saying, he rushed towards a sharp knife that was hanging up in the room, and would have plunged it into his heart had he not been held back by Pandaro who had taken hold of the wretched young man when he heard him thus express his despair with sobs and tears.

Troiolo cried: 'Now do not hold back, dear friend, I beg you in God's name. I am determined to do this, so let me follow my fierce desire. Let me go, unless you want to be the first to meet the sort of death I seek.

Let me go Pandaro – I shall hurt you if you do not – and then I shall kill myself.

(35) 'Let me release this most miserable of bodies from the world. Let me gladden with my death that deceitful lady of ours, whom I shall still pursue among the dark shades in the kingdom of woe.[8] Let me kill myself, for a life of sorrow is worse than death.' And saying this he struggled to reach the blade that Pandaro kept from him.

Pandaro himself was crying out too as he held him fast, and had Troiolo not grown so weak Pandaro's strength would have been overcome, such was the force that frenzy lent his struggles. Still, in the end Pandaro wrested the blade from his hand and made him tearfully and reluctantly sit down with him.

And after some bitter tears he turned and spoke to him sorrowfully in these terms: 'Troiolo, in our case I have always believed that if I dared to ask you for my sake or someone else's to kill yourself, you would courageously have done so without any delay – as I at any time would do for you.

'But you despite my pleas would not refrain from seeking a vile and dishonourable death – and had I not been stronger than you I should have seen you die here. I could not have believed this of you, and now consider the promises you made me worthless – although you can still make amends if you give good heed to what I say.

'It seems to me that you believe Criseida now belongs to Diomedes, and if I rightly understand what you have been saying, nothing but your dream is creating this impression – and you are finding a cause for fear in that because of the beast that wounds with its tusks. And without trying to find out anything further about it you want to put an end to your misery by dying.

(40) 'I have said before that it was foolish to put too much trust in dreams. No-one ever could or ever will be able to interpret clearly and surely the things that a man's imagination may conjure up in various forms during sleep. Many indeed have believed in one interpretation, and then another has come forward to contradict it.

'Such may eventually be the case with this; for although you see this beast as a threat to your love, it may be favourable to you and not mean harm as you suppose. Does it seem to you a noble deed for anyone – let alone a man of noble blood like you – to take his own life and make such an outcry about love?

'This problem needs to be met with a very different approach from the one you were taking. First, you should if possible have considered very carefully whether what you had seen was likely to be true. And if you had found it to be false and of no validity at all,[9] you should then have had no more to do with dreams and their tricks, for they may cause you trouble.

'If you had then discovered that Criseida had really deserted you for someone else, you should not just have wholly determined to die – for I know of no-one who would fail to condemn you for that. But you should resolve instead to treat her with contempt as she has treated you.

'And if indeed your thoughts depress you so much that they make you want to ease your pain by dying, you should not have chosen to do in such a way. There were other means by which you could have fulfilled that wish, as your grim thoughts should have made you well aware. For there, before the threshold of Troy's gates, are the Greeks who will kill you and not ask forgiveness for doing so.

(45) 'When you wish to die, then, let us both go forth armed against the Greeks, and let us, like young men of honour, join battle with them and avenge our own deaths by valiantly striking them down. I should not then refuse to do that for you if I were sure you were seeking death in such a venture for the right reasons.'

Troiolo, who was still trembling as a result of the frenzy that had gripped him, gave him as much of a hearing as his grief would allow. And when he had listened to him for a long time, seeing how he also in his grief was shedding bitter tears, he turned towards Pandaro, who stood there watching to see if he would abandon his mad attempt, and spoke to him thus, weeping and in words that were constantly broken by sobs:

'Pandaro, you may always be sure of this: that I shall be with you in every way I can, and, as long as it pleases you, neither life nor death will be hard for me to bear. And if just now, when you were struggling to rescue me, passion had made me lose sight of wiser considerations, do not let your wisdom find that a cause for wonder.

'That error was prompted by too hasty a belief in my wretched dream. But now my passion is subsiding I can clearly see how wrong I was, and how foolish was what I meant to do. But if you know for sure how I can find out the truth about what I suspect, I beg you in God's name to tell me, for I am all confused and cannot see it for myself.'

Pandaro said to him: 'In my opinion it would be best to try her out with a letter, for if she no longer cares for you I do not think we shall get a reply from her; and if we do have one we shall be able to see clearly from what she writes whether you can continue to hope for her return, or whether she has fallen in love with someone else.

(50) 'Since she left you have never written to her, nor she to you – and there may be such a good reason for her delay that you might say she was indeed right to remain; and it might be of such a sort that you would reproach her more for timidity than for any other fault. Write to her then, for if you do it properly, we shall find out for sure what you seek to know.'

Troiolo was already stricken with remorse, and was thus ready to believe him; and, going off by himself, he ordered writing materials to be brought to him, and that was done. Then, having thought for some time about what he should write and being no longer in an agitated state, he set about it and with no more delay wrote to his lady as follows:

(*Troiolo tells Criseida about the state his life is in, imploring her to return as she promised.*)

'Youthful lady in whose service Love placed and keeps me now and always for as long as I live – since by your departure you left me here in greater misery than anyone could conceive of, my confused spirit has placed all its hope and trust in the mighty power that stems from yours – and is unable to send you any other kind of greeting.

'Although you have almost become a Greek,[10] this letter of mine should still not fail to be accepted by you, for a love like ours, which has long united our affections, will not quickly be forgotten, and I pray it may last for ever. Take it, therefore, and read it through to the end.

'If there are any grounds that a servant may have for complaint against his lord, perhaps I then may have just cause to complain about you – considering your tender affection for me, the pledge you made, all your promises, and all the gods by whom you swore you would come back within ten days. And now, after forty, you have still not managed to return.

(55) 'But since I must rest content with what you wish, I dare not complain – but I will describe my thoughts as humbly as I can to you and also tell you of my passionate desire and my whole state, as I burn with love more than ever. And I am eager to know what sort of life you have been leading since you were exchanged for Antenor and sent to the Greeks.

'If I interpret your decision rightly, it seems that your father's persuasion or love for someone else may have influenced your thoughts. Or – since on rare occasions we do find an old man becoming bountiful – it could be that tight-fisted Calchas is behaving generously towards you, although, as you made clear to me during our last moments of bitter sorrow, you were firmly convinced that this would not be so.

'You have now stayed so much longer than we agreed, that you should feel compelled to redeem your promise and return at once. If it has been because of the first reason or the third,[11] you should have let me know, for you know I shall respect your every wish as I did before – and I would have endured that patiently, however hard it had been for me to bear.

'But I greatly fear that love for someone else may be the reason for your long delay – and if that is so, it will prove a deeper sorrow for me than any I have yet endured. You will now hardly need to ask yourself whether my devotion should have been thus rewarded. And for that reason I remain in such constant misery and fear that I am without any pleasure or hope.

'This fear makes me utter cries of anguish when I try to rest. This fear alone dominates all my thoughts, so that I do not know what I can do. This fear, alas, is about to destroy me, and I have neither the knowledge nor the power to defend myself against it. This fear has left me in such a state that I am of no use to either Venus or Mars.[12]

(60) 'My sorrowful eyes[13] have never ceased to weep since you left. Since then I have been unable to eat or drink, rest or sleep, and have given myself over to constant lamentation. And my voice can most of the time be heard continually uttering your name and appealing for help from you or Love – for that alone, I believe, can prevent my death.[14]

'You can well imagine what I would do now, were I to find out that what I suspect is true. Indeed, I think I should kill myself if I knew you to be guilty of such wickedness. And what reason would there be for me to remain in this life if I had lost hope of regaining you, dear heart, whom in this sorrowful state, I look to as my only comfort?

'Sweet songs and noble company – hawking, hunting and merry-making – the lovely ladies, temples and great festivities that I used to attend, I now shun entirely. And how distasteful they are to me, alas, whenever I begin to think of how you, my sweet joy and supreme source of hope, still remain so far from me.

'The brightly coloured flowers and the fresh grass which lend the meadows a thousand different hues have no power to charm a spirit that is wrung by a torment of desire for you, my lady; and I take pleasure only in the part of the heavens beneath which I think you now dwell.[15] I gaze up to it, saying: "She from whom I seek reward can see that."

'I look at the mountains surrounding the place that hides you from me, and say with a sigh: "They, though they do not know it, have before them the enchanting sight of those fair eyes, for which, far away, I languish in a life of sorrow. If only I could be one of them or upon one of them; if only I could be there to see it!"

(65) 'I look at the waves in the rivers going down to the sea beside which you now are, saying: "They after flowing for a while will reach the place where the light that is sacred to my eyes has gone to dwell, and they will be seen by her. Alas for my miserable state – why can I not take their place and go on the same journey?"

'When the sun goes down I look at it enviously, because it seems that, drawn by desire for you, who are my delight, it is crossing the sky to see you again more quickly than usual. And having lamented for a while I begin to hate it and my sufferings increase; and fearing thus that it may take you from me, I pray the night to drive it downwards quickly.

'When I hear at times the name of the place where you are, or see at times someone coming from there, it re-kindles the flame in a heart that has been made weak by extreme sorrow – and I seem to feel some stirrings of joy in this soul that is kept captive by your charm, and say to myself: "If only, my sweet heart's desire,[16] I could go to the place from which they come!"

'But what are you doing among knights in arms, among warlike men and noises of battle – in tents continually open to sudden attack, and constantly terrified by alarums, the sounds of weapons and storms on the sea, to which you are now so close? Does that not distress you greatly my lady – you who used to value your comforts so highly when in Troy?

'Indeed, I have, as I should, more pity for you than I have for myself. Come back then, and make good your promise before things grow worse for me. I will pardon all the suffering you have caused me by your delay, and I ask for no compensation but that of seeing your lovely face, which is my paradise, sole and entire.

(70) 'Ah, I beg you, for the sake of all that drew and bound me to you and you to me, and likewise for the pleasure that kindled both our hearts in like degree; and then also for the sake of that beauty you possess, my noble lady – for the sake of the sighs and piteous tears that we once shed so plentifully together – / (71) for the sake of the sweet kisses and those embraces that once made us cling so closely together – for the sake of the great gladness and sweet speeches that gave our pleasures a keener delight – and for the sake also of that faith which once with tearful vows you were pleased to pledge, that time when we last parted from each other, never since to meet again – / (72) that you should remember me and return. And if you happen to be delayed, write and tell me who has prevented you from returning until after those ten days. Ah, let it not be too much trouble for you, eloquent as you are, to satisfy me to this extent at least, and to let me know, my sweet joy, whether I can ever dare to hope for you again.

'If you give me hope I shall wait, even if I find it utterly unbearable. If you rob me of that, I shall put an end to this troublesome life by killing myself. But however much I may suffer for it, the guilt of having inflicted such a grim death upon one of your innocent servants will remain with you.

'Forgive me if I have failed to follow the proper form in setting things down – or if you find this letter I send you covered with blots. My anguish is the main reason for both of these things – for I spend my time in constant weeping, from which nothing that happens can distract me; and these frequent blots are therefore made by tears of grief.

(75) 'And although there is much more that I could say, I say no more than that you should come back to us. Ah, do that, dear heart of mine, for you will be able to do so if only you put your mind to finding a way. Alas, you would not know me, for I am so plunged once again in bitter grief. And I say no more than may God be with you and soon let you be with me.'

Thereupon he gave the letter sealed to Pandaro who sent it off and for a number of days they vainly awaited a reply. At this Troiolo's sorrow passed beyond the limits of what could be borne, and he felt certain of the unfavourable meaning of his dream – yet nonetheless he kept on hoping that Criseida might even now still love him.

(Deiphebus realizes the reason for Troiolo's grief, encourages him to take part in the coming battles, and tells his brothers what he has found out.)

From day to day as hope faded his grief increased, and he was forced to take to his bed, for there was nothing else that he could do. But purely by chance one day Deiphebus,[17] of whom he was very fond, came to see him. And Troiolo, not noticing him in his grief, began to say softly: 'Criseida, I beg you, do not let me die of sorrow like this.'

Deiphebus then realized what was afflicting him, and making it seem that he had not heard, he said: 'Brother, why do you not now give your sad spirits some relief? The season of delight is with us and is lovely to see. The fields have grown green again and make a gladdening sight, and the day has now arrived when the truce comes to an end – / (79) so that we can show our courage in battle to the Greeks just as we used to. Do you no longer wish to appear with us in arms – you who would always be there to strike the first blow, and you whose valour they always feared so greatly that you used to drive them all before you? Hector has urged us to join him tomorrow on the other side of the moat.'

(80) As when the famished lion hunting prey rests from its task, then suddenly rises up with quivering mane if it scents a stag, a bull or other creature it desires, and makes that the sole object of its desire – so also did Troiolo find his heart suddenly aroused and invigorated when he heard that the as yet undecided war was about to start again.

And he raised his head, saying: 'I am indeed rather weak, brother, but I have such a desire for battle that I will at once rise from this bed with my strength renewed. And I swear to you that whereas I once struck at the Greeks with a stout and valiant heart, I shall now strike them harder than ever I did, for I bear such hatred towards them.'

Deiphebus well understood the force of what he was saying and gave him much encouragement – saying that this was what they would have expected of him, and that he should no longer delay his recovery. Then they parted, and Troiolo remained in his usual melancholy state, whilst Deiphebus quickly went to find his brothers and told them all that had happened.

They at once believed him because of the behaviour they had already witnessed, but in order not to add thus to Troiolo's grief they decided among themselves to say nothing about it. They therefore at once had all their ladies instructed to visit him, bringing musicians and singers, and provide him with the kind of entertainment that might make him forget what was making his life a misery.

(The royal ladies of Troy visit Troiolo. Cassandra reproaches him, and he, defending Criseida, sharply rebukes her.)

In a short time his chamber was filled with ladies and with music and song. On one side of him was Polyxena whose looks seemed those of an angel,[18] and on the other sat the lovely Helen – whilst Cassandra[19] was also there before him, as were Hecuba and Andromache, together with a throng of his sisters-in-law and kinswomen.

(85) They all tried their best to console him, and someone asked what was troubling him. He made no reply, but gazing from one to the other his sad thoughts turned once again to Criseida, although he gave no sign of that save a sigh. But nonetheless he took some pleasure in the music and in their beauty.

Cassandra, who had happened to hear what Diephebus had told his brothers, said, as if mocking him to his face for appearing so distracted: 'I can see, brother, that it was an ill day for you when you were affected by that cursed passion which brings us to destruction, as we can see if we will.

'And since it had to be so, why did you not fall in love with a woman of noble birth? Instead, you have taken to pining for the daughter of a depraved and vicious priest of low rank. Look now at this son of a mighty and revered monarch, leading a life of misery and woe because Criseida has left him!'

Troiolo was troubled by this revelation, both because of hearing the woman he loved most spoken of disparagingly, and because he knew then that his secret had reached her ears, but he could not tell how. He thought that she might have found out from the way the gods had replied to her, but nonetheless he said: 'This will be thought true if I remain silent about it'.

So he went on to say: 'Cassandra, your desire to surpass others in gaining foreknowledge about all secret matters has already brought you to grief on many occasions. It might, perhaps, have been more sensible for you to keep quiet than to indulge in such reckless talk. You throw your words about in front of everyone, and I have no idea of what you mean about Criseida.

(90) 'And so, because of your wild talk, I am going to do something I have never done till now, and expose your folly. You claim that an overwhelming love for Criseida is sapping my strength, and you want to turn that into a matter of great dishonour to me. But thus far your Apollo

has not quite shown you the truth about the question – so admit[20] that you have taken his name in vain.

'I have never been drawn towards Criseida by a passion of that kind, and I do not believe there is or ever has been anyone in the world who would dare to maintain such a falsehood. And if it were so – as you persist in claiming – I swear upon my honour that I should never have let her go from here. Priam would have had to kill me first.

'And I do not think anyway that he would have agreed to it as he agreed to Paris's abduction of Helen which brought us the rewards we are now reaping – so keep your wagging tongue in check. But let us just suppose that this really was the case, and that I was enduring all this suffering for her sake – why then should Criseida not be thought worthy in every respect of any noble man that you could think of?

'I do not wish to speak of her beauty (although in everyone's opinion it excels that of celestial beings), for a fallen flower quickly fades. But let us turn simply to her nobility, upon which you have cast such aspersions. And if I am telling the truth about this let all who will agree – and let the rest deny it, yet give me their reasons for doing so, I pray.

'Nobility exists wherever virtues do,[21] as no-one with sense will deny. And they are clearly apparent in her, if a cause can be inferred from its effects. But we, nonetheless, have to scrutinize all aspects of such a blessing, just to satisfy this woman who talks so much about everyone else's business, without knowing what she is babbling about.

(95) 'Unless I am much deceived by my own eyes and by what others say of her, there neither can be nor has been any woman more honourable than her. And if what I hear is true she is far more temperate and modest than any other woman, as her appearance clearly shows; and she is, when necessary, quiet and retiring – which, in a woman, suggests nobility of soul.

'She shows prudence both in her behaviour and in her speech, which is grave, judicious and full of good sense. And I recently witnessed something of that when she was exonerating herself from her father's treachery; for with her well-chosen words she displayed a noble and truly royal indigation in the midst of her grief.

'Her behaviour is well enough known and thus I think needs no defending by me or anyone else. And I know of no courteous knight from amongst all those there may be in the world whom her courtesy and nobility of manner would not easily let her outshine[22] if only she had sufficient opportunity.

'And I am certain of that, for I was once present when she treated me and others with such graciousness that there are many now occupying royal thrones who by comparison would have appeared clumsy and looked as if they were neglecting us because we were inferior. Although here she has always behaved modestly, her reputation proclaims her worthy of praise.

'What more, lady Cassandra, do you now require of a woman – your royal blood? Not all of those you see bearing crowns, sceptres or royal robes are really kings, for you must often have heard before that a king is made worthy of the name through merit, not might. And if she is thus endowed, do you not think she has as much right to rule as you have?[23]

(100) 'And she would certainly know much better than you how to wear

one – I mean the crown, if you understand me. And she would not behave like you, you foolish woman, giving offence to everyone. I should have been what you call favoured by God to have had her as my lady, for I should value most highly what Lady Cassandra despises.

'Now go, and ill luck go with you since you are unable to talk sense. Be off[24] and attend to your own defects, but leave the virtues of others as they are. What a sad thing and what a strange calamity it is when a madwoman foolishly tries to find fault where she ought to give praise, and complains about it if she is not listened to.'

Cassandra fell silent and would willingly have been somewhere else at that time. She rejoined the throng of ladies without saying anything more, and when she was out of his sight she quickly went off to the king's palace and never came back to see him again, for she had hardly been well received on that occasion.

Hecuba, Helen and the rest approved of what Troiolo had said and within a while they had all pleasantly consoled him with their conversation, entertainment and cheerful company. Then they all left together, each returning to her own home. But they afterwards visited him again frequently while he remained bedridden.

Troiolo by thus continuing to suffer pain grew strong enough to bear it patiently – and moreover, because of his fierce resolve to prove his courage against the Greeks, this also enabled him soon to regain the powers he had lost in the course of such bitter anguish.

(105) And furthermore Criseida had written to him pretending she loved him more than ever, offering a number of false excuses for staying where she was so long without returning, and asking for yet another postponement of her return, which would never take place. This he granted her, for he hoped to see her again but did not know when it would be.

Thereafter in a number of battles with their enemies he showed what he could do as a soldier. And he made them pay more dearly than anyone could have thought for the sighs and other bitter lamentations they had cost him – yet not as dearly as his anger would have wished. But finally death, which destroys all, laid his passion and its struggles to rest.

Part VIII

(Here begins the eighth part of the Filostrato *in which, to begin with, Troiolo approaches Criseida again with letters and messages, and she leads him on with fair words. Then, as a result of Deiphebus's capturing a garment from Diomedes, Troiolo realizes from a brooch upon it that Criseida must have given herself to Diomedes. He laments this fact with Pandaro, falling into utter despair, and his sufferings are at last brought to an end when he is killed by Achilles.*

And to begin with Troiolo tests Criseida's loyalty and affection again by means of letters and messages.)

(1) He had, as we have said, already become accustomed to suffering, and it was further increased for him by the deep and inexpressible grief that he, his father and his brothers felt at the death of Hector,[1] to whose supreme bravery they had entrusted[2] the bulwarks, walls and gates of Troy; for that brought them enduring woe and misery.

But love, nonetheless, would not leave him, however much hope had faded. Indeed, as lovers usually do, he tried by all possible ways and means to regain the lady who had once been the sole object of his delight and love. And he constantly made up excuses for her failure to return, believing it was because she was not able to do so.

He sent her a number of letters, telling her what he was suffering for her sake night and day, reminding her of their past happiness and of her pledge to return – and often gently rebuking her also for delaying so long. He sent Pandaro to her whenever any truce or pact had been agreed on between the armies.

And likewise he also thought of trying to go there in the simple guise of a pilgrim;[3] but indeed he could think of no device that he believed would well enough conceal the truth of the matter, nor did he think he could find a suitable explanation if he happened to be recognized in such inappropriate dress.

(5) And from her he received nothing but fine words and large but empty promises. Hence he began to distrust each and every one of them and to gain a suspicion of the truth, as will often happen when someone takes a really good look at what he is dealing with. For his suspicions were not unjustified.

And he well knew that love for someone else was behind all this pretence, and declared to himself that neither her father's persuasion nor filial affection could ever have governed her heart to such a degree – and there was no reason for him to continue seeking evidence to confirm what his ominous dream had already revealed to him.

Yet love had greatly diminished his faith in that dream, for it is usual for a lover to be loth[4] to believe anything that will add to his sufferings in love. But not long after that something occurred which revealed to him that what he had suspected about Diomedes was indeed true – and this removed all his illusions and forced him to believe it.

(Deiphebus was showing Troiolo a garment which he had captured from Diomedes in battle when Troiolo recognized upon it a brooch that he had given to Criseida.)

Troiolo was fearful and uncertain and still tormented by his passion when he heard that, following a very hard-fought battle between the Greeks and Trojans, Deiphebus had come back with a magnificent garment he had captured from Diomedes after severely wounding him, and was exulting and rejoicing greatly over the spoils.

And as he was having it borne before him through Troy Troiolo arrived and together with all the rest admired it greatly, taking hold of it for a moment in order to look at it more closely. And while he was examining it and his eyes were glancing up and down all over it he chanced to see on the breast a gold brooch that might have been put there as a fastening.

(10) And this he recognized at once as the one he had given to Criseida

when, parting from her in grief, he had said farewell the morning after that last night he had spent with her. And at that he said: 'Now I see that my dream and suspicions and thoughts were indeed true.'

(*Troiolo, together with Pandaro, laments Criseida's treachery which is now plainly apparent.*)

Having come away from there, Troiolo sent for Pandaro and, when he had come, began with tears to bewail the continual devotion he had shown for his Criseida; and he went on to reveal exactly how he had been betrayed, bitterly lamenting the fact and appealing for death alone as his remedy.

Then in tears he continued: 'O Criseida my love – where is that faith, the love and desire – where is that loving pity you proclaimed so earnestly before God, alas, when you left? Diomedes now has it all – whilst I who loved you more have been left in grief and affliction by your betrayal.

'Who from now on will trust any kind of vow, and who will trust love or women when they can clearly see how you have treacherously broken your word? Alas, I do not know, and I never thought you would be so hard-hearted and cruel as to let me ever vanish from your thoughts for the sake of some other man – for I loved you more than myself and, misguidedly continued to wait for you.

'And did you then have no other jewel to give your new lover, Diomedes, than the one I had given you with so many tears, to remind you of my wretched state while you were staying with Calchas? It was sheer contempt and the wish to show quite clearly what you thought[5] that has led you to do this.

(15) 'I can see that you have banished me utterly from your heart, whilst in mine, despite myself, I still preserve the image of your lovely face with grief and affliction. Alas for me, what an evil hour it was when I was born! Thoughts like this are destroying me, robbing me of any hope of future happiness, and leaving me in anguish and distress.

'You have unjustly banished me from your heart where I had hoped to dwell for ever, and have falsely set Diomedes in my place. But I swear to you by Venus herself that the way I wield my sword in the very next battle will soon make you regret that, if I manage to find him and provided I have the strength to overcome him.

'Or he may kill me, and that would make you happy. But I still hope that divine justice will consider both my bitter grief and your great wickedness. O most exalted Jupiter, whom I acknowledge as the sure refuge of righteousness, and from whom alone stems that mighty power by which things live and move – are the eyes of your justice turned elsewhere?[6]

'What has happened to your fiery[7] thunderbolts? Are they at rest, or do you no longer keep your gaze upon mankind's wrongdoings? O true light and radiance of the skies, delighting earthly spirits – do away with this woman whose breast is full of falsehood, cunning and treachery, and let her no longer merit forgiveness.

'O Pandaro, my friend – you rebuked me so firmly for trusting in dreams, but now you can see what may be foretold by them, as your Criseida will make you well aware. The gods take pity upon us mortals, and in various ways they show us things of which we know nothing – often revealing them to us for our own good.

(20) 'And this is one of the ways they are sometimes revealed during sleep, as I have often found before, now I come to think of it. I wish I had died then,[8] since from now on I can expect no happiness, joy, pleasure or delight – but at your bidding I will remain to meet death in battle with my enemies.

'May God send Diomedes to meet me the first time I go out to fight. I long for that in the midst of all my woes, for then I should let him feel how my sword can bite and make him die a miserable death on the battlefield. And then it would not matter if he killed me, so long as, when I died, I could find him suffering in the realms of darkness.'

Pandaro sorrowfully listened to all this, and, realizing the truth of it, could find nothing to say. And whilst, on the one hand, love for his friend drew him to remain there, on the other shame at Criseida's wrongdoing kept prompting him to leave; and since he did not know what to do for the best, both these impulses caused him much misery.

At last, in tears, he uttered these words: 'Troiolo, I do not know what I can say to you. If it is as you say, I shall denounce her as strongly and as often as I can. And I shall not attempt to put forward any excuses for this great wickedness of hers, nor shall I ever try to visit her again, wherever she may be. What I did before, I did out of love for you, leaving aside all concern for my reputation.

'And if I did what you wanted, that is reward enough for me. I can do nothing about what is now happening and am just as distressed about it as you – and if I could see some means of setting it right, you may be sure I would embrace it eagerly. Leave it to God, who may act as he thinks fit,[9] and whom I pray as earnestly as I can to punish her in such a way that she will not be able to commit another crime of this sort.'

(Troiolo seeks out Diomedes on the battlefield and they exchange insults; and finally Troiolo is killed by Achilles.)

(25) There was much lamenting and complaining, but Fortune remained fixed in her course. She set her heart wholly upon Diomedes whilst Troiolo was left to grieve; and Diomedes gave thanks to God, whilst Troiolo bewailed his misfortune.[10] And Troiolo continually took part in battles, looking above all others for Diomedes.

And they often came face to face, to the accompaniment of vile and bitter insults;[11] and they exchanged mighty blows – sometimes charging at each other on horseback, sometimes wielding their swords – and most furiously defending their right to love.[12] But Fortune had not ordained that either of them should carry through what he intended against the other.

There is no doubt that the Greeks were at various times made keenly aware of Troiolo's wrath, to such an extent that there were few opponents that he did not hurl from their horses dead, if only they gave him time to do so – such deadly blows did he deal. And having endured a great while and slain more than a thousand of them he was sadly one day killed by Achilles.[13]

That was the end of Troiolo's ill-conceived love for Criseida, and that was the end of his pitiful sorrow, unmatched by any since. That was the end of the bright glory that made him worthy of the throne; and that was the end of his vain hopes for wretched Criseida.

(The author speaks very briefly to young men who are in love, showing how it is better to offer one's love to mature women rather than younger ones.)

You young men whose amorous desires keep growing with your years, I beg you in God's name to restrain your eager steps from this wretched pursuit and see yourselves mirrored in Troiolo and his love, thus set before you by these verses of mine. For if you take them to heart as you read, you will not lightly place your trust in any woman.[14]

(30) A young woman is both inconstant and eager for many lovers, and prizes her beauty more than her mirror warrants. She is full of vanity about her youthfulness, and the more attractive and desirable it is the more she prides herself upon it. She has no sense of merit or judgment and is forever fickle like a leaf in the wind.[15]

And many of them also, because they are nobly descended and can list their ancestors, are convinced that they have the right to take precedence over others where love is concerned, and think it shows good breeding to be arrogant and turn up their noses and walk around haughtily. You should shun and despise such women, for they are not ladies of rank, but brutes.

A mature woman has a more constant need to be loved and takes pleasure in loving, distinguishes clearly what is to be avoided, acts carefully in choosing what to do or not to do, and keeps her promises. These are the ones to follow, but you should not, however, decide in haste – for not all women are made wise by advancing years when they are anyway of less worth.

So look about you, be warned, and take pity at once on Troiolo and yourselves, for it would be well to do so. And beseech Love earnestly on his behalf to set him at rest in the place where he dwells, and graciously grant you such clearsightedness in loving that you will not end up by dying for the sake of a wicked woman.

Part IX

(Here begins the ninth and last part of the Filostrato, *in which the author addresses his work, instructing it whom to seek, in whose company to go, and what to do – and that is all.)*

(1) Sweet verses, my sad song, usually spring from moments of happiness – but you have been wrenched unnaturally from my sorrowful soul in the midst of deep affliction. And I do not know the reason for that, unless it lies in the mysterious power my lady's high nobility engenders and sends forth into my stricken heart.

She, as I know and often realize, can reduce me to nothing or make me far greater than I am. This, I believe, is the real subject of your long discourse, and I am pleased it should stem from that rather than from my bitter sorrows. But however it has happened, we have now reached the end I desired.

We have reached the harbour we sought, sailing through breeze and tempest, sometimes past rocks and sometimes on the open sea,[1] following through the unknown ocean the celestial light and sacred image of that star which makes all my thoughts able to attain their true goal, and has done since first I sighted it.[2]

I thus see fit to drop anchor now and put an end to the voyage, whilst we here wholeheartedly offer up the thanks the grateful pilgrim owes to the one that has guided us. And on the shore we are now approaching we shall deck the vessel that has borne our love with due garlands and other offerings.[3]

(5) And when you have rested for a while you will go to seek the noble mistress of my heart. What happiness you will find in seeing her as I in my misery alas cannot do! And when you have been welcomed into her hands humbly express my devotedness before that mighty power of hers which alone can restore me to health.

And in the mournful guise you now wear I beg you by means of this other man's[4] woes to let her know of my afflicted state, and of the laments, sighs and bitter weeping I have endured, and still suffer from, since her departure hid from me the bright beams of her lovely eyes. For it was their presence alone that brightened my life.

If you find that listening to you makes her show any pity at all in her angelic looks, or that she grieves for my distress – then beg her with all your might either to consent to return or to command my soul to depart. For, wherever it may have to go, my present life is such that I should far prefer to die.

Yet take care not to go on such a high errand without Love – for without him you might perhaps be very ill received, and without him you would not even know how best to perform your task. But if you go with him I think you will be treated with respect. Go then – and I pray Apollo to lend you such grace that you may be given a hearing and come back with an answer that will bring me joy.

TESEIDA

and the Marriage of Emilia

Prologue: To Fiammetta

[The poet has fallen from his lady's favour, but in the midst of his sufferings and regrets finds consolation in thinking of her, and resolves to continue in humble and faithful service to her.][1]

And wishing to make my work bear the most faithful witness to my words, I remembered that earlier, in those happy if short-lived days, I had found you eager to listen to and at times to read various kinds of stories especially those about love – since you were then kindled with the same kind of ardour as that which now consumes me. For that, perhaps was how you sought to prevent moments of boredom and idleness giving rise to more dangerous thoughts. Hence, like a willing servant who not only waits upon his master's bidding but anticipates it by doing what he thinks will be approved, I discovered a most ancient story[2] which was unknown to most people and was attractive both in the subject it dealt with – namely love – and those it spoke of, who were noble youths of royal blood. And taking such care as my other more oppressive cares would allow, I sought to please you by setting it down in the vernacular and in verse to make it more appealing – especially to you who once gave my poems their highest claim to fame.[3]

And two features among others make it plain that I have composed this for your sake. One is that what the story relates concerning one of the two lovers and the young woman he loves may be taken by you, if you well recall and were sincere, to correspond to what was said and done by both of us, I shall not reveal which of the two I mean, for I am sure you will know. And if perhaps some superfluous matters are included, they are occasioned by a desire to conceal things that it is not honourable to make public, and to be faithful to the story. Moreover you should know that only when the ploughshare is supported by many other contrivances can it cleave the soil.[4] You can thus perceive what my life was like before, and how it has been since you refused to have anything more to do with me.

The second is that I have never avoided speaking allegorically in a story, fable or other form just because women, being of little intelligence, will usually make fun of it. But since I know you are distinguished from the rest of that crowd by virtue of your understanding and knowledge of the things I have mentioned, I feel free to set them down as I wish . . .

[To prevent Fiammetta from being discouraged by the apparent length of the work, and to 'incline her heart to look upon it kindly', the writer then offers a brief summary of the poem's contents.]

. . . And if, most noble lady, you consider these features separately and together with a balanced judgment, you will be able to understand what I was speaking about earlier on, and thus, recognizing my love, will abandon the disdain you have shown; and having done so you will be able to change my misery back into the happiness I seek . . .

[Failing this, the writer asks Fiammetta to grant him the lesser consolation of accepting the 'present small book'; and he concludes his prologue with the prayer that 'he who made me yours the first moment I saw you may, if he possesses the power he once had, rekindle the flame that has died in you and restore to me one of whom I have for some reason been deprived through the enmity of Fortune.' Then follows a sonnet containing a briefer account of the contents of the whole work.]

Book I

[The book, like all the rest, begins with a sonnet summarizing its contents. Then follows the author's invocation to the Muses, the gods and Fiammetta.]

(1) Castalian sisters dwelling in bliss upon Mount Helicon beside the sacred Gorgonian spring,[1] beneath the shade of those leaves beloved of Phoebus,[2] with which I yet hope, if only you will grant it, to deck my brows – incline your holy ears to my prayers and listen to them as it befits you to.

It is now my wish to re-tell in melancholy verse an ancient tale which the years have rendered so remote and obscure that no Latin author to my knowledge seems to mention it. Make this work of mine therefore find favour with those who read it or come to hear it in any other way.

Be with me, fiery Mars, fierce and unyielding in battle, and you, mother of Love[3] with your joyful and happy appearance, and your speedy son whose arrows show their power throughout the universe[4] – and assist both my hand and my tongue for I mean to show how your actions brought little happiness and were fraught with great suffering.

And you before whom I hope my present utterance will perhaps appear – I once again, as humbly as I can, entreat your whole-hearted attention, in the name of that lord who inspires noble souls with love. You will hear how he makes all his followers languish in misfortune, and how after their tribulations he brings them peace.

(5) And this you will understand in the clearest possible way when you hear tell of the deeds of Arcita and noble Palemone, who were born of royal blood and were both Thebans as will be shown. For, though kinsmen, they came into conflict through their exceedingly great love for the lovely Amazon Emilia; and as the result of that one of them lost his life.

[The Amazons of Scythia under their Queen Hippolyta maltreat the Greeks who land upon their shores, and Theseus, duke of Athens, having decided to take vengeance sets out to invade their country (6–20). Hippolyta, on receiving the news of his approach, addresses her followers and garrisons her cities (21–39). Theseus arrives in Scythia, eventually wins a battle with the Amazons on the seashore and besieges Hippolyta (40–95), who after an exchange of letters agrees to surrender (96–126). Theseus then marries her, and, with a number of other weddings taking place between Greek knights and Amazon ladies, he decides to make a match between Hippolyta's young sister Emilia and his cousin Acates (127–38).]

BOCCACCIO'S GLOSS ON STANZA 6 OF THIS BOOK

Bearing in mind that the main purpose of this little book's author is, as his prologue shows, to deal with the love of the two young Thebans Arcita and Palemone for the Amazon Emilia, and with the events that followed as a result of it – someone might justifiably ask what the function is here of the war between Theseus and the Amazon women that occupies only the first book of this work. I would say briefly, then, that the author has written about these things for no other purpose than to show from what place Emilia came to Athens. And because the subject – that is, the behaviour of these Amazon women – is rather strange to most people, and therefore more interesting,[5] he wanted to portray it somewhat more detail than was perhaps necessary. And he does the same kind of thing with the defeat which Theseus inflicted upon Creon, King of Thebes – in order to show whence and how Arcita and Palemone came into the hands of Theseus. Once these two things have been explained, much of what follows will become a great deal clearer to my readers.

Book II

[After the introductory sonnet the second book begins by describing how Theseus came to return to Athens together with Hippolyta and Emilia (1–9). Then follows what the author calls 'a digression from the main subject, in order to explain the reason for Theseus's campaign against Creon.']

(10) But Mars had stirred up the Lernean[1] people to make a violent attack upon the Thebans,[2] and had already often yielded them wretched spoils from princes, who in some cases were still held by the common people and in some cases ransomed; and with his bloody spear he had cruelly brought sorrow to one nation and another.

For, following Amphiaraus, Tydeus and the noble Hippomedon had been killed, together with the fair Parthenopaeus and many Thebans of whom I make no mention, both before and after fierce Capaneus. And following all these Eteocles and Polynices in their sad struggle had been wounded and died, and Adrastus had fled to Argos.

This left the wretched kingdom unpeopled and prey to all kinds of woe. But in a short while it was invaded by Creon, who with dire consequences made himself its king and ruler – winning both his throne and his triumph by means of a savage cruelty that no-one before him had ever contemplated.

He hated the Greeks fiercely from his heart and maintained his hatred towards them after they were dead. For by strict decree he had forbidden all who wished to remain in his favour to burn any of the dead bodies lying there; and those that had not previously been devoured by wild beasts he left unburied to corrupt and putrefy.

Hence the women of Argos,[3] who, making a solemn show of all their suffering, had sorrowfully come to perform the final rites, were informed about that cruel edict before they arrived; and thus, deploring such wickedness, they resolved to entreat Theseus with tears to avenge this outrage.

(15) And thence, aided in their task by grief, they turned their steps towards Athens, and on arriving there they made their misfortunes known through a display of bitter grief. The Athenians were much astonished at the sight of that desolate company and asked what reason there was for this, why they had come and from what country.

And when they learnt of the noble rank of these ladies and the reason for their grief they were overcome with tender compassion on seeing this great torment of theirs; and the nobler citizens overwhelmed them with offers of houses ready for their use until Theseus, who was expected at any moment, should return to Athens.

They would accept no favours from anyone, and seeking nowhere but the temple of Clemency they wearily, wretchedly and in deepest grief made their dwelling there, while in great torment at his absence they mournfully awaited the sovereign's return; and Athenian ladies remained to keep them company there all the time.

(*How Theseus returned in triumph to Athens and what celebrations took place there.*)

Theseus, sped on his way by a brisk breeze, was returning well pleased towards Athens, together with a large retinue of noble knights and Queen Hippolyta, the lady who possessed and ruled his heart. His crossing was made quickly and without difficulty, and the very morning he touched shore the news became known in Athens.

The Athenians, who were so eagerly expecting him, had prepared magnificent celebrations to mark his return, and these were at once begun. Drawing on all their resources, which were indeed great, they adorned their whole city with cloth of gold and other hangings, together with innumerable singers and musicians.

(20) My words cannot express how fine the ladies then appeared as they displayed their beauty in the public buildings[4] and temples, on balconies and along the streets; for their presence enhanced such festivities in various ways. And to be brief, people everywhere were singing and rejoicing in the highest of spirits.

His nobler citizens had prepared for him a magnificent triumphal chariot, the like of which had never been seen by anyone, and they had it brought to the place where he was. And, in addition, they had provided him with imperial robes and a crown of laurel, to show that he came in triumph as a conqueror.

Theseus therefore, once he had come ashore and was decked in this regalia, mounted the chariot. And there his beloved Hippolyta stood next to him on one side, and on the other I believe was Emilia. And the other ladies and knights attending them followed on horseback without delay.

Various festive groups of Athenians, finely dressed in different costumes, had come on horseback or on foot to greet him with songs, all of them rejoicing to the accompaniment of innumerable musical instruments. And they escorted him back to Athens, where he went straight to the temple of Pallas to honour her divinity.

Here he reverently presented a number of things, including his own weapons and the others he had captured; and then, turning the chariot in another direction he went about the city for a while, greeted by vast throngs of people wherever he went. And his magnificent exploits were loudly proclaimed and celebrated as worthy of everlasting remembrance.

(How the Greek ladies in mourning came before Theseus.)

(25) And whilst he was thus continuing in his progress he chanced to pass by the temple of Mercy where the company of Achaean ladies mournfully remained. And when they heard that he had come to that place they roused themselves to desperate action; and with loud cries, wails and a great deal of noise they set themselves in the way of the Sovereign's chariot.

'Who are these appearing at our joyful celebrations with dishevelled hair, beating their breasts, in black clothing, full of gloom and all in tears – as if they resented my glory which I know gives joy to others?' So said Theseus as he stood there in amazement, and one of them answered him weeping:

'My lord, do not wonder at our sad appearance which makes us contemptible to everyone, and do not think that we are bewailing your achievements or resenting your glory in any way – even though to see you thus in triumph moves us to mourn more perhaps than we did when it was simply our first grief that assailed us.'

'Who are you then?' Theseus asked them 'and why are you the only ones to be weeping like this at a public festival?' Then Evadne, who was more stricken with grief than the rest, came forward and said: 'I was the wife of Capaneus,[5] and each of the others that you see in this company was the wife, the mother, the sister or daughter of a king. And I shall explain to you what it is that afflicts us.

'The deceitful wickedness of the tyrannical son of Oedipus towards his only brother Polynices and his cruel deception over the kingship led the wretched army of the Argives to its great defeat at Thebes – a defeat that was much heavier than men say. And there a grim destiny claimed each of the noble lords in death.

(30) 'And whereas we vainly hoped to see them return to their cities with such glory as that in which we now find you triumphant and crowned with laurel – we are obliged in the mourning garb we now wear to go and bury them. But the harsh tyranny of him who seized the kingdom after those two has prevented us from doing so.

'Treacherous Creon, whose hatred lasts longer than life did in those who died, is denying the Greek corpses burial – an act of cruelty that I think is truly unheard of – and he is keeping their shades back on this side of the dark swamp of the Styx.[6] And because of that, endless pain in addition to all our other sorrows afflicts us when we hear that beasts are devouring them.

'Hence, moved by compassion, we came from Achaea in order to perform this final service. But when the terms of that edict were reported to us we turned our steps in this direction and resolved to make our plea about this outrage before you, merciful lord. And that[7] is what our looks may offer on our behalf, first to you and then to your lords.

'If high nobility, as we believe, dwells within you, take pity upon us now. You will thus also gain high renown, and will, furthermore, be doing what every virtuous man should do. And, if anyone other than you were to try to do this, you would rightly be angered about it and prevent him, so that you might have the honour of punishing such offences.

'Ah, if our appearance and our tears do not move you, nor our pleas, nor our right to do what we can through that pious ritual – at least let the sad plight of those who once were kings move you. Do not let their future reputation turn to mockery; they were indeed born of the same blood as yourself, and like you they also bear the name of Greeks.'

(35) The flow of tears from this woman's eyes never ceased while she spoke but continued to increase apace. And this was also the case with the others following her – making them powerfully affect all those Attic[8] lords with such pity that each of them in his heart roundly condemned the cruelty inflicted by Creon.

Theseus gave careful heed to the words that had been spoken as he dwelt upon the appearance of those ladies. And although he could see how unkempt they were, his own judgment led him very clearly to acknowledge their underlying nobility. And sharp sorrow affected his heart when he heard of the death of those kings; and after a moment he answered their sad plea thus:

(*Theseus's reply to the Greek ladies.*)

'Your sombre garb and anguished lamentations, recognition of you through knowing those who were your lords, remembrance of the splendour of your state, your comforts and delights, your kingdoms and followers and the glorious reigns of your kings, and the way your fortunes have been turned from happiness into grief – have gained a hearing for your pleas in the midst of my supreme triumph.

'I indeed wish I could restore your kings to life and to their former state as easily as I think I shall be able to have proper funerals granted to those you wish. And the pride of him who would refuse you this will be humbled. Hence if vengeance can offer consolation for an injury, you may achieve your purpose through me.

'Revive your fainting hearts with glad hopes – for I swear to you that before I and my mighty lords take our rest again within the walls of Athens we shall have made trial of this to the utmost. And I am already confident of victory, trusting not so much in my own strength as in the injustice of Creon's cause.'

[Theseus thereupon leaves Hippolyta and Emilia in Athens, addresses his followers and sets out against Creon (40–53), bringing him to battle, killing him in single combat, routing his followers and capturing Thebes (54–73). He then allows the ladies of Argos to perform the funeral rites for their kinsmen and places Thebes at their disposal. They burn both the corpses and the city and return to their own country (74–84). Then follows a description of 'how Arcita⁹ and Palemone were found and brought to Theseus.']

(85) Whilst the Greeks were searching through that bloodstained field and turning over the corpses to find their dead, they happened to come across two wounded young men who were in a critical state and enduring constant pain. And both of them begged to be killed because of the suffering that afflicted them from their injuries.

They were lying not far from one another still fully armed, and, when examined by those who had first laid hands on them after hearing them cry out in pain, it was plain that they must be of princely rank. This was also apparent from the splendour of their equipment and the haughtiness of their expression, which made them seem in their anger to be defying God.[10]

They approached them humbly, as if they were indeed sure of their rank, and did not disarm them as they had done with the other enemy soldiers they had sent into captivity. Then, gently raising them in their arms they reasoned with them, recalling them from despair, and brought them to Theseus without delay.

As soon as Theseus saw them he judged them to be men of great importance, and he asked them if they were of the blood of Cadmus. And one of them proudly answered him: 'We were born and grew up within his house and are descended from him; and when Creon defended his unjust cause against you we and our followers were with him as supporters.

Theseus was very conscious of their regal disdain but did not respond in the way their hostility justified. Instead he took pity on them further, and making use of all the skill his physicians possessed he had all their wounds dressed and then kept them as prisoners in readiness for his solemn triumph.

[Theseus returns to Athens with Palemone and Arcita as prisoners in his triumphal processions and offers up sacrifices in the temple of Mars (90–6). The second book then ends with a brief account of 'how Theseus had Palemone and Arcita put in prison'.]

(97) When noble Theseus had rested and refreshed himself for a number of days he had Palemone of Thebes and fair Arcita brought before him. He thought they were both most worthy of honour and courageous in appearance. He therefore considered putting them both to death, for he feared that if he let them go they might yet cause him a great deal of trouble.

But then he said to himself: 'That would be a great injustice on my part, since neither of them is a traitor.' And he decided that the best thing would be to keep them in prison; so he at once ordered the gaoler to guard them well and treat them honourably. In this way Arcita and Palemone were condemned by him to perpetual imprisonment.

The prisoners were all locked up and placed in the charge of a man who knew his duty well. But these two were accorded somewhat easier treatment since they were of royal blood. Theseus had them lodged within the palace and kept them thus inside a chamber with all their wants attended to.

(*Here ends the second book*)

Book III

[After the introductory sonnet follows 'the beginning of the third book of the *Teseida*']

(1) After Juno's fury had been somewhat assuaged by the destruction of Thebes, Mars returned to his cold homeland,[1] together with his Furies. Now therefore my verse will speak in gentler terms of Cupid and his battles, and I beg for his assistance in what I have to say about him.

Let him exercise his power upon my verses as he did upon the hearts of those Theban prisoners, so that they may reflect their distracted conduct. For they, far from remaining duly patient, were led eventually into a conflict of a sort that was repugnant to both, and was sadly for one of them the cause of his death.

The two Thebans therefore – being thus imprisoned, plunged in gloom and having almost nothing else to do but weep – utterly despaired of ever being able to find happiness again and continually inveighed against the injustice of their misfortune, repeatedly cursing the time and the moment when they came into the world,[2] / (4) frequently calling upon Death to take their lives if that were worthwhile. And they had already undergone nearly a year in this dolefule state when Venus in her bright sphere prepared to give them further cause for sighs; and no sooner had she fixed upon this thought than her decision went into effect.

(*The season is first described, and then how Arcita and Palemone fell in love with Emilia.*)

(5) Phoebus, as he ascended with his steeds, was following the celestial sign of the humble beast[3] which without resting bore Europa to the place

that bears her name to-day. And within it the degrees by which Venus ascends were bringing her into a favourable position, so that the sphere of Ammon, which was meanwhile in Pisces,[4] was disposed to be completely benign.

From this propitious state of the heavens the earth received benign effects and re-clothed its pleasant places with fresh new grass and lovely flowers. The saplings had re-clothed their branches with leaves, and the weather encouraged the trees to blossom and yield fruit and the world to grow fair again.

And the small birds also had begun joyfully and gaily to proclaim their love in song amid the leaves and flowers; and the animals were unable to conceal theirs either, but revealed it clearly through their behaviour. And those lively youths whose thoughts were turned to loving felt love grow more ardent than ever within their hearts.

At this time the lovely young Emilia – drawn to do so by her own inclination and not impelled by any kind of passion – would go alone each morning into a garden that lay outside her chamber, and would amuse herself there wandering about barefoot and clad in a tunic, singing songs of love.

And when this lovely innocent maiden had followed this custom for a number of days – plucking the fresh rose with her white hands from the midst of its thorns and then weaving many other flowers with it into a garland for her golden hair – a strange thing occurred one morning because of her girlish beauty.

(10) One fine morning, when she had risen and bound up her golden hair, she went down into the garden as usual, and singing gaily she was joyfully and deftly making herself a garland of many flowers as she sat there upon the grass – all the while singing beautiful love-songs with an angelic voice and a glad heart.

At the sound of that charming voice Arcita, who was in the prison beside the lovely garden, rose without saying anything to Palemone and eagerly opened a small window in order to hear the song better. And in order to see who could be singing it he put his head out some way between the bars.

The day was still somewhat dark, for the sun shone upon only a part of the horizon. But nonetheless by straining his eyes he could glimpse what that as yet unknown young girl was doing there with such extreme delight. And gazing fixedly upon her face he declared to himself: 'She is from Heaven!'

And drawing back within he said softly: 'Palemone, come and see: Venus herself has descended here! Do you not hear her singing? Ah, if you care for me at all come here quickly! I know you will be delighted to see what a celestial beauty has come down here below from the highest heavens.'

Palemone, whose joy in listening to her was already greater than he would have thought possible, arose and went with him towards the window, so that they might both silently behold the goddess. And when he saw her he declared fervently: 'This must indeed be Cytheraea,[5] for I have never before seen any creature so lovely, charming or graceful.'

(15) As they both with rapt attention delighted their eyes and ears alike

by keeping them fixed on her alone – marvelling greatly at her and lamenting to themselves the time that had previously passed by in vain when they had not seen her – Arcita said: 'Palemone, do you behold what I see within those fair celestial eyes?'

'What is it?' Palemone then asked in reply. Arcita said: 'If I am not mistaken I can see within them the god who once wounded Phaeton's father by means of Daphne,[6] and in his hand he holds two gilded arrows. And already he is setting one of them against the bowstring and fixing his gaze on none but me.[7] It may be that I am angering him by gazing at this women who gives me such delight.'

'Indeed,' Palemone then answered, 'I can see him, but it may be that he has shot one of them, for he has no more than one in his hand now.' Arcita said: 'Yes, he has given me such a wound that I shall be racked with pain unless the goddess comes to my aid.' Then Palemone cried out in utter dismay: 'Alas, the other one has struck me!'

At the sound of that 'alas' the young girl quickly turned to her left and her eyes flew straight away nowhere else but to that little window – and that made the white on her cheeks grow red with shame, for she did not know who these men could be. Then, regaining confidence, she rose to her feet with the flowers she had gathered and made ready to leave.

But as she went she was not unmindful of that 'alas', and although she was a maiden as yet unready for love's fulfilment, she was nonetheless aware of what it implied. And thinking that she knew the truth of the matter, she rejoiced in being found attractive and thought herself lovelier and made herself look fairer the next time she went into that garden.

(20) The two squires drew back within once they saw that Emilia had gone, and when they had remained for some time dwelling upon fresh thoughts Arcita began thus to speak first: 'That fierce archer has lodged within my heart something that is draining away my life, and I feel myself succumbing little by little – burning, alas, in some kind of fire.

'And the image of that person will not depart from my mind, nor do I have a single thought about anything else. Her form is so engraved upon my heart and so delights my spirit that I should think it the height of good fortune if I could please her the way she pleases me. And failing that I do not think I shall ever be at peace.'

Palemone said: 'The very thing you speak of is happening to me, and I have certainly not experienced it before. For I feel strange pangs within my heart which I do not think have ever yet been felt. Indeed, I believe that lord of whom I have often heard tell holds us in his power – namely Love, the cunning stealer of all noble hearts.

'And I tell you that his prison is already more oppressive to me than that of Theseus is. Already I feel more anguish of spirit than I thought this god could inflict. It was great folly on our part that made us go to that little window while that lady was singing so beautifully, for already my heart feels faint because of her.

'I feel captivated and enthralled by her and can find no hope for myself; indeed, I know that I am a prisoner here, bereft of all my power. So what can I do that would gain her favour? Nothing – instead I shall surely die of this, and would God that I were already dead! That would be the greatest solace of all for me.

(25) 'How good and restorative for us would be Aesculapius's remedies for such wounds! He, they say, could by means of herbs bring mutilated human bodies back to life. But what am I saying? For Apollo, who knew about all the herbal essences in the world could not find any effective remedy for himself when struck by an arrow like this.'[8]

This is how these two new lovers converse, each consoling the other with his words. They do not know whether this woman is a goddess come from the kingdoms of the blessed to dwell here below – or whether she is an earthly lady.[9] And her voice and beauty bewilder them, so that – not knowing who it is that has them thus in her power – they suffer greatly from the effects of these pangs.

Nor do the wild winds released by Aeolus so furiously rush from their Sicilian caverns – seeking now the lower regions and now the higher ones – as these two heaved forth their fiercely burning sighs from deep within. But their voices were weak, for the wound that afflicted them was still fresh.

Thus continuing to visit that beautiful garden sometimes alone and sometimes with others to entertain her, the girl would repeatedly let her gaze stray towards the window from which she had first heard Palemone's cry – being drawn to do so not out of love but in order to see if anyone was looking at her.

And if she saw that she was being watched, she would, as if unaware of it, begin to amuse herself by singing in a beautiful clear-toned voice. And she would slowly wander across the grass and among the shrubs in a graceful yet modest way and contrive to make herself appeal more strongly to anyone who was looking on.

(30) It was not any thought of love that made her do this, but rather the vain desire that women are born with in their hearts, to make others gaze at their beauty. For, being more or less barren of any other virtue they are content to be praised for that one; and contriving by means of it to make themselves attractive, they ensnare others whilst retaining their own freedom.

[Palemone and Arcita grow increasingly infatuated with Emilia as the days go by and find out her name from one of their attendants (31–42). The weather changes, and Emilia, to the dismay of the lovers, stops coming to the garden (43–6). Then Pirithous,[10] a close friend of Theseus, comes to visit him and asks to see the two prisoners (47–8). At this point brief portraits of them are presented, beginning with 'the appearance and character of Palemone'.]

(49) Palemone was tall, with well-knit limbs, somewhat dark-haired, cheerful in appearance, pleasant-looking and well-spoken; but since he fell in love he had become modest and gentle in manner. He was of excellent intelligence and discreet in conduct; rosy-complexioned, extremely graceful, dignified in stance and abounding in courage.

(The appearance and character of Arcita.)

(50) Arcita was very tall, slim (but not excessively so) and cheerful in expression. He was as white and red as an April rose, with blond curly

hair, a modest manner and an air of nobility. He had fine eyes and a steady gaze, but showed great vigour in his speech, and anyone could see how agile and nimble he was.

[Pirithous, having greeted Arcita as an old friend, begs Theseus to release him. Theseus does so, but forbids him on pain of death to return to Athens (51–4). Arcita expresses his gratitude for this but is nonetheless mainly concerned about being deprived of the sight of Emilia, and even considers asking to be kept in prison rather than sent into exile (55–73). The book ends with an account of 'how Arcita took leave of Palemone and departed from Athens'.]

(74) Having parted from Pirithous he went to where Palemone was kept prisoner and spoke thus to him: 'My dear friend, I must now against my will take leave of you and depart as one who has been banished and cast out from this place. I may not, I think, ever venture to return, and that will bring me in misery and anguish to my death.

(75) 'As I depart, dear comrade, I abandon my reins to Fortune, and should indeed prefer to be in this prison than to have my freedom as an exile. Then at least when the season changed I should see the lady who has my heart in her power. But if I leave I can never hope to look on her again, and the pain of that will surely kill me.

'I leave my loving heart behind me here and go on my wanderings as a mournful exile from myself, not knowing where Fortune will lead me in my misery. I beg you therefore if at any time you see that lady who has set me afire and aflame – gently remind her of one who for her sake is dying of grief.'

All the time that Arcita was speaking in this fashion Palemone was weeping bitterly and saying: 'How wretched and desolate my life is! Why does Death not destroy me at once so that my miserable destiny could be brought to an end before you leave? For without you, alas, I shall remain in sharp torment, woeful and disconsolate.

'But you, if you are as wise as you usually are, must look for much better fortune and for some relief from your woes – seeing that you when free will be able to achieve much of what you desire, whilst I am forced to remain in idleness. And in your travels you will come across many things that will alleviate your love-sickness.

'But I, left to myself, shall little by little melt away like burning wax. And although the sight of that sweet and lovely face may at times bring me joy, it will nevertheless kindle yet more flames within me since it will not remain before my eyes. And so I do not now know what I can do, and feel as if my heart were breaking within me.'

(80) And thus these two companions who were so deeply in love lamented with bitter sighs and seemed to have become two wells of abounding tears,[11] so drenched were they with them. And since they thus made each other's suffering worse, they had to be aided by their servants and were much rebuked for their folly in showing how inflamed with passion they were.

Then, on hearing the words of their squires, the two companions arose and embraced each other closely with sincere affection and heart felt goodwill. And shortly after that they kissed each other on the lips and started weeping more bitterly than before, and in broken voices bade each other farewell. And thus Arcita went away from there.

Nothing further remained for Arcita to do but leave, and already he was mounted ready to depart, saying to himself: 'Poor wretch that I am – if only God cared enough about my existence to let me see Emilia's exquisite face for a moment before leaving, then I might be able to depart with less sorrow.'

That prayer then rose up to the heavens, and Arcita's wish was at once granted. For that fresh lily of the spring appeared with a waiting-woman, leaning with her bosom against the edge of a balcony,[12] gazing at the charming young man who was going off so sadly into exile and showing a certain sympathy for him.

But he, having uttered his prayer, raised his face without knowing what was to happen, and then set eyes on that angelic and celestial beauty. And that made him say to himself: 'Now even though Fortune tears me away, I believe I can come to no harm.' And then he looked at her once again, saying: 'Dear heart – without you I go weeping on my way.'

(85) Thus saying he began to ride away in obedience to Theseus's decree. But it grieved him to leave his love behind, and he looked back at her as long as he could see her, making frequent halts with the pretence of setting himself to rights. But when there was no more use in further delay, he rode away weeping out of Athens.

(*Here ends the third book of the* Teseida)

Book IV

[After the sonnet the beginning of Arcita's exile is described. He changes his name to Pentheus,[1] continuing to grieve over his separation from Emilia, and visiting Thebes he laments the desolation of the city (1–16). He visits Corinth and Mycenae, subsequently entering the service of King Peleus on the island of Aegina. One day he sees there a ship bound for Athens and hears that Acates, whom Emilia was to marry, has just died. Thinking that his appearance has changed so much as to be unrecognizable, he decides to return to Theseus's court as a servant and immediately does so (17–41). On arriving there he goes to pray for help at the temple of Apollo and finds no difficulty being accepted at Theseus unrecognized by all except Emilia, who remembers him as soon as they see each other at a festival (42–56).]

(57) She no sooner saw him than she said to herself with a smile: 'This is that Arcita whom I saw departing in tears. Alas, what a sad and wretched life he must be leading! But what is he doing here? What can he be looking for? Does he not know that if Theseus comes to hear of his return he will have to be put to death or go back to prison?'

Nevertheless she was so discreet and prudent that she said nothing further about this to anyone, and behaved towards him as if she had never seen him anywhere before. But she was most curious to know what kind of illness had made his fair face so dark and lean as to give him simply a look of hunger and yearning.

Noble Pentheus, under the sway of his passionate devotion, became so assiduous in his duty towards Theseus, and to all the rest according to their qualities, that he placed complete confidence in him and held him dearer than any other servant. And the queen likewise had a warm affection for him, as did the young girl.

[Arcita continues in his secret devotion, not daring to reveal his love to Emilia (60–3). During the hot weather he frequents a grove outside the city, to sleep and make his appeals to the God of Love, Apollo and Venus (63–78). During one of these visits he is moved to utter the following complaint to Fortune.]

(80) 'Wretched Fortune – what great changes you continue to wreak in the human lives that are subject to you! Alas, what families and nations have you brought low, whilst exalting the basest ones as you pleased and refusing to let such occurrences be bound by any principle. For I myself can be seen as a clear witness to your treacherous mutability.

'Born, alas, of royal blood I came into a world that was fraught with all kinds of trouble;[2] and having been most lovingly brought up in great wealth, I dwelt, poor young wretch that I was, in the city of Bacchus,[3] happily occupying a position of power without any thought of your cruel effects. And then through the fault of someone else my happiness, my kingdom and my family were destroyed.

'And I was sorely wounded and left for dead upon the battle-field, then taken and brought to Theseus who, mighty lord that he is, had me kept prisoner during his pleasure. There, to make things worse for me, the cruel burning dart of love pierced my heart because of sweet Emilia's beauty, but she has never given me a single thought.'

[Arcita then briefly describes the events of his exile and the sufferings he has endured for the sake of Emilia (83–5).]

(86) 'And she, alas, has no concern for my bitter anguish and considers none of these things; so that serving her is much less use to me than serving the wind, and I thus remain in continual torment. If only those lights of love had just favoured me with one pleasant glance! But you, cruel Fortune, are my enemy here, for all the while you fan fresh flames in me.

'You have aided me only in keeping my name completely secret, and have favoured me furthermore by making me humble enough to be a servant. You have also gained me the good graces of Theseus which have made my life much more pleasant. But all this is as nothing unless you now make Emilia aware of how much I love her.'

[Arcita's complaint is overheard by Pamphilus one of Palemone's servants, who recognizes him and returns to tell his master in prison – at which point the fourth book ends (88–91).]

Book V

[After the sonnet comes a description of Palemone's hopes and fears as he lies in prison and of how Pamphilus brings him the news about Arcita's return (1–8). Then follows an account of 'how Palemone became determined to escape from prison and how Pamphilus found the means'.]

(9) Then he began to brood over Arcita's conduct as a lover, and came to believe that he had indeed won Emilia's sweet love. Hence he exclaimed: 'Woeful wretch that I am – what an evil moment it was when I came into the world! For here I am a prisoner and in love, whilst someone else is doing what I might do to find bliss.

(10) 'And if only I could still hold or gain the slightest hope of escaping from this place! Then, released from this sorrow of mine, I should rejoice and be confident, too, of reaching my supreme goal. But Fortune is so fiercely hostile to me that I shall not be out of here until the moon stands still!

'And if I should manage to escape, I would have to dispute with Arcita on a fine steed and in stout armour about what he and I are to do concerning our love for that noble person who keeps me in such constant suffering. And she would surely become mine, or else one of us would have to die upon that battlefield.

'But how can I defy him thus when I have never attempted to escape from here? He, in order to see her, did not shrink from associating with one who was his enemy, and he has never ceased serving someone else for the sake of serving her. And I have been wasting my time in lamentations, whilst I ought to have sought death rather than remain here in continual concealment.'

And just as Tisiphone,[1] when summoned by Oedipus in that dark place where he was living in perpetual night, used her cunning to kindle the two brothers' desire for the kingdom – so also through the poison that she has the power to convey, she made desire for Emilia to take root in him, saying: 'Neither power nor love can well be shared with others.'[2]

[Pamphilus contrives Palemone's escape by having him feign illness and disguise himself in the clothing of Alimeto, a Theban physician who is called to attend him (making the guards meanwhile befuddled with drink). Accompanied by Alimeto, who has disguised himself as Pamphilus, Palemone then makes his way out of the prison, equips himself with armour and a horse, and set out for the grove where he finds Arcita-Pentheus asleep (14–36). There follows an account of 'how Pentheus on waking made much of Palemone and what they then spoke about'.]

(37) Meanwhile it was already about to become day and the birds had begun to sing – and thus Pentheus awoke and quickly rose to his feet. He

at once turned in surprise towards Palemone who was approaching, and said: 'Knight, what do you go through these woods in armour to seek?'

Palemone at once replied: 'I was searching for nothing else in the world but you, my comrade. That was what I wanted and longed for, and that was why I have escaped from prison.' Thereupon he greeted him warmly, and Pentheus recognizing him immediately, returned his greeting.

And they both wholeheartedly rejoiced and told each other all that had happened to them. But Palemone, who was all aflame with passion, said: 'Now listen to me, my dear sweet friend. I am so much under the sway of fair Emilia and her radiant looks that I can find no rest, day or night, but am always ablaze with passion.

(40) 'And you will know about that, for you likewise love her also. But she cannot belong to more than one of us; so I earnestly entreat you to let her be mine. If you will do that, I am ready to take action that will at once gain from her what my heart desires. Let her then be my lady alone.'

When Pentheus heard this he became all flushed with anger and his heart blazed furiously within. And he answered, saying: 'Palemone, it must surely be quite clear to you that I put my life at risk solely in order to serve Emilia whom I love more than I can say.

'I therefore beg you, if you have any concern at all for my life, to grant what you yourself are asking to your kinsman Arcita, who has faced great perils in order to attain full happiness with her. And you who have heard me tell of these will know if they deserve to be wondered at. So, my dear friend, grant what I ask.'

Palemone then said: 'Indeed it is no mark of the friendship I thought you bore me to refuse so forthrightly the favour I asked of you. But I swear to you, by the all-powerful heavenly Jupiter and the divinity of Venus, that before I depart from this place we shall have settled such differences with our swords.

'So arm yourself as you think best, and defend your cause – for as long as you deny me what I ask and my heart consumes itself within me our conflict can never be resolved. Why are you so loth to take up your guard against me – seeing that I am eager to triumph or die for the sake of my lady?'

[Arcita attempts with various arguments to dissuade Palemone from fighting, but without success (45–54).]

(55) Then Pentheus said with a sigh: 'Alas, I see in this the wrath of the gods who still remain fiercely opposed to all our desires. And Fortune, not Love, has with a show of favour and sympathy beguiled us into this position, in order to make us die at each other's hands, as we mortals so often do.

'Alas, it was indeed a great surprise to me that Juno let us lead our lives in such peace without tormenting us as she had our fellows, of whom none ever met a glorious or praiseworthy end. I may well grieve therefore as I see us being drawn towards a similar fate.

'Our ancestors who sprang from the teeth planted by Cadmus the son of Agenor were so implacable towards one another that with no thought for brotherly love they slew each other;[3] and the keen-toothed hounds of

Actaeon tore their master to pieces.[4] And Athamas killed his own children – such was the cruel power that Tisiphone wielded over him.[5]

'Latona killed Amphion's children before Niobe's eyes,[6] woeful mother that she was – and Juno's ruthless hatred led Semele to be wretchedly consumed by fire.[7] And everyone knows of the mad frenzy of Agave and her kinsfolk,[8] and likewise that of Oedipus, who killed his father and took his mother as wife.

'There is no need to tell what took place between the two brothers who were sons of Oedipus;[9] the pyre on which they were laid after all their evil deeds itself bore witness to that. And after them wretched Creon had no great cause to give praise to Bacchus.[10] Now we alone are left as the last of the line of Thebes, to kill each other.

(60) 'And since you so desire it, I am willing for there to be battle between us two alone. I shall be ready to do as you wish, but first let me don my armour and fetch my good charger. Then what this frenzied spirit prompts you to seek will be accomplished – and let him who has the worst of it lament his loss.'

Pentheus quickly armed himself, looked to see if anything was missing, quickly fetched his horse and nimbly mounted it. And turning towards Palemone who was boldly and most eagerly awaiting him he addressed him thus: 'Now choose whether you will be at war or at peace with me.

'But let the heavens that behold these actions, Apollo as he rises, and the Fauns and Dryads (if any are known to rule over this place) bear me true witness. And let the stars I behold testify to my grief over this conflict – and Priapus also,[11] whose ground we are about to stain with blood.

'No-one can ever reproach me with having been the cause of this strife between us. You brought it about; you alone sought it and scorned to be reconciled to me. God knows indeed that I could never cease to love that lady who has my heart in her possession; but whilst loving her so, I would dearly love to make peace with you and am eager to do so.'

[Palemone's only reply to this is a brief repetition of his challenge, and the duel begins. Arcita stuns him with a blow upon the helmet and thinking he has killed him begins to lament. But Palemone revives and insists on continuing the fight (64–76). But by a coincidence 'that might not happen in a thousand years' Theseus and Emilia have come to hunt in this same grove (77). Emilia by herself first discovers the two knights fighting and returns to bring Theseus, who, having gazed in wonder at them for some time, interrupts the battle and asks them to tell him their names (78–82). Arcita offers to do so on condition that they are granted pardon, and Theseus agrees (83–5).]

(86) Then he answered at once: 'It is I, your servant Pentheus who am speaking to you, and it was the overwhelming power of love that led me to do battle with this valiant knight in the hope of defeating him. And he likewise hopes to defeat me, for I am his rival in love. As for his name – here he is and can tell you it much better than anyone else.

Palemone looked ill at ease, but nonetheless banished his fears and said: 'My lord, I cannot disguise who I am, and furthermore your nobility assures me that you would not wish to judge severely my innocent intention in escaping from prison for the sake of love. For I am your servant Palemone.'

Theseus was at first angry when he heard them give their names, but then he thanked them heartily for doing so and said to them: 'Now let it not offend you if I ask you to tell me how Cupid made his golden arrow strike you both equally hard – seeing that one of you comes from Aegina and the other was captured at the woeful city of Thebes.

'And if I may know the lady's name, I beg you to tell me.' Palemone then with a sigh told him all that had happened, and Theseus, being much more deeply affected by that than by the rest of what he had been told, said: 'Love has given you great courage, since for his sake you do not fear to die.'

(90) Palemone said to him: 'Noble lord, you have learnt all that you wanted to know, and I have been encouraged to tell you by the desire for death, which would put an end to the bitter suffering that continues to afflict my sorrowful heart. And having escaped from your prison I do most richly deserve to die.'

(How Theseus replied by pardoning them and what terms he imposed upon them.)

Then Theseus said: 'God forbid that it should be as you ask, even though through your folly you have deserved it. For one of you has returned in defiance of my decree and the other broken out of my prison – so that if I did so I should never be blamed, nor should I be doing wrong but following old established practice.

'But since I have been in love before and often made a fool of myself as a result, I am very eager to forgive others. For I on several occasions gained forgiveness, not through my own actions but through the kindness of one whose daughter I abducted.[12] You thus stand assured of forgiveness, for my great compassion will outweigh your offence.

'But this forgiveness will not be absolute, for I shall attach an easy condition to it which you must promise to fulfil if I pardon your wrongdoing.' They pledged themselves to do this, and he made them swear to observe such conditions conscientiously, and solemnly made peace between them. Then he made the following arrangements with them.

He began by saying: 'Fair lords, I had given some consideration to the young girl you both love, and had thought to make her a good match for Acates our cousin.[13] But evil fortune has frustrated these plans through death – and she, lovely as she looks, is yet unmarried.

(95) 'I am thus compelled to take others into consideration, for her age now requires me to do so. And I certainly cannot well imagine giving her to anyone who would love and honour her more truly than would one of you – if indeed you love her as much as my heart leads me to believe. But since both of you cannot have her, she must needs fall to one alone.

'She would be well bestowed on either of you, since you are royal in blood, exalted in rank and noble in conduct. And she likewise possesses those qualities and is also sister of the brave queen who shares the imperial throne with me. So you ought not to look down upon her as a wife, if you can get her.

'But in order to put an end to all your strife you will have to arm yourselves and put matters to the test in the way I shall describe. Palemone is to set about finding a hundred picked companions and you will have to do the same. Then you and your followers will join battle in our amphitheatre.

'Whichever one of you puts the other to flight through force of arms shall become her husband; whilst the other, deprived both of her and of his honour, will have to submit to such judgment as shall please that lady at whose mercy he will be from that moment on. And the space of time allowed you for this will be one whole year.' And so it was agreed.

[Arcita and Palemone eagerly agree to this proposal, whilst Emilia's only response is a blush (99–102). The company then joyfully return to Athens and Theseus entertains the Thebans in his palace, restoring to them their castles and possessions (103–5).]

Book VI

[After the sonnet 'the sixth book of the *Teseida* begins. And first there are some words from the author.']

(1) Fortune, the mighty ruler of the world, inconstantly and frequently altering everything one way and another – giving and taking away – now turning bright, now dark, as, when and how she thought best – had through her treatment of the two Thebans displayed what power she has over earthly affairs.[1]

For they had been born and brought up under her favour, and she had already changed her appearance when they were found upon the battle-field. Thereafter, having deprived them both of wealth and happiness, she left them desolate in prison, shut away from all pleasant prospects. Then she released one of them and nearly restored him to happiness – and this one was Arcita.

And when the other one had, as it pleased her, also escaped from there, she threw him into such a frenzy of wild imaginings that he almost brought himself and his comrade back from newly won happiness to deep grief. Then, being close at hand and familiar with her changeful ways, Theseus pardoned them and raised them to favour.

And she not only gave them hopes of possessing what they both desired, but furthermore, as we have said, she restored each of their inheritances undiminished, so that they both returned from their former penury to a life of wealth. To such a happy state did she bring them after rescuing them from death or wretched imprisonment.

Now who would ever claim that human foresight can make any proper provision in the face of her mutability? If it were not wrong to say so I should declare all such attempts wholly worthless – bearing in mind both this case and those that we continue to read, hear of and witness all the time – even though how she does such things is a mystery to us.

[After spending some time in courtly pursuits the two Thebans set about recruiting supporters for the tournament (6–12). The day appointed by Theseus approaches (13) and a large number of princes arrive, headed by the Nemean King Lycurgus.]

(14) The first to appear, still in mourning for the death of Opheltes[2] and clad in black, was King Lycurgus – mighty, strong and powerful, great in wisdom and bold in spirit. He brought with him the very pick of his kingdom's knighthood, and offered his support to Arcita on whose behalf he had come from Nemea.

[Lycurgus is followed by, among others, Agamemnon, Menelaus, Castor, Pollux, Nestor, Pirithous, Ulysses, Diomedes and Admetus King of Thessaly (15–57) – as well as a number of supporters of either side from Boeotia (58–60). The author also explains why a number of well-known mythical figures were absent. Thus Narcissus would have come if he had not been turned into a flower, Leander had he not been drowned, and Erysichthon were he not dying of hunger as the result of a feud with Ceres (61–4).[3] All those who appear are nobly welcomed by Theseus, Hippolyta and Emilia and by their prospective leaders, Palemone and Arcita (65–9), and the book ends with a brief description of their entertainment at the Athenian court.]

(70) Fine banquets and gifts fit for kings were constantly provided there; and there was talk only of love, accompanied by condemnation of those who were vicious and disdainful. And their skills were exercised most of the time in youthful sports and frequent jousting, or in keeping company with ladies in the gardens. Both the greater and the lesser among them were kept happy and the true lovers set at ease.

And indeed, since the time when Pallas disputed with Neptune over the naming of the city,[4] so many high-ranking people of such great nobility had never been found gathered together there at any time. And Theseus regarded this as a supreme honour, placing it among his most memorable achievements.

(*Here ends the sixth book of the* Teseida.)

Book VII

[After the sonnet the seventh book opens with Theseus's address to the Greek princes assembled in his amphitheatre. He begins (3) by assuming that they know what has caused them to be summoned there, and goes on to describe the development of his plans for settling the lovers' rivalry.]

(4) 'But indeed, when I made a truce between them and left it to a hundred men on each side to fight for the love of the lady they so desire I did not think that lances or spears, large numbers of bright or dull weapons, great

horses or mighty foot-soldiers would be called for to quench this conflagration – for I thought it would be more like a formal wrestling match.

(5) 'Nor did I think the whole of Lernea[1] under its Achaean kings would be stirred by such a slight affair – but that each of them with his vassals would have been concerned to put an end to this sort of strife, and would have preferred that after only a brief struggle one of these men should gain the love they seem to desire so much.

'But these two, thinking me, perhaps, to be ignorant of the power they wielded, grew eager to make me aware of it; and they have brought you here with your followers to pay tribute to the love that breeds such extreme ardour within them. And I am well pleased that you have come and that they have shown such strength.

'But nonetheless I beg you to conduct matters differently, and in the way I shall describe. We are not faced here with any struggle to gain a throne or recapture a lost inheritance. No deadly hatred exists between these two, and no-one is seeking here to avenge any injury that has been committed. But love alone, as I have said, is the cause of the dispute.

'Hence, if I judge rightly, this battle should be friendly rather than malevolent. For those of a malevolent sort are waged by people seeking to cause trouble or having other ends in mind, or by the savage Centaurs of Thessaly who never have any thought of peace[2] – and not by us who, although we may have been bred in one place or another, are still descended from the same stock.

'And how could I ever bear to see Larissan[3] blood being shed and each of us falling at the hands of the others as the seed of Cadmus chose to do?[4] To-day there are neither the same circumstances nor the same issues, so let us leave them to men of that sort, and dwell in harmony as we ought – lightheartedly doing battle for the sake of love.

(10) 'Whoever could wish for such a reason to place so many nations at risk of losing such noble people as those I see before me? It would be ill-advised and most repugnant to the gods to find a son attacking his father here, and kinsmen viciously striking at each other with weapons in their hands.

'But since you have gathered here for this purpose, and in order that you may not have come in vain – let each of you choose, then, whichever of the two lovers he loves best, and let a hundred of you be numbered on each side, just as my judgment decreed that day when I found them thus in the grip of grief, anger and love.

'And in order that hatred may not be bred between you, leave aside your lances, as they are more dangerous, and make trial of your own strength to your hearts' delight with swords and maces. And let those who wish wield two-headed axes, but no other kinds; weapons of that sort will suffice for you. And he whose courage yields him victory will win both the lady and the glory.

'These will be like ceremonial games in honour of Mars, whose sacrifices we perform on the appointed day; and hence the skill we have in wielding arms will be displayed. And since I have to remain here where we are sitting as judge rather than participant, I shall, unarmed as I am, give close heed to your actions; so take care to conduct yourselves well.'

The acclamation of the nobles and the populace was so loud and strong that it rose up to the heavens. 'May the gods' they said 'protect such a lord, who seeks to prevent the deaths of those he loves, and through his kind and gracious concern let our conflicts be resolved less bitterly!' And without leaving that place each hundred of them chose their party and joined it.

[Arcita and Palemone both choose ten of the princes who have joined them, asking each of them to pick nine of his best men for the tournament. They then return to the court, having sworn to keep the peace meanwhile (15–21). On the eve of the appointed day the two Thebans go to ask the gods for their help (22–3) – Arcita first lighting votive flames and pouring libations, and then offering his 'prayer to Mars'.]

(24) 'O mighty god, maintaining your sacred dwellings amid the snowy realms of the Bistones[5] in regions that are dark, hostile to the sun and dominated by that power of yours through which the proud sons of Earth had their boldness tamed and all lay cold and dead once you and your father Jupiter had shown your strength[6] – / (25) if, as I devoutly wish my age and powers make me fit to be numbered among your followers, then for the sake of that pity Neptune had for you when you were ensnared by Vulcan whilst enjoying Cytheraea's beauty and shown to all the gods,[7] I humbly beg you not to reject my prayers.

'I am a young man as you see, and Love has so overcome me through the power of a miraculous beauty that I shall need to call upon all my strength and courage if I am to enjoy what my heart most desires. And without your help I am capable of little, or rather can achieve nothing at all.

'Assist me then, for the sake of that sacred fire which once inflamed you as it now does me, and grant me your strength in this ritual contest in which I am to take part. That would indeed not be a small favour but a supreme blessing for me. Help me then to accomplish this aim, for if I triumph in the struggle it will yield me joy and you honour.

'Your eternal temples will be decked with the arms of my conquered comrade and will also receive my own – and the reasons for that will be commemorated there. Everlasting flames shall burn there, and if you grant me the victory I have spoken of, I vow to offer you my beard and hair which have never yet felt the attack of steel.'

(How Arcita's prayer reached Mars; what his temple is like and where it is.)

Mars was perhaps at that time burnishing the rusty places in his huge and terrible dwelling[8] when Arcita's fervent Prayer, all tearful in appearance, arrived there to perform her given task.[9] She grew dumb with terror when she saw the house of Mars, / (30) there upon the plains of Thrace under wintry skies, racked by continual tempest, in which during the rainy winters troops of perpetual storm clouds are blown hither and thither to different quarters and drops of water fall frozen by the cold, together with snow that gradually hardens and turns to ice.

And it stood there amid a barren wood of stout turkey-oaks, which grew thickly and very tall, knotty, rough, hardy and ancient, and cast eternal shadow upon the face of that grim land. And there amid those aged trunks a mighty sound could be heard, forever whirling around, borne by more than a thousand furies – and neither beast nor herdsman was to be found.

Here she saw the house of the martial god which was built entirely of bright and polished steel, reflecting the light of the sun which loathed that evil place. The narrow entrance was all of iron and the doors were braced all over with everlasting adamant.

And she saw the iron columns that supported the building. She thought she saw demented Assaults there, wildly emerging from the entrance. Blind Wrongdoing and every kind of Woe were likewise to be seen there, and in that place she saw Rages red as fire and pale Fear.

And she saw Betrayals with their hidden weapons and Plots with an honest appearance. Strife was sitting there holding bloodstained weapons, together with all sorts of Quarrel – and every part of the building seemed to roar with harsh Threats and fierce Animosity. And in the midst of this place Strength was most wretchedly seated, bereft of honourable praise.

She also saw exultant Frenzy there, as well as armed Death with his bloody face, and Amazement. All the altars ran with the blood that had been shed by human bodies in battle alone, and each was lit by flames taken from lands burnt and ravaged in the course of grim wars.

And the whole temple, both up above and all around, was cunningly adorned with historical scenes, in which the first thing she saw were the spoils taken from cities by night and day. Whatever had been conquered by force of arms appeared sombrely there: people in chains, gates of iron and battered fortresses were there to be seen.

And there she also saw warships, empty chariots, mangled faces, wretched, pitiful cries and every kind of army, triumphant in appearance. All manner of wounds were also to be seen there, with blood drenching the earth. And grim, proud Mars displayed his cruel countenance in every place.

BOCCACCIO'S GLOSSES ON THE TEMPLE OF MARS (EXCERPTS)

... He [the author] thus says first that the temple of Mars is in Thrace in cold and misty regions that abound in rain, winds and frost,[10] and are wild and covered with barren trees – and is in gloomy surroundings that are hostile to the sun and full of turbulence. In order to comprehend this, it must be known that in every man there are two main appetites. Of these one is called the 'concupiscible' appetite, which leads a man to desire and rejoice in having those things which, wisely or misguidedly, he considers to be enjoyable and pleasant. The other is called the 'irascible' appetite, which troubles a man when he loses or is prevented from gaining the objects of his enjoyment, or when they cannot be attained. This irascible appetite is most commonly found in men who have a superabundance of blood, because the blood is naturally hot, and hot things through any slight movement are easily kindled. And so it is that men of a very sanguine constitution are quick to become angry, although some of them, through the strenuous exercise of reason, bridle and suppress their anger. And since, as we have stated elsewhere,[11] men in cold countries are more sanguine in constitution than is the case in others, the author here makes clear that the temple of Mars (that is, this irascible appetite) is in Thrace – which is a very cold region situated under the pole star, where the men are extremely fierce and contentious and wrathful because of the great abundance of blood in them . . .

He then says that in this house of Mars there are demented Assaults which he says emerge from the entrance; and thus he shows that the first action of a man enraged is to attack – for as we know angry people are quick to rush to arms or assault others. And he calls these assaults demented – that is, mad – as they obviously are. Next he says that blind Wrongdoing is there as the result of such an assault; for anyone who rushes into action without rational consideration sins blindly. He says that all kinds of Woe are also present – that is, all kinds of lamentation. And that is reasonable enough, for after deeds of madness lamentations necessarily follow, either from those who are unjustly made to endure them or from those who are known to have performed them. Next he states that Rages red as fire are there – and through this detail he refers to the appearance of the angry man whom, we usually find, becomes flushed to begin with. He speaks of Rages in the plural to make clear that there are two sorts of anger, each of which causes the angry man to become flushed. One takes the form of unreasonable rage which is vicious and is what we speak of here. The other may be reasonable, as is indignation about some injustice which takes its counsel from reason in denouncing and setting right whatever has been wrongfully done – and the author means this to be in the house of Mars because many just wars have sprung and always may spring from it . . .

He also says that all parts of the building roar – that is, resound – with harsh Threats and cruel Animosity – that is, railing – and these as we well know are the actions of angry men. Furthermore, he says that there Strength is most wretched. By this he means bodily strength which, when it is abused in killing and maiming the innocent, is a kind of strength that is most wretched and poor – that is, without any honourable praise. Next he says that exultant Frenzy is there – as we regularly find in every action of those who are unjustly angry, for they are all frenzied. He calls it exultant because they enter wildly upon all their ventures in a spirit of impiety and with noise and display. He next says that armed Death and Amazement are there, as the twin effects of wars born of anger. For either people perish in battle at the hands of armed men, or if they survive are struck with wonder at the great effects which take shape from small beginnings, as we have often found . . .

(38) And cunning Mulciber[12] had devoted his skill to building this sanctuary in days before the sun's beams showed him Cytheraea[13] lying with Mars. And Mars from a long way off heard what she[14] sought and knew whence she had come to entreat his aid. He therefore received her and attended to her concerns.

Then having listened to her whom Arcita had humbly sent from afar, he quickly went without delay to the place to which he had been secretly summoned. And no sooner had the temples sensed the presence of their sovereign deity than they at once trembled and all their doors creaked together – and at that Arcita was struck with fear.

(40) The flames burned much brighter, the ground gave forth a marvellous fragrance, and the incense-burners sent out smoke towards the image places there in honour of Mars, whose armour all clashed against itself as it stirred – thus showing the awestruck Arcita that his prayer had been heard.

The young man then rested content in hope of winning victory, and he did not emerge from the temple that night but spent the whole time in prayer. And several signs he was vouchsafed during that time made him more confident of the truth. But when the new day had dawned this fair youth had his armour put on him.

(How Palemone went to offer prayers at the temple of Venus.)

Palemone also had made every temple in Athens reek with smoke, and there was not a single god or goddess left in Heaven to whom he did not appeal for help. But above all others he chose that day to offer worship to Cytheraea with incense and humble sacrifices, and remained in her temple to pray.

And reverently he uttered the following prayer: 'O fair goddess, noble Vulcan's wife on whose behalf Mount Cithaeron rejoices – I beg you now to take pity on me for the sake of the love you had for Adonis.[15] Fulfil this desire of mine that you have made so passionate, and lend my right arm strength tomorrow, so that I may thus be made happy.

'No-one can know how much I am in love, no-one can tell how great is my desire, and no-one can understand how much I yearn for the lovely Emilia, the mistress of my heart, whose name I call upon night and day. No-one, that is, except you and your divine son who well know what mighty pangs of love I, as her servant, endure.

(45) 'I could never express my desire in words, nor tell how much I feel. You alone, O goddess, know of it, and by granting this wish lasting fulfilment can turn my suffering into joy again – if you do what I so earnestly entreat by letting me regain possession of my lady Emilia.

'I do not ask for victory in battle in order to deck the temples of Mars with arms. I do not seek to win glory from those I shall encounter tomorrow – nor do I desire that my deeds should be long remembered. I desire only Emilia, and her, O goddess, you can grant me if only you will.

'Choose your own way of doing so, for I have no preference. It little matters to me whether I win or lose, if I cannot be sure of attaining my heart's desire. Therefore, O goddess, take whichever way is easier and allow me to win her. Do so, I beg you, O Cytheraea, and do not deny me, all-powerful goddess.

'Your temples will always be honoured by me as places worthy of constant worship, and they will always be decked with myrtles. I shall make all your altars bright with flames, and sacrifices will be offered as surely befits such a goddess. And I shall always revere your name beyond that of any other god, because of its surpassing power.

'And if it does not please you to do as I ask, make sure to take the first sword you find in the arena, and by piercing my heart force my soul and vital spirits to issue forth while my blood drenches the battlefield. For such a death would be far more welcome to me than a life in which, bereft of her, I was forced to see her given to Arcita instead.

(How the prayer reached Venus, what her temple is like and where it is.)

(50) Just as the prayer of Arcita had sought out Mars, so that of Palemone went away to tender-hearted Venus up on Mount Cithaeron, where Cytheraea's temple and dwelling place stands in a rather shaded spot amongst very tall pines. And, as she approached, Desire was what she first saw in that lofty place.

Accompanying her she found the surroundings in every way mild and pleasant, for they were like a leafy and lovely garden, full of the greenest plants, short new grass and all sorts of newly-opened flowers. She also saw clear springs flowing there, and amongst the other plants with which the place abounded there seemed to her to be more myrtles than anything else.

She saw nearly every kind of bird singing sweetly there amid the branches, upon which she also saw them happily building their nests. Then she saw rabbits[16] scuttling to and fro upon the new grass, together with timid young red-deer, roe-deer and many other kinds of small animal.

She also thought that she could hear all kinds of musical instrument and pleasant song there. Moving along with unslackened pace and marvelling somewhat bemusedly at the noble place and its beauties, she saw that in virtually every part it was thronged with spirits flying hither and thither to their places. And while gazing at these / (54) she saw Cupid, who had laid down his bow at his feet and was among the shrubs beside a spring making arrows, some of which his daughter Pleasure was picking out to temper in the water. Sitting with them she saw Idleness, who, together with Memory, was fitting the shafts with the steel that Pleasure had tempered.

(55) Then she saw Grace pass by with Elegance and Friendliness, and Courtesy completely at a loss.[17] She saw the magic Arts which can force people to act foolishly, and which reflect our likeness in a grossly distorted form.[18] And she saw Imaginary Delight standing to one side with Nobility.

Then she saw unadorned Beauty pass close by, gazing at herself, and saw Charm accompanying her – each of them praising the other. With them she saw Youth who was agile, well-dressed and high-spirited, and at a distance she saw Foolhardiness keeping company with Flattery and Procurement.

And in the centre of this she saw a temple supported upon tall columns of copper, and around it she saw dancing finely dressed young men and ladies, lovely in themselves – barefoot and with hair and gowns flowing free; for they spent the day in no other way but this. Then above the temple she saw flocks of sparrows fluttering and doves cooing.

And close by the entrance she saw Lady Peace sitting, quietly and gently holding a curtain in front of the door. Near her Patience was modestly sitting, with her pale face and utterly dejected appearance, and all around her she saw Promises and Strategies.

Then entering the temple she heard gales of sighs kindled by fierce Desires blowing around the place. These lit all the altars with fresh flames born of Pining and each of them ran with tears caused by a harsh and wicked lady called Jealousy whom she saw there.

(60) And there she saw Priapus occupying the most exalted position, clad just as he was when any who wished could see him, that night when the laziest of animals by its braying awoke Vesta, who was not a little favoured by him and to whom he was making his approach in such a guise.[19] Likewise throughout the temple she saw garlands of many different flowers.

She saw many of Diana's followers' bows hanging up broken there – amongst them being that of Callisto who was turned into the northern Bear.[20] There also were the apples of proud Atalanta who excelled at running – together with the weapons of that other haughty woman who gave birth to the beautiful Parthenopaeus, grandson of Oeneus of Calydon.[21]

She saw famous stories depicted everywhere, and among them she found all the deeds of Ninus's wife[22] portrayed with the finest craftsmanship. She saw Pyramus and Thisbe at the foot of the tree, with the mulberries already stained,[23] and along with these she saw great Hercules in Iole's lap,[24] and sad Byblis pitifully pursuing Caunus.[25]

But being unable to see Venus, she was told – she knew not by whom – 'She takes her delight in the most secret part of the temple. If you want her you must go quietly through this door.' So without further delay she went forward humbly in order to enter and perform the mission entrusted to her.

But as soon as she came there she found Wealth on watch at the door and thought she should be treated with great respect. When allowed in by her she discovered the place to be dark on first entering; but having been there a while she perceived a little light and saw her lying naked upon a great bed which was most beautiful to behold.

Her hair was golden and was bound unbraided about her head. Her face was such that those most highly praised have by comparison no beauty. Her arms and bosom and firm breasts were fully revealed, and the rest of her covered by a garment so fine it hid almost nothing.

The place was redolent with a thousand perfumes. On one side of her sat Bacchus and on the other Ceres with her pleasant flavours.[26] She herself held Wantonness by one hand and in the other the apple she had won in the Vale of Ida through being preferred to her sisters.[27] And having seen all this she put forward her plea, which was granted without demur.

BOCCACCIO'S GLOSSES ON THE TEMPLE OF VENUS (EXCERPTS)

. . . Attention should first be given then to the nature of the place. The author says that it is on Mount Cithaeron, amongst pines etc., as the text shows. In order to explain this is must be known that whilst Mars above is said to stand for the 'irascible' appetite, so Venus stands for the 'concupiscible'. This Venus is twofold in character.[28] In one form she can and should be seen to represent all worthy and legitimate desires – such as the desire to have a wife in order to have children, and so on – but this Venus is not involved here. The second Venus is the one who causes all kinds of lust to be desired, and she is commonly called the goddess of love. And the author here describes the temple of this goddess and the other things surrounding it, as the text shows. There are two reasons why the author therefore speaks of the Temple of Venus as being upon Mount Cithaeron. The first is that it was in fact there – for Mount Cithaeron is close to Thebes, and at certain times of year the Thebans used to hold the most sacred rites upon it, offering up frequent sacrifices in honour of Venus. And the second is that the nature of the place is very suitable for Venus, for it is a region that is very moderate in its degrees of heat and cold – as will be very clearly perceived by anyone who considers the matter carefully. For that part of Greece in which Mount Cithaeron is situated is neither too far to the north nor too far to the south, but just about mid-way between. And this moderation is very necessary for sexual activity, for if we consider the question carefully, a man who is frigid in temperament or happens to have become chilled cannot without great difficulty engage in such activities, since his energies are subdued by the cold. Likewise the man who is either constitutionally too hot or has become heated through excess of wine or exertion will have so dissipated his energies that they cannot be employed in this way. Moderation is therefore essential to this kind of pursuit, and because of that the author rightly situates the temple of this goddess in a temperate place . . .

He also speaks of the place as being shady and full of springs. He means this shade to signify two things. One is the refreshing coolness so welcome to those who are too hot – and that is also the reason for the springs. The other is the kind of place that is necessary for Venus's purposes, which require comfort and darkness. He makes a similar point when describing the place where Venus dwells. And having described those things which can usually, when combined with natural impulses, excite people to sexual activity, he then describes those that excite the people we commonly call lovers. He presents these things in personal form and in various ways since he sees some of them as natural forces and some as artificial stimulants . . .

He says that Pleasure tempers them [Cupid's arrows] in a spring. Here it should be understood that Love took as his wife a girl called Psyche and had by her a daughter, namely Pleasure herself.[29] By this Psyche the author here means Hope – and whenever she, together with Love, enters or remains in the mind of the lover they beget between them this daughter Pleasure, who here stands for the particular delight the mind feels within itself because of its hopes of gaining the object of its love. This kind of gratification is what tempers the arrows of love, making them powerful enough to inflame the heart throughout. And it tempers them in the fount of our false judgment since through this gratification that is bred of love and hope we come to think that the object of our delight is to be preferred to all other things whether worldly or divine. But since the forces thus spoken of cannot establish themselves without the recollection of their cause and a certain lapse of time, he therefore brings in Memory and

131

Idleness to tip these arrows that have been forged by the heat of love and tempered by the inner gratification born of hope. And is it not obvious that if we did not recall the form and actions of what we delight in, we should be unable to love it? And similarly if we did remember such things but were encumbered with many different concerns, would not this pleasure be unable to establish itself in our minds but pass away, giving place to other preoccupations? . . .

Within [the temple of Venus] he portrays a tumult of sighs, saying that the flames upon the altars bathed in tears are nourished by them – and he asserts that they are caused by Jealousy. By this the author means to say that sighs are not caused and tears are not shed until we are inside the temple – that is, in love and affected by jealousy. For the sighs of some-one who is in love, yet not jealous, are easy and usually pleasant. But jealousy brings endless and exceedingly bitter anxieties, which often draw sighs, tears and anguished groans from the breasts of those who are jealous – as those who experience or have experienced it know . . .

Having seen these legends and perhaps many others illustrating the power of Venus, Palemone's prayer, according to the author, reached the spot where Venus was. In this place, as is very clear to those who look at the details carefully, he portrays very fully the pleasurable state in which we find all those who through skill, intelligence or expense have attained their desires and remain devoted to them. He then says that Venus was in the most secret part of the temple, over which Wealth kept guard – and by this he means that the life of pleasure cannot be had or maintained for long without wealth. Then he speaks of the place as being dark – and that is because those who are doing evil hate the light. Next he describes the beauty of Venus whom he portrays reclining, partly naked and partly draped with a rich purple cloth so fine that it conceals hardly anything of those parts it covers. Through this reclining he represents the languor characteristic of pleasure-lovers and the life of ease. Through Venus's beauty, which we know to be a frail and transient thing, he represents that false judgment of pleasure-lovers which through true reason we can very easily recognise and prove to be baseless. Through the partial nakedness of Venus he represents the appearance of things, which holds the atten-tion of those whose understandings cannot grasp the truth about them. Through the part of her that is visible under the fine garment he seeks to portray the secret belief of those who judge by appearances. For such people, when they see a woman with a lovely face, immediately leap to the conclusion that the parts concealed by her clothes must possess some measure of beauty and attractiveness greater than those of a woman who has a less beautiful face. And they almost believe they can see such parts, even though later experience proves to them that all women, lovely and unlovely, are made after the same fashion. He then says that on one side of her was sitting Bacchus the god of wine and on the other Ceres, goddess of crops; and through these two he portrays gluttony which is much indulged in by pleasure-lovers. He also says she was holding Wantonness by the hand – by which he means to show that the actions of pleasure-lovers are characterized not only by lust but also by wantonness. And he sees such wantonness as consisting in kisses, touching, trifling, badinage and the other foolish things that are done at such times. The perfuming of the place is essential for those who indulge in such pursuits. For since the activity itself is so malodorous, if the sense of smell were not soothed by perfumes the stomach and the mind would easily be put off, and so would all the other functions. By means of the apple he shows in Venus's hand he seeks to represent the foolish choice of those who prefer this kind of existence to any other.

(67) Once she had heard Palemone's words the goddess quickly went to the place to which she had been summoned, and thus strange sounds were heard in that holy building. And hence also there arose in Heaven a fresh cause of strife between Venus and Mars; but with masterly skill they found a way to satisfy the prayers of both sides.

Whilst Apollo kept the world deprived of light Palemone thus remained shut within the temple continuing in his devotions, just as the custom at that time may have been for those were to change a squire's livery for that of a knight – for he, being one of the former, was going to do so.

And certainly the lovers I have spoken of were because of their general amiability beloved by all the people of Athens. Hence every single god was implored by all with equal fervour to keep them from suffering and injury and to satisfy both in such a way that neither might ever find fault with it.

[There follows a description of how Emilia goes to worship at the temple of Diana – first washing herself, then purifying the temple, lighting two equal sacrificial fires upon the altar and offering up turtle-doves and lambs (70–6). Then begins 'Emilia's prayer to Diana'.]

(77) 'O goddess, to whom the earth, the heavens, the sea and the kingdoms of Pluto are revealed whenever you choose to visit them – accept my humble sacrifices with such ceremony as I am able to provide. I know indeed that you are worthy of greater things – but on this occasion, O goddess, let good intentions make up for my being unable to provide more.'

Saying this she fell silent until she saw the sacrificial fires fully alight. Then, stricken with grief, the maiden knelt before Diana, with tears bathing the fair face she turned towards the goddess. And having remained bowed in grief for a while she raised it again most tearfully, / (79) and began in broken tones to say: 'O chaste goddess – you who haunt the woods, set yourself to watch over virgins and are most vengeful in your wrath, as Actaeon came to know[30] when he, being more youthful than lucky, was stricken alas not by your bowstring but your wrath and turned into a stag – / (80) hear these words of mine, and though I am unworthy grant them your favour I pray, in the name of your mighty threefold deity. And unless it is too difficult for you, seek to bring them to fulfilment, if your chaste breast was ever pierced by pity for any maiden praying to you or asking for your aid.

'I am still one of your company of maidens for I am much more suited to archery and woodland pursuits than to delight a husband with my love.

And if your memory looks back in time, you will also recall how we set out wills firmer than rock in the face of wanton Venus to whom the desires of fools are so irrationally devoted.[31]

'Hence if it is best for me as a young maiden still to remain among your fellowship, then quench those fierce and fiery spirits that kindle a desire I find so troublesome in those young men, who are in love with me and both seek to enjoy my love. And put an end to the strife between them, for as you know it does indeed grieve me greatly.

'And if the Fates have nonetheless determined that I must submit to Juno's law, you ought surely to grant me your pardon and not for that reason reject my prayers. For you must know that I am subject to another law, and must do as they wish. Lend me your aid therefore and listen to my prayers, O goddess, if I am now worthy of that.

'I earnestly entreat your aid for those who with their keen-edged weapons are so rashly going to assail each other tomorrow. And I beg you to put an end to the grief I endure because of their sufferings in love, and let their strife he peacefully resolved or diverted to another end that will yield their reputations more glory.

(85) 'And if perhaps the gods have already immutably decreed that these two may fulfil their purpose – make sure that he whom I should most willingly receive and he who has the deep-rooted desire for me is the one to enter my arms. For they both seem so pleasant to me that I cannot choose for myself.

'And let the other suffer no further injury at all than the disgrace of losing me. And if I may ask as much, O goddess, let these fires whose incense rises towards your divine throne show me whose I shall be. For one of them stands for Arcita and the other for Palemone.

'My sad heart will then at least learn to show less grief for the loser and will more easily be able to bear it when I see him fleeing from the amphitheatre. My choice which is now uncertain will thus also incline to one side, and I shall be able to witness the other's defeat more calmly if I know what has to happen.'

(What was shown to Emilia as she prayed, and how she left the temple.)

Whilst Emilia prayed the fires went on burning and spreading their pleasant fragrance throughout the splendid temple. And Emilia was still gazing on them, as if bound at once to find in them what she sought, when Diana with her company of archers appeared to her, saying: 'Maiden, you will soon see what lies in store for you.

'For it has already been decided among the gods in Heaven that you are to marry one of these men, and Diana is content that it should be so.[32] But which of the two it is will be concealed from you yet a while, although you may observe what is to happen within the temple and in this very place. Fix your gaze closely then upon the altars, and you will find out what your heart yearns to know.'

(90) And after this was said the arrows in fair Diana's quiver clashed, and her bow moved of its own accord. And none of those followers remained there any longer, but each quickly returned to the woods from which she had come. Hounds bayed and her horn was heard resounding – all of which Emilia took as signs that her prayer had been heard.

The maiden wiped away the tears from her lovely eyes, and still attending to the fires she fixed her gaze most closely upon them.[33] And she had not been doing so long when one went out and then rekindled itself; and the other turned the colour a flame is sometimes given by sulphur – its tongues flickering this way and that and roaring loudly as it burned.[34]

And the burning brands became bloody, and from all their unlighted ends they shed drops that extinguished the coals.[35] And as she witnessed this Emilia did not properly understand either the behaviour or the appearance of the fire that had first gone out and then been rekindled – for she saw in it only what she chose to see.

And she thus returned to her chamber as uncertain as she had been when she left it – even though she might say she had seen something that showed what lay in store for her. She passed that night in great distress until the stars had all vanished; then she arose and made herself look fairer than the morning star had ever appeared.

[Arcita and Palemone summon their followers and leave the temples to join Theseus at his court (94–102). Theseus invests them with the order of knighthood and they both set off in procession to the amphitheatre, where the sound of trumpets and the roar of the crowd makes those involved feel 'less keen enthusiasm' for the coming battle (103–5).]

(106) And each for his part felt like the hunter[36] approaching a gap in the cliffs in the Gaetulian[37] forests – who waits for the lion that has been roused by the continuing noise,[38] and rapidly musters his courage whilst his face grows chill with fear. He grips his weapons tightly with sweating hands, and each step is taken with a shudder.

He does not know what is coming or what sort of creature it may be. But he forms a fearful impression of the roaring creature in his mind, while wishing that he had not deployed his skills in this way. And he, nonetheless, in his blind anxiety seems to interpret the roaring he hears, making it sometimes allay his fears and sometimes increase it further.

(*The author describes the amphitheatre and how Aegeus and many others entered it.*)

The circular amphitheatre was situated a little way outside the city. It was not an inch less than a mile all around; its marble wall with its tablets of polished carving rose so high into the sky that it almost strained the eye to look at; and it had two entrances with strong and most finely wrought gates.

Of these one with its great columns was set to face the rising sun; whilst the other looked towards the west and was made exactly like the first. All had to enter through these and not from any other side, for there was no entrance on those. In the middle there was a perfectly circular arena, spacious enough for any noble festival / (110) and surrounded by terraces which made, I believe, more than five hundred circles before reaching the summit of the wall. And there were broad steps of marvellously fine stone upon which people sat to watch the fierce gladiators or others engaged in any sport, without at any point getting in each other's way.

[Aegeus, Theseus and the Athenian populace, followed by Hippolyta and Emilia, enter the amphitheatre (111–13). The two Thebans then make their appearance – Arcita entering through the eastern gate and Palemone through the western one (114–21). Seeing Emilia there, Arcita addresses an inward appeal to her – as also does Palemone, although his words are not recorded (122–9). Theseus then addresses the contestants, and the book ends with the Thebans encouraging their own followers – although here again only Arcita's speech is given (130–45).]

Book VIII

[After the sonnet 'the eighth book of the *Teseida* begins, with an invocation first and then the opening of the battle.']

(1) The entire audience in the amphitheatre was silent as it awaited the third signal from the Tyrrhenian instrument.[1] They gazed up, down and around and discussed their private opinions of one or the other – some of them backing this side and some that. And while they were busy watching them the third blast suddenly broke upon their ears.

Now let the Muse I honour most compose and rhyme on my behalf, describing the warlike sport in which the two lovers fiercely engaged, whilst they both deployed equal companies of brave and trustworthy knights; for on my own I should never be able to express the violence of the conflict and the bitterness of its consequences.

If the sound of a raging sea, whipped by fierce strong winds, were added to all that which sailors made when gaining harbour, or that which is said to have been made when Caesar encountered Pompey in Thessaly – it would not equal this by far, for nothing louder had ever been heard.

Nor would it have, if amplified by that which Lipari made, or Etna, or Stromboli, or Vulcano at his hottest – or when Jupiter at his angriest struck most terror into fierce Typhoeus with his mighty thunder. So now let all those who have any understanding at all consider how mighty it was, and perhaps they will grasp what I have been saying about the noise / (5) of weapons, horns, drums and trumpets[2] and the cries in foreign tongues – all of which, they say, could be heard as far away as Corinth, so greatly did it fill the air. All birds ceased to fly; beasts in the forest grew fearful; and all who were not there to see thought that part of the sky had fallen.

And as at the point where the Apennines find themselves severed from Mount Peloro,[3] the opposing winds make the great billows dash against each other and turn from dark purple to white – so did these forces surge against each other faster and more fiercely than when, after a sudden storm, the high mountain torrent rushes headlong down to seek its lowland bed.

Thus this courageous company spurred on their mighty chargers, and not having lances they fiercely drove their horses bodily against each other. The mounting dust concealed them completely, and many then fell from their saddles without mounting their horses again or rising from where they lay.

[The battle then proceeds in a series of epic combats, and one of Arcita's followers is the first of many fatal casualties (15). Diomedes and Minos, supporters of Palemone are captured (29–37), Evander, Sychaeus and Peleus are in various ways put out of action (38–50), and there is an encounter between Arcita and Admetus (51–7). Idas is taken after attempting to capture Arcita (58–65), and Admetus leads an assault upon Arcita's standard (66–77). Arcita after resting a while is impelled, on glancing at Emilia, to return to the fray with even greater energy (78–85). The state of the battlefield and the reactions of the noble onlookers are then described (86–93), and particular attention is given to Emilia's dismay at what is happening and her anxiety on behalf of both contestants (94–5).]

(96) She would at moments say to herself: 'Alas, Love, what trouble you have wrought! Neither you nor these two had entered my thoughts at all; I did not come here for their sake and was not meant to be bestowed on them – nor did Theseus ever consider doing so. But you and Fortune together have placed me in this predicament.

'And if you still meant through my beauty to inflame anyone with your ardour, you could have done so by making him confidently woo me by virtue of his rank. For I am not so great a prize that for my sake so many should have to display all the prowess of which they are capable. Alas for me; I was not meant to be sold so dear.

'Ah, what a curse it was that Nature gave me this beauty,[4] whose price is this terrible, cruel and ferocious battle being waged here for the sake of my looks alone! And to stop it happening I would gladly let my beauty dwell for ever in obscurity, rather than have it bring such bloodshed as I see down there in the arena.

'Alas, Love, what omens but everlasting lamentation will escort me into the chamber of either of these two? The sorrowing souls of those being unjustly slain for my sake will never be sated with my sorrow and grief, but will always continue to haunt me and rejoice over all my misfortunes.'

[Emilia continues to grieve over her responsibility for the bereavements that will result from the battle. She wishes that Palemone and Arcita could fight for her in single combat, that she herself could decide between them, or that Theseus had let them settle matters in the grove (100–10). Meanwhile Mars, seeing that the combatants are tiring, descends to the arena in the form of Theseus in order to spur Arcita and his followers on to further efforts, and the battle is thus rekindled (111–19). Eventually Palemone is dragged down by a man-eating horse belonging to the son of Hercules, and is immediately disarmed by Arcita (120–3). Then follows 'the author's description of Emilia when she saw that Palemone had been captured.']

(124) She was watching all this with great sadness, and when she saw how things had gone between them and knew for sure that she was to be Arcita's, her heart at once inclined in his favour and she became passionately enamoured of him. And already the effects of love were

137

making her anxiously beg for him to be acknowledged victor – and she felt no more concern for Palemone.

(125) In such a way was her mind altered by the sudden sight of him who she thought would win her! If anyone is perhaps not keen to know who his friends are and who only seem to be, let him take care not to fall without being able to rise again quickly; for he that was loved earlier while the battle was undecided is forsaken now its outcome is assured.

Now Emilia admires all Arcita's good looks and his noble bearing; now his valour seems most excellent to her and his boldness far superior. Now she believes he possesses greater nobility, and now she considers him a hundred times more courtly. And whereas before she thought them both equal, they now seem utterly unalike.

Now she has decided, and contented with the judgment of the gods she resolves to accept the better one. And she already thinks of herself as wedded to Arcita; already she secretly harbours an unaccustomed passion for him, and already she begs the gods again and again to let him be her husband. And she goes on looking at him with unwonted desire, admiring his conduct above all others.

Already she resents the continuation of the struggle, desiring an immediate end to it; and showing a new kind of concern, she already fears injury to Arcita more than she did before. Into her heart come new ideas about him, of a kind that she has never yet entertained. And with her mind fixed only upon the image of Arcita, she yields herself without resistance.

[Palemone's followers give up the struggle, and the book ends with a description of Arcita riding about the arena in triumph – thanking the few companions of his who remain in the field, and challenging the rest to dispute his victory (129–31).]

Book IX

[After the sonnet 'the ninth book of the *Teseida* begins and describes first how Venus sends Erinis,[1] a fury from Hell, to startle Arcita's horse and make it fall backwards upon him.']

(1) Already his sad fate was at hand and was the harder for him to bear because the glory he had won through that victory had raised him so high. But such is the way of this world that a man comes nearer to falling, and falls the more heavily, the higher he soars above the verdant ground.

Up on the lofty fortress of Minerva, Venus and Mars stood carefully watching these two and were both content with the agreement they had reached regarding the prayers. But then Venus, seeing that Palemone's men could no longer keep the battle going, turned to Mars and said: 'Now you have performed your part.

'You have wholly fulfilled Arcita's prayer, and as you see he is the victor. It now remains for me to grant that of Palemone, whom you see standing there dejected and defeated.' Mars, behaving courteously, answered: 'What you say is true, my dear – so do just as you please.'

Shortly before she had visited the gloomy realms of burning Dis[2] and made her wishes known to their dark ruler.[3] Thereupon a number of Furies emerged ready for great tasks – but she, having chosen Erinis, said to the others: 'Go where you please.' And she then made all her wishes plain to her.

(5) This fury appeared crowned with serpents,[4] and her ornaments were green hydras which she had restored to life in the River Ilissos.[5] These, when licked by the sulphureous flames that came stinking out of her mouth, made her yet more ferocious. This goddess was holding in her hand a scourge made of snakes.

Her arrival struck the onlookers in the amphitheatre with such horror that each trembled in his heart, but none could tell why.[6] The winds made a strange noise and the sky grew darker; the amphitheatre shook and all the doors twisted on their hinges and creaked loudly.

When she had grown used to the light of day she did not change her shape or expression but straight away went down into the arena where Arcita was triumphantly riding around,[7] and terrible as she was set herself suddenly in front of his galloping horse, which reared up in fright and fell right over backwards.

Beneath it fell the once happy Arcita, and the stout saddle-bow bore down upon his chest and crushed it, so that his whole body appeared to be one wound. And the young man, who in the throes of great agony was on the very verge of yielding up his life, was then at once assisted by many people who ran towards him.

With much difficulty they freed him from the cruel saddle-bows, and very laboriously they lifted him in pain off the back of the horse, which feeling itself set free did not look at all tired – so fast did its legs go as it fled, and so fiercely did the fury threaten it with her grim, cruel and gloomy looks.

BOCCACCIO'S GLOSS TO STANZA 5

The author at this stage relates what took place to his fictional pretence – that is, to the agreement reached by Mars and Venus, who each wanted to help the knight that had prayed to them. Hence, as can be read above, Mars in the shape of Theseus spurred Arcita on to victory and struck fear into Palemone's followers as a result of which Arcita won. Now, in order to make clear how Venus had arranged for Palemone to win Emilia, he shows her bringing about Arcita's death at the moment of his victory, so that once he is dead Emilia may be left to Palemone; hence as we find in the text Arcita's horse shied, reared up and fell back on top of his chest. It is indeed a fact that animals can be made to shy by something frightening that they appear to see – but what it is they see, or think they see, no-one knows. The author thus supposes it was Erinis, one of the furies of Hell, that frightened the horse, and in order to explain the horse's wild behaviour he makes her very fearful in appearance.

[Emilia is overcome with horror at what has happened, and sees what has happened as one more disaster for which she bears responsibility (10–12). Meanwhile Agamemnon and Menelaus retain control of the field, and Arcita is attended to by many of the nobles including Emilia (13–21). Theseus then orders all but the combatants to leave the amphitheatre, and summons physicians to revive Arcita, whose recovery is however more rapidly assisted by words of comfort from Emilia (22–8). Then follows a description of 'how Arcita returned to Athens upon a triumphal chariot.']

(29) The sun had already passed the eighth hour of the day when the battle, which had begun at the third hour, came to an end; and already the cupbearer of Jupiter[8] who had taken Hebe's place was visible above the horizon, and Venus's twin fishes[9] were making haste to display the starry sky. Hence both Aegeus and Theseus thought it was time to leave.

(30) And Arcita was already about to request that when Theseus gave orders to bring the triumphal chariot, which he had had prepared for whoever might be the victor. There he had it richly decorated and begged Arcita to travel back to the palace in it, if it did not displease him to do so. Arcita answered that on the contrary it would be a pleasure.

And indeed when Rome paid the highest of honours to Scipio with a triumphal chariot it was not like this. Nor was it surpassed in splendour by the one Phaeton in his overwhelming panic abandoned on that occasion when both Libra and Scorpio were scorched,[10] and he, struck down by Jupiter's thunderbolt, fell into the River Po, as an inscription there shows.

And although Arcita was still very dazed after falling from his fierce charger, he was not yet so weakened that he failed to look impressive as he sat there fully arrayed in his triumphal robes and crowned with green laurel as the custom was. And the lovely Emilia mounted the chariot with him and sat beside him there.

[A procession is then assembled in the amphitheatre, including both Arcita's followers and his defeated opponents whose weapons and armour are to be presented to Mars (33–7).]

(38) When the procession had been marshalled Theseus had the gates of the amphitheatre opened and Arcita thus emerged in triumph to be greeted by all with great acclamation. He had those arms presented to mighty Mars and humbly offered thanks for the victory he had been granted. Then he quickly left the temple.

And thus he rode most joyfully in triumph about the city, often turning his gaze upon Emilia and admiring her beauty more than ever. It seemed to him like a thousand years before he could be granted the joy of possessing her, and he bitterly regretted the accident that had occurred and was consumed with sorrow because of it.

(40) She bore herself with dignity and modesty, lowering her eyes before everyone's gaze as a newly-wedded bride, blushing with shame, is wont to do. She behaved pleasantly and graciously to all, and everyone alike admired her just as noble Arcita did, although he looked pale and troubled.

[The onlookers continue to marvel at the procession and especially at

Palemone and his followers marching as captives before Arcita's chariot (41–7). Arcita is brought to Theseus's palace where he is placed in bed, with Hippolyta and Emilia attending to him (48–9). Meanwhile Palemone and his men remain in gloom and despair until Theseus rises to address them (50–1).]

(52) 'My lords, I am not unacquainted with a belief that some people hold true – namely that Divine Providence when it created the world clearly foresaw what would become of all the seeds of human and animal life that it held, and decreed everlastingly that what it had thus foreseen should remain so.

'I do not know whether this is true, but if so then we are ruled by the will of the Fates whose power has always been exercised through the eternal circling of the heavenly spheres.[11] Hence it is useless for men to strive against them, and those who attempt through strength or cunning to resist them are deluding themselves.'

[Theseus goes on to praise the bravery shown by Palemone and his followers, and to declare the gods alone responsible for their defeat. He invites them to join in the celebrations, and some of them do so immediately whilst others return to their lodgings to change clothes and recover from their wounds (54–62). Palemone then, according to the terms of the agreement, presents himself as a prisoner to Emilia. She, after some words of comfort and reassurance, releases him and presents him with a ring, new weapons and armour and a horse – advising him to follow Mars rather than Cupid for the time being. Palemone in return expresses his gratitude and continuing devotion (63–80). Arcita, having rested, asks Theseus to fulfil his promise and the book ends with his wedding to Emilia, although the celebrations are to be postponed until he has recovered (80–3).]

Book X

[After the sonnet follows an account of the funeral ceremonies for all those who have died in the battle (1–9). Meanwhile all the wounded have recovered except for Arcita, so Theseus sends for Idmon, a famous physician from Epidaurus,[1] and has him examine the Theban's wounds. Idmon quickly diagnoses his patient's condition (10–11.]

(12) He thus answered Theseus immediately as follows: 'Noble lord, your friend Arcita is as good as dead, and there is nothing the skill of a physician can do. Jupiter alone could keep him alive if he wished to, for he is above nature and can accomplish much more than nature can.

'But leaving miracles aside, I declare that Aesculapius himself could do nothing at all to cure him. Nor could radiant Apollo, even though he had every kind of skill at his command and knew the properties of dryness and cold, moisture and heat,[2] and the virtues of every plant and root; for the wounds within him extend both down and across his body.

141

'Hence any attempt to achieve a cure would in my opinion be wasted. Try to cheer and console him so that his soul may depart as peacefully as possible to that eternal prison where Dis keeps all light extinguished and where we shall follow him when we can no longer remain here.'

[Theseus is grieved at this news, but Arcita acknowledges himself to be on the verge of death. He asks to see Theseus and after describing the history of his past life, and especially of his devotion to Emilia, he requests that she may after his death become Palemone's wife (15–31). Theseus promises to ensure this and tries to offer some words of hope and encouragement, but Arcita takes no notice; and after remaining silent for a while he asks to see Palemone (32–7).]

(38) And when he saw him before him and had gazed closely at him for a long while as if he had not known him before, he said in a sorrowful voice: 'O Palemone, the heavens have decreed that I am to remain here no longer – and so before my sad departure I wanted to see you, touch you and hear your voice.

'Juno has been so implacable in her hatred towards us[3] that of Cadmus's line only Arcita and you, Palemone, are known to survive. Now, my kinsman, friend and companion, I must depart from you in anguish, to appease that goddess who has begrudged me my life when she could have made it happier had she wished to.

(40) 'At the moment when I should be received as one of her followers she makes me leave this happy world to go and join those who have gone before us. If only she had let me enter those dear sanctuaries of hers for just three days![4] I should then have let her slay or destroy me without resistance.

'But she would not allow that, and I can do no more. Hence I entreat you, who with myself are the only survivor from the noble line of our ancestors, that when the sad moment comes for me to leave this life and my lamentations behind, you will close my eyes, mouth and gaping nostrils and enable me quickly to pass over the Acheron.

'And since, like me, you have long loved graceful Emilia, I have earnestly entreated Theseus to let her be your wife for ever. I beg you not to deny me this, even though you know she has pitied and shown love for me, as it was just and honourable for her to do.

'And I swear to you in the name of that sorrowful realm I go to, never to return – that, to tell the truth, I have never in all my life robbed you of anything save a few kisses, and have loved her only as much as you yourself have done. So I beg you out of generosity to take her and be good to her.'

[Arcita goes on to implore Palemone to restore the reputation of Thebes and console Emilia after his death (44–7). Palemone answers by urging him not to think of dying, but Arcita repeats his plea and they are both overcome with tears (48–51). At this point Hippolyta and Emilia appear and Arcita speaks of his grief at having to leave the woman he has just married (52–7). Emilia pledges devotion to him and he then tells her what he wishes her to do after his death – explaining that the gods really meant her for Palemone, and asking her to kiss him for the last time (58–66). She eventually does so – lamenting once again the misfortunes the gods have brought to and through her,[5] and expressing a wish to remain chaste in the service of Diana if Arcita should die, or to be married to one of Theseus's enemies and bring her bad luck upon him (67–85). In an atmosphere of universal grief Arcita, now sensing that he is close to death, decides sacrifice to Mercury, the companion of dying souls – praying that since he deserves to be placed neither among the damned nor in Heaven, he may be allowed a place in the Elysian fields (85–99). Then he begins to lament his approaching death.]

(101) 'Now Arcita's life is failing; now his nobility will be seen no more; and now his doomed but unconquerable passion will come to an end. Now he will gaze upon the gloomy shores beside the Acheron. Now he will understand the despair of those dark shades in their misery and wretchedness. Now, whilst still in love, Arcita is forced to flee from the world as an exile.

'Alas that I must so soon take leave of my youthful life in which I yet hoped to show my powers to the full – for that was what my courage led me to aspire to. Alas, death comes to me too soon and more unjustly than to anyone else – assailing and tormenting me, and turning the full force of its savagery upon me.

'Where has your strength gone, Arcita? Where are the weapons you once loved so dearly? Why do you not take them up now, and rescue your miserable life from the clutches of death? Alas, my strength has all vanished and I can no longer wield them. I must then, alas, accept defeat and since I can do no more, must pass over into the next world.

'O fair Emilia, my heart's desire – O fair Emilia, my only love – O sweet Emilia, my own dear heart, I must now relinquish you. Alas, I know not which of the gods is thus venting his hatred upon me; but it is because of you alone that death gives me pain, and for your sake I shall never cease to pine.'

[He then imagines what his future existence will be in the world of the dead, and concludes by bewailing the loss not only of Emilia but also of his friends and patrons (105–10). The book ends with a brief account of 'how Arcita departed from this life'.]

(111) After he had uttered these words he heaved a bitter sigh from deep within his breast and said no more. And turning towards Emilia, he opened his eyes to gaze at her; and having remained gazing at her for a while, he then turned them away and saw all the people round him weeping bitterly because his death was at hand.

For it had laid hold on every limb, spreading from his feet towards his breast; and the vital spirits had also fled from his arms. A little life yet remained within his consciousness[6] and in his heart, but already the chill of death was falling upon his sorrowful breast and fast drawing darkness down upon his eyes.

But having lost his sight he began to murmur to himself while his strength continued to ebb away. And he did not stay long in that state, but forming such murmurs into clearer speech he said in a very low voice: 'Farewell, Emilia' and no more – for his spirit was forced to depart.

(*Here ends the tenth book of the* Teseida.)

Book XI

[After the sonnet, 'the eleventh book of the *Teseida* begins, showing first how Arcita's soul, having left his body, admires what it finds up in the heavens and despises what it leaves down here.']

(1) When Arcita had thus ended by calling upon her whom he loved more than any other in the world his free spirit flew away towards the inner surface of the eighth sphere, leaving behind it the outer bounds of the others. From there he gazed in wonder at the orderliness and supreme beauty of the moving stars[1] and heard sounds that were full of the utmost sweetness.[2]

Then he turned downwards to look again at what he had left behind him.[3] And he saw the little globe of earth with the sea and air encircling it and the fire above, and he judged it all to be worthless by comparison with Heaven. But then, looking backwards for a while, he let his eyes linger upon the place in which his body remained.

And he smiled to himself, thinking of all the Greeks and their lamentations, and greatly deplored the futile behaviour of earthly men whose minds are so darkened and befogged as to make them frenziedly pursue the false attractions of the world and turn away from Heaven. Then he departed to the place that Mercury allotted him.

[Emilia, after a brief appeal to Arcita's departing soul helps Palemone to perform the final offices for him (4–6), and there follows a description of 'how everyone wept for Arcita'.]

(7) The daughters-in-law of Priam, the wives and the daughters did not raise such an outcry when the ransomed corpse of Hector, their joy, their lord and their dearest delight, was brought back to them,[4] as did Hippolyta in the midst of the grief which she was indeed right to feel. So did Emilia and many other Greek ladies who were there with them.

The kings were overcome with pity and sorrow, and wept – as did Palemone. And the rest of whatever rank, old or young, also wept. And whereas Athens had formerly been filled with happiness, it now appeared everywhere a place of tearful desolation and of gloomy and sombre lamentations.

No-one could console Theseus, for he had been so entirely devoted to him. And the same was true of Peleus, noble Pirithous, Nestor and many others – including Aegeus whose white beard was bathed in tears of grief for Arcita who had just abandoned this sorrowful existence.

(10) But since he was a wise man who understood the ways of the world and the course of events, and had a great deal of experience, he resolutely restrained his grief in order to demonstrate to all who saw him how to be reconciled to what had happened. Then he sat down beside Palemone, who was weeping uncontrollably, /(11) and by means of a few words offered

whenever he could find a pause, he made attempts to stem this grievous weeping – reminding him of ancient and true examples of deaths and changes in fortune, sorrows and joys,[5] and of how everyone often meets with the one after the other. But whilst he spoke they all went on weeping and giving little heed to what he was saying.

[The courtiers' mourning continues unabated for the rest of the day and through the night (12). Theseus then decides to build Arcita's funeral pyre in the grove that he earlier used to frequent, and he orders a wood nearby to be felled for that purpose (13–14). He then has Arcita robed, crowned with laurel and placed upon a bier whilst all sorts of trees in the wood are felled (to the great distress of birds, beasts, gods, nymphs and fauns), raised into a pyre, together with layers of flowers and scented woods, and topped with a gold-embroidered Tyrian cloth (15–29). Then follows a description of 'how the Greek Kings came to bear Arcita to the pyre, what mourning there was beside it and how it was embellished by Theseus.']

(30) Everywhere already there was nothing but weeping to be heard, and already the royal court so resounded with it that far away amid her valleys sad Echo answered with as loud a voice. And Palemone appeared at the court wrapped in a cloak of mourning, with his beard unkempt and his pitiful locks covered in dust and altogether dishevelled.

And over Arcita's sad corpse Emilia with her face all pale and desolate was weeping no less bitterly, and augmenting the grief of those who stood around. And she could not be made to part from the body for anything Theseus mighty say, but it seemed that her greatest pleasure was to gaze upon her dead Arcita.

When the Achaeans arrayed in mourning came weeping into the court, the grief on all sides was much more bitterly renewed – more than it was even when that sad spirit left this uncertain world. And it rose and fell many times, for their hearts within were so wrung with grief.

Nor was there a moment's pause in the uproar in that afflicted household, whilst Aegeus did his best to comfort Palemone somewhat by speaking to him often – showing him how life in this evil world is beset with troubles and how, unfortunately, the worst kinds of hardship fall all the time upon those who live here.

And although Palemone may perhaps have been silent, he gave no more heed than Actaeon's pack is thought to have given to him. But he persisted in weeping, and no amount of pleading could ever win him away from it, for his heart was so full of pity for that dearest departed friend of his, whom he had so unjustly treated as an enemy.

(35) And there the mighty horses he had kept appeared magnificently caparisoned, and on each of them was a young squire bearing his arms. And there his ancestral heirlooms were likewise displayed; and there quivers and bows with arrows were to be seen, with several of his choicest and most splendid robes.

And in order to render full homage to his noble ancestry Theseus had all the royal regalia brought to adorn him. Finely made purple robes could there be seen enfolding him, and for his sake Theseus consigned his sceptre, orb and magnificent crown to the flames of his funeral pyre.

The noblest of the Achaeans went before him lamenting bitterly and bearing aloft precious vessels full of honey, blood and new milk. And they did not quicken their pace at all, but with their fair faces much altered they marched gently on, one after the other, in the order that had been assigned them.

The noblest of the Greeks, weeping, lifted the bier on to their shoulders and bore it out of Athens, whilst the people all cried out in grief, loudly and frequently cursing the injustice and folly of the gods. And at length these leaders brought that pitiful bed to the place that had been chosen for the pyre.

Finding it there already prepared and enriched with all kinds of wood, they set the bier down upon it; and it was soon completely surrounded by a milling throng of all those people who had followed to watch. Then the leaders drew back to await the arrival of the others.

Palemone appeared sadly escorted by Aegeus on his right, with Theseus on his left and the other Greeks then forming a group all around him. Next Emilia appeared sorrowfully accompanied by those of the weaker sex, and bearing the funeral flame towards that woeful place.

[Emilia addresses her final lament to Arcita and reproaches the gods once more. She kindles the pyre, casts upon it the ring Arcita had given her and her other jewels, and then swoons. Palemone meanwhile has had his beard and head shaved, and consigns the hair from these, with weapons and other precious objects to the flames (41–8). There follows an account of 'the rituals observed by those present while the pyre was burning.']

(49) The fire that had been kindled was already making the first boughs crackle, and tongues of flame were taking hold everywhere and blazing brighter all the time. And indeed a more splendid pyre had not been known in distant or recent times than the one that was there provided for Arcita as the crowning glory of his life.

(50) The gems splintered and the silver upon the great vessels and jewellery all melted, and all the garments dripped gold into the fierce flames. And all the wood streamed with precious resin and burned up brighter, and the burning boughs whistled in the flames, as did all the other things committed to them.

And the bowls of foaming wine, dark blood and fair white milk all gave off steam as well, in response to the intense heat of the fire. And the noblest of the Greeks stood before Palemone to shield his eyes from the distressing sight of the pyre, and the ladies placed themselves in front of Emilia for the same purpose.

Then Aegeus divided the knights into seven companies with ten men in each – all armed and mounted upon great chargers. Each of them had on the kind of surcoat that was proper to wear upon that sombre occasion; and seven of the noblest Greeks took command of them.

And turning to the left they went all around the pyre three times. The dust they raised diverted the grim ascent of the flames, and the lances resounded as they clashed together during the frequent turns they sadly executed there, moving ceaselessly round and round with flying hooves.

Four times those weapons made a terrible clashing sound, and the ladies uttered as many wails of grief, striking their hands together now and then. Next, following the order they had observed all this time, with each of them keeping behind his leader, they all turned to the right, and began wheeling around again, grieving and lamenting.

(55) And whatever they had on over their armour and may have been wearing perhaps as surcoats they each at once took off and cast into the fierce blaze. They also stripped their horses of their trappings and armour, and in this way, as you have heard, the fourth circuit was completed by these people.

And furthermore some threw on harnesses, some lances, some shields, some belts, some helmets, some visors, and others quivers full of arrows. And some offered up the best bows they could find; and some also had their cuirasses placed there; and some had triumphal chariots, and some horses – so eager were they all to do him honour.

[The pyre burns down and the next day Aegeus collects Arcita's ashes in an urn (57–8). Funeral games then take place and prizes are awarded for running, wrestling, fighting with maces and throwing (59–68). Palemone then raises a temple to Juno on the spot where the pyre had been and places the ashes within (69), decorating it with sculptured scenes showing all of Arcita's experiences that have been described in the poem – beginning with the return of Theseus from Scythia, and ending with the funeral that has just taken place (70–87). Only his fatal fall is destined to be left out, although the author declares that the Greeks' love for Arcita would never let them forget this (88). The temple is richly ornamented and endowed (89), and the ashes are placed there on a marble column (90) within an urn that bears the following 'epitaph for Arcita':]

(91) 'I guard the honoured ashes of noble Arcita, for whom due sacrifices are offered here. And let those who are lovers take warning from him if love sets them too fiercely aflame. For he might well say: "As you are now I once was,[6] and through devoting my prowess to Emilia I met my death: so shield yourself from love." '

(*Here ends the eleventh book of the* Teseida.)

Book XII

[After the sonnet the twelfth and last book begins with a brief description of Emilia's continued mourning for Arcita (1–2). Then follows an account of 'how Theseus after making a long speech decrees that Palemone is to marry Emilia and that the garments of black are to be put aside.']

(3) But when a number of days had gone by following that unhappy event, he and the Greeks in council with him seemed of one mind that this deep mourning should now be brought to an end, and that Arcita's wish for Palemone to marry his beloved Emilia should put into effect.

Hence Palemone, summoned by Theseus but not knowing why, attended upon him then in the company of those Kings, dressed in black and dejected as he was. And Theseus himself, accompanied by his barons, entered the place where Emilia, still weeping, sat together with a number of ladies.

(5) And then when all had quietly taken their places Theseus remained for a long time without saying anything. But seeing that every ear was humbly bent upon him alone, he restrained the tears of grief that rose to his eyes, and began to speak in this manner:

'Since no-one who has not lived can ever have died, it is just as clear that no-one who ever lived did not die. And hence when it pleases Him who set bounds to this world, we who are now living will die. We must thus cheerfully submit to the will of the gods, since we cannot resist it.

'Those oaks which take so long to mature, and which we know to live so long, still at some time perish. The hard stones we tread upon we know for sure will eventually be worn away by various effects. And we find ancient rivers running dry, and new ones springing from them.[1]

'There is no need to speak of men, for it is quite clear that Nature leads and has ever led them to one of two ends: either to a gloomy old age, full of infinite woe, and surer then to be ended by death – or else to death while still young and taking most pleasure in life.

'And indeed I think it is better to die at the moment when life is still happy. And a man of any worth will not concern himself about the manner and place of his death, for wherever that may be Fame will render him the honour that is due. His body which remains is not affected by dying in one place rather than another – nor does the soul for that reason gain more torment or less bliss.

(10) 'I take this to be true also of the form of death; for although one man may be drowned in the sea, another die while still in his bed, another through shedding his blood in battle or by whatever means one may imagine – yet all must still come to the banks of the Acheron, whether they make a good end or a bad.

'Hence it is wise to make a virtue of necessity when we have to. To do otherwise is plain folly, and more especially so in those who have experience of life than those who yet have none. And indeed this true saying of mine may well apply to us who miserably live out our lives amid contingencies.[2]

'Yet events that are entirely certain, on the other hand, include the death of one whose nobility was such that it bore the delectable fruit of fame after its blossoming time. And if we paid good heed to that we would set aside our miserable grief and address ourselves to the kind of noble actions that would gain us a glorious reputation.

'Indeed on such occasions it hardly seems right to try to repress our grief and lamentations, so we must yield to them yet to some extent. But we should then restrain ourselves, since the impulse to indulge grief to such an extent is harmful to those who succumb to it, and is also foolish, for no-one will thus regain what he yearns for.

'And surely if there was ever mourning in Greece for a valorous man, it has duly been observed for Arcita by many kings and countless people. He has been commemorated with great honour and placed upon a magnificent pyre, and every rite that is due to the dead has been properly performed.

(15) 'And mourning as we can see, has continued for many days in Athens. Because of that everyone has until now duly been wearing sombre clothing – especially those of us assembled here, who set an example that others must always follow, especially where good deeds are concerned.

'Thus since whatever is given life here likewise dies, whatever may befall – and since we have rendered due honour to him for whom we now grieve – I accordingly judge it best that we should change these gloomy clothes and leave aside these lamentations which are more suitable for women than they are for men.

'If I believed we might regain Arcita with our tears, I should say that we all ought to weep – and I would implore you to do so. But that would not be of any use; so from now on let everyone be cheerful and leave off weeping and wailing if you wish to please me, as you should seek to do at all times.

'Moreover, we should think about complying with Arcita's last request. For Phoroneus, who first gave us laws,[3] said that each man's final wish ought duly and solemnly to be observed; and Arcita asked that Emilia should be given to Palemone who loved her so much.

'Hence, when these dark garments have been abandoned and weeping and sorrow have ceased let our joyful and brilliant festivities begin. And before any of these lords take their leave let us publicly and with due magnificence celebrate the marriage of the two I have just named. Be ready then, I beg you, to do as I wish without demur.'

[Theseus's words are generally approved and supported, but Palemone, acknowledging a conflict between his reason and desire, asserts that to marry Emilia would be a betrayal of his loyalty to Arcita who had made this request only out of generosity and without meaning to invest it with the force of law (20–8). Theseus acknowledges the strength of Palemone's feelings, but reminds him that all the assembled Greek kings would defend him against any charges of acting dishonourably, and once more calls upon him to obey (29–32). Palemone, after appealing to the gods and begging for pardon from the shade of Arcita complies out of respect for Theseus (33–7). Theseus then turns to Emilia, who claims that what has happened to Acates and Arcita was due to Diana's displeasure and expresses fears about the possible consequences of marrying Palemone (39–42). A brief indication is then given of 'how Theseus answered Emilia'.]

(43) Theseus then said to her: 'That argument cannot be sustained – for if Diana had been displeased her wrath would have been visited upon you and not upon those to whom you were betrothed. And so start raising your spirits and altering your appearance straight away. Your beauty is not suited to the service of Diana, either in her temples or in the mountain forests.'

[Emilia and all those present then discard their mourning in obedience to Theseus (44–6). There follows a description of 'how, when the day assigned for Emilia's wedding had arrived, the kings together with Theseus and Palemone went to the temple of Venus where it was to be solemnized.']

(47) Theseus and his counsellors decided when the wedding should take place and had it proclaimed throughout Athens that all should be ready to take part in the celebrations. Hence, when that day drew near, they all according to their station prepared to offer wholehearted congratulations to young Emilia.

And Arcita had already been forgotten by everyone, and they gave no more thought to him, for they were all solely concerned with the celebrations and with looking forward to the day of the wedding. When this dawned bright and clear everyone's high spirits were enhanced, and Theseus had the temple of Venus opened up in order to go there.

And he also had the priests go there bearing the fair image of Hymen. And, attended by old Aegeus in noble and costly robes and by all the other kings, he went there with them. And Palemone accompanied them – his joy surpassing the power of any to describe it.

(50) And who could describe in common language the gold, the gems and the costly jewels that adorned the Greek kings? They were of such size, beauty and brilliance that if we tried to give an account of them here, most people would not credit it. And when they had arrived at that joyful temple they waited for the ladies to appear.

[Hippolyta meanwhile has been helping to adorn the bride, and a long description of Emilia's beauty follows, beginning with her hair, forehead, eyes, nose and cheeks (51–8).]

(59) She had a tiny mouth, full of smiles and lovely to kiss. With its delicate lips it was brighter than carmine, and when she spoke those who saw her thought she was an angel. And her teeth could have been compared to pearls, for they were well-proportioned, close-set, regular and small.

(60) And furthermore her chin was delicately rounded in harmony with her face; and in the middle of it she had a dimple which thus made her yet more charming. It was tinged with pink, which made her look still more beautiful, and below it was her white, scarcely lined throat,[4] which was fair and delicate and not too long.

Her neck was full and long and well set upon shapely white shoulders, which were soft, not too thin and well suited to receive eager embraces. Her bosom had begun to develop and her charming breasts seemed well-rounded and were so firm that the nipples were always forcing themselves outwards against what she wore over them.

Her arms were plump and well-proportioned, her hands long, her fingers slender, nimble in all their movements and nobly shaped. And in brief, no other lady in the whole country was so finely endowed as she in that respect; and she was straight, slender and well-proportioned about the waist.

She was plump and shapely around the hips and had small feet; but only he whom she had earlier made burn with love for her a long while could tell what the unseen parts of her body were like. I cannot imagine that my powers would suffice to describe them even had I seen them – so full of joys must they have been.

And since her birth Apollo had not yet returned thrice five times to the position he held when she was born,[5] although many people would perhaps have come to a different conclusion, to judge from the shapeliness of her body which in a short time had grown much more developed than usual and possibly more than other women's ever had.

(65) When she first appeared richly adorned as we think she was then, and dressed in the very finest green cloth – all the people who then saw her, from first to last, believed her to be Venus and none of them could have enough of gazing at her.

[The crowds gather to watch Emilia on her way to the temple, where the aid of Juno and Hymen is invoked and the marriage solemnized (66–9). The nobles then return to the palace for the wedding feast and the accompanying celebrations (70–4). There follows a description of 'how Palemone slept with Emilia'.]

(75) The day, which Palemone thought too long, moved towards evening. And then when the sky had become filled with stars and Juno had been called on for her blessing, Emilia went with Palemone into a splendid chamber – one where a bed was prepared in a manner we might think fitting for such magnificent nuptials.

What that night was like for the two lovers cannot be spoken of here. He who at some time has been overcome by passion will know, if he ever achieved joy after all his fierce yearning. And I well believe that through imagination anyone who has not yet had this experience might understand it, for it was happier far than any other.

Indeed, it may be reckoned from the offerings sent next morning to the temple that before day dawned Venus had been seven times kindled and as often quenched by the well of passion in which a good fisherman rarely retains his usefulness. And when morning came he arose brighter and fresher than a rose upon its thorny stem.[6]

Then he summoned Pamphilus and, just as he had earlier vowed, made him take magnificent offerings to fair Cytheraea's temple – glorifying, honouring and giving thanks to her by whose means he had gained the beautiful Emilia whom he deeply loved and had so long desired.

[The celebrations continue for fifteen days, after which the Greek Kings return home (79–83) and the author concludes by addressing 'some words to his book'.]

(84) Since the Muses began to walk naked in the sight of men,[7] there have already been those who have employed them in fine style for moral discourse – and others have enlisted them in the service of love. But you, my work, may be seen as the first ever to have had them celebrate the peformance of martial feats in the vulgar tongue.[8]

(85) And since you have been the first to cleave these waters which no other craft before you has ever furrowed, you may yet, lowly as you are, be placed perhaps amongst others to whom some measure of praise is due. And should you find yourself in their company, honour as forbears those

who have gone before you, thus setting a precedent for those you leave behind.

And since we have already attained the harbour we yearned for during this long voyage,[9] sped thither by various winds – we here furl our roving sails and having dropped anchor here await the garlands and gifts that are our due, whilst praising that pole star[10] whose light has led us hither acting as our guide.

(*Here ends the twelfth and last book of the* Teseida *and the marriage of* Emilia. Deo gratias. *Amen.*)

[There follow, as epilogue, two sonnets, in the first of which the author asks the Muses to requite his loyalty by conveying the poem to Fiammetta and deciding with her about its name and future fate. In the second the Muses reply that the lady has been much impressed by the power of love as revealed in the story of the two Thebans (lines 1–8)].

(9–15) Then, all aglow with the flame of love she entreated us that such fine accounts of bravery and beauty might not remain without a name, and chose, O poet, to call them *The Teseida and the marriage of Emilia*; and we with our clear notes will claim boundless fame for them in every age. We have thus baptized them in the sacred spring and given them leave to travel everywhere.

IL FILOCOLO

Menedon's Question

[Florio-Filocolo, the hero of the romance, has come to Naples in the course of his quest for Biancifiore. Here he and his companions (including Menedon) are present at a gathering in a garden, where thirteen questions of love are presented in the form of stories and debated in the presence of Fiammetta, who presides as 'queen'[1]. Menedon's question is the fourth of the sequence.]

(31) The noble lady appeared content when Menedon, who was sitting next to her, said: 'Most noble queen, it is now my turn to put a question before you, so with your permission I will state it. And if I subsequently make too much of what I have to say, I beg forgiveness from you and then from the rest of the company – for the question I mean to put forward cannot be made completely clear unless it is preceded by a story which will not perhaps be a short one.' And after these words he began to speak as follows:

'I recall that in the city where I was born there was a very wealthy and noble knight who loved a noblewoman of that city with a most perfect love[2] and made her his wife. This lady was so beautiful that another knight, called Tarolfo, fell in love with her and had such great love for her that he had no eyes for anything else and desired nothing more than her. And by various means – whether by frequently going past in front of her house, or jousting, displays of arms[3] or other kinds of action – he devoted his skill to gaining her love. And he kept sending her messengers, perhaps to promise her immense gifts, as well as to find out how she was disposed. The lady bore all this in silence and gave no favourable sign or reply to the knight, saying to herself: "Once this man becomes aware that he can get no favourable response or action out of me, perhaps he will give up loving me and pestering me[4] in this way." But indeed, for all this, Tarolfo did not desist – following as he did the teachings of Ovid, who says that a man should not fail to persevere on account of his lady's obduracy, since through sheer persistence soft water will pierce hard rock.[5]

'But the lady, fearing that these matters might reach her husband's ears and that he might think that this was happening with her consent, decided to tell him about it; but then a better idea occurred to her and she said: "If I spoke about it I might cause such trouble between them that I should never live in peace. This must be dealt with by other means" – and she devised a cunning stratagem. She sent the following message to Tarolfo: that if he loved her as much as he protested she would like a gift from him, and she swore by her gods and by the fidelity[6] that should reside in a noble lady that when she had received it she would do whatever he desired; but if he was unwilling to give her what she asked, he should resolve to trouble her no further unless he wished her to reveal the matter to her husband. And the gift she asked for was this: she said that in that city and in the month of January she wanted to have a fine large garden with an abundance of herbs, flowers, trees and fruits, just as if it were the month of May. And she said to herself: "It is an impossible thing to do, and that is how I shall get free of him".[7] On hearing this, Tarolfo, although he thought it impossible and knew well why the lady had asked it of him, replied that he would never rest nor return to her presence until he was able to give her the gift she had asked for.

'And having left the country with such companions as he chose to take, he searched through all the lands of the west in order to gain someone's advice about how he might achieve this desire, but, failing to find anyone, he then searched through the hottest regions and arrived in Thessaly, which was where a wise man had told him to go for this purpose. And when he had been there many days, still not finding what he sought, it happened that, more or less in despair about his mission, he arose one morning before the sun was ready to come up in the east and began to walk all on his own across the wretched plain that had once been stained with Roman blood.[8] And having gone a considerable distance he saw in front of him, at the foot of a mountain, a man who was neither young nor of very great age, bearded, in clothing that suggested he must be poor, and small of build and thin. He was picking herbs and using a small knife to dig up the various roots with which he had filled a corner of his gown.

'When Tarolfo saw him he was amazed and greatly feared that this might be something other than a man, but when his judgment confirmed that it was indeed a man he approached him, greeted him and then asked him who he was and from where, and what he was doing in that place at such an hour. The little old man answered him: "I am from Thebes and my name is Tebano, and I am going through this plain picking these herbs, so that by making from their juices certain preparations that are necessary and useful for various illnesses I can earn a living – and it is necessity, and not pleasure, that compels me to come here at this hour. But who are you that seem of noble appearance and are travelling here thus alone?" Tarolfo answered him: "I am a very wealthy knight from far in the west, and, being afflicted and troubled by thoughts about a task of mine which I cannot fulfil, I am walking here thus alone in order to have more opportunity to express my grief without restraint." Tebano said to him: "Do you know what kind of a place this is? Why did you not go by a different path? You could easily be set upon by angry spirits here." Tarolfo answered: "God has power over all places equally – here as well as elsewhere. He has my life and reputation in his hands; let him deal with me according to his will. For me, indeed, death would be a precious treasure." Then Tebano said: "What is this undertaking of yours which makes you so sad to have failed in?" Tarolfo answered him: "It is of a kind that I now consider to be impossible to fulfil, for I have so far found no advice." Tebano said: "Can it be talked about?" Tarolfo answered: "Yes, but what's the use?" "Perhaps none," said Tebano, "but what can you lose?" Then Tarolfo said: "I am in search of advice about how in the coldest month of the year it may be possible to have a garden full of flowers, fruits, and herbs, as lovely as if it were the month of May – and I can find no-one to give me the proper kind of help or advice about that." Tebano was lost in thought for a while before he replied, and then he said: "You and many others judge the wisdom and capacities of men by their clothing. If my gown had been like yours, or, if maybe, you had found me amongst wealthy princes rather than gathering herbs, you would not have found it so difficult to tell me your business. But often the greatest treasures of knowledge lie hidden beneath shabby coverings, and therefore no-one should conceal his needs from anyone who proffers advice or aid, so long as it does not harm him to have them revealed. But what would you give to anyone who enabled you to achieve what you seek?" Tarolfo stared him in the face as he said this, wondering whether he might be making fun of him, for it seemed incredible to him that this man could have the power to work miracles unless he were God. Nonetheless he gave this answer: "In my country I command a number of castles, together with a great deal of treasure – all of which I would divide in half with anyone who would do me such a favour." "Clearly," said Tebano, "if I were to do this I would not need to go gathering herbs any more." "Certainly" said Tarolfo, "if you are indeed the one who will undertake to accomplish this for me, and if you manage to do so, you will no longer need to struggle in order to become rich. But how and when will you be able to provide me with this?" Tebano said: "When will be up to you, and do not trouble yourself as to how. I shall come along with you, trusting in the pledged word that you have given me, and when we are in the place you choose, say what you require and I shall provide it all without fail." Tarolfo was so wholly delighted with what had happened that he could scarcely have been more pleased had he been at that moment holding his lady in his arms, and he said: "My friend, I feel that time is getting short to accomplish what you have promised me, so let us leave without delay and go where this is to be done." Tebano, having thrown away his herbs and collected his books and other things needed for the practice of his art, set out with Tarolfo, and in a short time they had arrived at the town they sought very close to the month in which the garden had been asked for. There they rested quietly out of the way until the time was ripe; and once that month had indeed begun Tarolfo ordered the garden to be prepared so that he could present it to his lady.

'When Tebano had received this order he waited for nightfall, and when it came he saw that the moon's horns had grown once more into a complete circle and that it was shedding its full radiance over the familiar countryside. He then went out of the city all alone, unclothed, unshod and with his hair flowing loose over his bare shoulders. Night's wheeling motion continued;[9] birds, beasts and men were quietly at rest; on the trees unfallen leaves remained motionless and the damp air was undisturbed. The stars alone were shining when, after walking around the city a number of times, he arrived at the place beside a stream which he settled upon as the site for the garden. There he stretched out his arms towards the stars, turning his face to them three times, plunging his white hair as often into the flowing water, and calling loudly for their aid the same number of times . . .'

[Here follows a description of Tebano's invocation of various powers and deities, of his journey, in a chariot drawn by two dragons, in search of exotic materials, and then of the actual rituals he performs. Like the preceding paragraph, it is substantially based upon the accounts of the sorcery by which Medea restores Aeson to youth in Book VII of Ovid's *Metamorphoses*, in particular lines 179–284.]

'. . . Then he took a branch of a withered olive tree, and with it began to stir all these things together. While he was doing so the dry branch began to turn green, rapidly putting forth leaves – and not long after it had been covered with these it appeared to be laden with black olives. When Tebano saw this he took the boiling mixture and began to pour and sprinkle it all over the chosen ground, in which he had planted as many sticks as he wished to make into different kinds of trees. And the earth no sooner felt it than it began to blossom all around, putting forth fine fresh shoots, and the dry sticks all turned into green saplings and fruit trees. When this was done Tebano went back to the city to rejoin Tarolfo, and since there was to be a very important festival in the city the following day, he went to present himself to his lady, whom he had not seen for a long time. He said to her: "Madam, with much difficulty I have provided what you required, and it awaits your pleasure when you wish to see it and take possession."

'The lady was highly surprised to see this man, and more so when she heard what he had to say; so in disbelief she replied: "That pleases me greatly; let us see it tomorrow." When the next day came Tarolfo went to the lady and said: "Madam, may it please you to walk in the garden which you ordered me to provide during this cold month?" Then the lady set out with a great following, and having arrived at the garden they went in through a fine gateway, and found the air inside mild and pleasant, not cold as it was outside. The lady walked admiringly all around picking plants and flowers which were, as she could see, abundant there; and the power of the potion that had been sprinkled on the place had been so far-reaching in its effects that the fruits which August usually brings forth adorned all their trees there in that harsh season, and many of the people who had come with the lady ate them. This seemed to the lady to be a most beautiful and marvellous place, nor did she think she had ever seen one so beautiful. And since she had many kinds of proof that this was a real garden and that the knight had accomplished what she had asked, she turned to Tarolfo and said: "Unquestionably, knight, you have earned my love, and I am ready to fulfil the promise I have made you. But I would truly ask you as a favour to agree to put off claiming what you desire of me until my lord goes hunting or somewhere else away from the city, so that you can take your pleasure more safely and without any fear." Tarolfo agreed to this, and leaving her the garden went away more or less satisfied.

'This garden became well-known to all people of the country, although nobody knew until a long time afterwards how it had come into being. But the noble lady to whom it had been presented went sadly away from it, going back to her room in a state of heavy dejection. And looking for some way of retracting what she had promised but finding no valid reason, she grew yet more despondent. Her husband, noticing this on several occasions, began to wonder very much about it and to ask her what was the matter; and the lady said that nothing was the matter, for she was ashamed to tell her husband about the promise she had made in exchange for the gift she had requested, and was afraid he might think her immoral. In the end she was unable to hold out against repeated questioning from her husband, who kept trying to find out the reason for her dejection; and she told him from beginning to end why she was in such a sad state. Hearing this, the knight pondered for a long while, and since he well knew the lady's virtuousness he spoke to her in this way: "Go, and fulfil your vow in secret, and grant Tarolfo freely what you promised him; he has justly and most painstakingly earned it." The lady began to weep, saying: "May the gods keep me from such a sin. On no account will I do so; I would sooner kill myself than do anything that would dishonour or displease you." The knight replied to her: "My lady, I certainly do not want you to kill yourself for this, nor to give yourself a single unhappy moment because of it. It does not displease me at all; go and do what you have promised, for I will not hold you any the less dear. But when this is done, beware of such promises another time, even if you think the gift you ask for is quite unobtainable."

'When the lady saw that this was her husband's wish, she adorned and beautified herself, and, taking some companions, went to where Tarolfo was staying and appeared before him blushing with shame. When Tarolfo saw her he rose from beside Tebano, with whom he was sitting, went to meet her full of wonder and joy, and greeted her respectfully, asking the reason for her coming. The lady answered him: "I have come to place myself wholly at your command; do what you please with me." Then Tarolfo said: "You give me great cause for wonder, considering the hour at which you have come and the companions you have brought. This cannot be, unless something unusual has happened between you and your husband; I beg you, let me know about it." The lady then told Tarolfo in full exactly how things had turned out. Upon hearing this Tarolfo was struck with greater wonder than before, and began to consider deeply, to acknowledge the great generosity[10] of the husband who had sent her to him, and to say to himself that anyone who contemplated a base action[11] towards such a generous man would deserve the greatest reproach. And he spoke to the lady in this way, saying: "Noble lady, you have fulfilled your obligations faithfully[12] and like a woman of great spirit, and I therefore consider what I desired of you to have been granted. And so when you wish you may return to your husband and thank him on my behalf for this great favour, begging him to pardon me for the folly that I have been committing till now, and assuring him that from now on no more actions of this kind will be performed by me. The lady gave Tarolfo

158

many thanks for this great kindness[13] and joyfully went away to rejoin her husband, to whom she related in turn everything that had happened to her.

'But when Tebano rejoined Tarolfo he asked how things had turned out for him. Tarolfo told him, and Tebano replied "So because of that am I going to lose what you promised me?" Tarolfo answered "No, on the contrary; go when you please and take half of my castles and my wealth as I promised you, for I consider that you have peformed your service to me in full." To this Tebano replied: "May the gods forbid, after the knight has been so generous to you with regard to his lady, and you were not churlish towards him – that I should be less than considerate.[14] To have served you contents me beyond anything else in the world, and what I was to receive as a reward for that service I want to remain yours as it always was" – and he refused to take anything belonging to Tarolfo.

'The question now is: which of these was the highest form of generosity – that of the knight who allowed his wife to go to Tarolfo; or that of Tarolfo who, when the lady, whom he had always desired and striven for up until then, came as he had wished, sent her back unharmed to her husband; or that of Tebano who already in his old age had forsaken his own country, come to that place to obtain the promised gifts and striven to accomplish what he had promised – and having obtained these gave back everything and continued to live in poverty as before?'

(32) 'Both the story and the question are excellent' said the queen. 'Indeed each was most generous, and, considering them closely, the first appears to have been generous with regard to his honour, the second with regard to his lustful desires, and the third with regard to the wealth he had gained. And therefore, in order to find out who showed the greatest generosity or graciousness,[15] we must consider which of these three things is the most precious. When we have found out this we shall clearly perceive who was the most generous – for he who gives most must be considered the most generous.

'Of these things, one is precious – that is, honour, which Paullus, when he had overcome Perseus, chose to have rather than the riches he had won.[16] The second – namely, lustful intercourse – is to be shunned, according to the opinions of Sophocles and Xenocrates, who say that lust should be fled from like a raging tyrant.[17] The third – namely wealth – is not to be desired, since it will in most cases be unfavourable to a life of virtue – and one can live virtuously in a state of moderate poverty, as we perceive from the actions of Marcus Curtius, Atillus Regulus, and Valerius Publicola.[18] Thus, if amongst these three only honour, and not the other things, is to be prized, then the one who gave up that performed the greatest act of generosity, although he behaved less than prudently. His also was the initial form of generosity which set the pattern for the others. Therefore in our opinion the one who gave up the lady, in whom his honour resided, was more generous than the others.'

(33) 'I am content' said Menedon, 'that it should be as you say, insofar as it is your pronouncement. But it seems to me, as you will hear, that each of the others was more generous. It is indeed true that the first gave up the lady, but in doing so he did not act so generously as you claim, because if he had wished to withold her he could not legitimately have done so. For

the lady had taken an oath which had to be kept – and he who yields what he cannot withhold acts well and seems generous to that extent, but gives little. And therefore, as I said, each of the others was more generous . . .'

[Here Menedon describes Tarolfo as deserving the lady because of all his efforts, yet being generous with regard to her husband's honour, her oath and his own "long desire".]

'. . . The third [Tebano] was yet more generous, for, bearing in mind that poverty is one of the cruellest things in the world to bear – driving away happiness and rest, banishing respect, destroying virtue and bringing bitter anxieties – everybody of course keenly desires and seeks to avoid it . . .'

[Here Menedon argues that Tebano has felt the effect of poverty, and by serving Tarolfo is seeking to free himself from such wretchedness and become rich.]

'. . . If, therefore, someone has gone from poverty to wealth and is enjoying the change, how great is the degree of generosity he shows by giving that up and agreeing to return to the condition from which he had taken so many pains to escape! Many significant and generous actions were performed here, but this seems greater to me than all of them, considering that the one who did the giving was advanced in years; for avarice usually has a more abiding hold upon the aged than upon the young. I therefore consider that both of the other two showed greater generosity than the first, whom you praised so highly – and the third more so than any of them.'

(34) 'You have defended your case as well as it can be defended by anyone,' said the queen. 'But we mean to show you in brief why you should abide by our judgment rather than yours. You assert that the man in question did nothing generous in surrendering his wife, since he was bound in justice to do so because of the oath taken by the lady – and this would indeed be so if the oath were valid. But since the wife is a limb of her husband – or rather, joined as one body with him – she could not have taken that oath without her husband's consent. And if she did so it was of no validity, for if a previous oath has been lawfully made none that follows can contravene it – particularly not one which is improperly made without legitimate cause.[19] In the process of joining together in marriage it is customary for the man to swear to be always content with the woman and the woman with the man, neither of them exchanging the other for anyone else. Therefore the lady was not in a position to take that oath, and if she did so she took it without legitimate cause; and since it ran contrary to her previous vow it could not be valid. Since it was invalid he was not bound to give her up to Tarolfo against his will, and if he did thus surrender her, it was he who was being generous, with regard to his honour, and not Tarolfo as you maintain. Nor could Tarolfo have shown great generosity in setting the oath aside, as it was of no validity; therefore he remained generous only with regard to his lustful desires – which is what everyone is bound out of pure duty to do, for we are all obliged by every just standard to abandon vices and follow virtue. And if anyone does what, as you describe it, justice compels him to do, he is in no way

generous; but any good action that goes beyond this is rightly to be called generosity. But since, perhaps, you are silently wondering what it is about a chaste wife's honour that should be so dear to her husband, we will extend our discussion somewhat, so that you may see more clearly that neither Tarolfo nor Tebano (whom we mean to consider afterwards) acted at all generously by comparison with the knight.

'It should be recognized that neither chastity nor the other virtues yield their possessors any reward save that of honour, and such honour renders them pre-eminent among other less virtuous men. This honour, humbly maintained, enables them to gain the friendship of God,[20] thus living and dying in happiness and afterwards inheriting everlasting bliss . . .'

[Here Fiammetta goes on to describe the temporal and spiritual benefits that the honour of a chaste wife brings to her husband, and conversely the sufferings of a husband whose wife is not this way inclined.]

'. . . But to return to the subject, you can thus see how much the knight gave up. Yet we have not lost sight of what you said about Tebano being more generous, since, having toiled to become wealthy, he did not hesitate to return to the wretchedness of poverty through giving up what he had gained. It seems clear that you are ill-acquainted with poverty, which surpasses all kinds of wealth if it is cheerfully encountered. Perhaps Tebano already felt himself oppressed by various nagging anxieties about the riches he had won . . .'

[Here Fiammetta gives examples of the kinds of fear to which Tebano might have been subject on this account.]

'. . . Because of all this, remembering his past life and how pleasant it had been for him without all these anxieties, he said to himself: 'I wanted wealth to bring me comfort, but I now see that it increases troubles and cares and banishes peace of mind.' And becoming eager again for his previous way of life he restored that wealth to the person who had given it to him. Poverty is a kind of unprized wealth, an unrecognized good and the deliverer from care,[21] as Diogenes fully recognized.[22] Poverty needs no more than what nature requires, and he that patiently accepts it is freed from all dangers, nor is he prevented from attaining great honours if, as we said, he lives a life of virtue. Therefore if Tebano freed himself from this kind of anxiety, he was not generous but wise. He showed favour to Tarolfo in choosing to give this to him rather than someone else, since he could have given it to many others.

'Thus the knight who surrendered his honour was more generous than any of the others. And bear in mind that the kind of honour he gave up is irrecoverable – which is not the case with such other kinds as derive from battles, trials of strength and other affairs; these if lost on one occasion can always be redeemed on another. And let this be all that we need to say about your question.'

APPENDICES

Appendix A

The Fortunes of Troilus

Neither Chaucer nor Boccaccio had direct knowledge of the early Greek sources for the story of Troilus, and the information that these offer on the subject is in any case rather fragmentary. In the *Iliad* Troilus is simply spoken of by Priam as a son who has, like Hector and Mestor, become a casualty of the war (XXIV, 257). Elsewhere in the Greek epic cycle it is made clear that his death, like Hector's, was at the hands of Achilles,[1] and Sophocles also refers to the circumstances in which it took place.[2] Achilles's ambushing of Troilus beside a spring and the subsequent slaughter of the young prince on the altar of the Thymbraean Apollo were a frequent subject for vase-paintings from the sixth century B.C. onwards.[3] The episode is also alluded to later by Apollodorus in the course of his summary of Greek myths and legends.[4]

The pathos of Troilus's early death is dwelt upon by several classical Latin writers.[5] Virgil (*Aen.* I, 474–8) describes a scene in which:

'Troilus, an unfortunate youth and ill-matched against Achilles, having flung down his weapons in flight is borne away by his horses; and falling backwards he remains attached to his empty chariot still holding the reins. He is dragged along with his hair and the back of his neck on the ground, and his downturned spear scrawls in the dust.'[6]

Horace cites Troilus as an example of a young man whose death is greatly mourned (*Odes* II, ix, 13–16), and Cicero likewise mentions him in the course of a discussion about premature death (*Tusculan Disputations*, I, xxxix).

Of the other main characters that Chaucer and Boccaccio associate with Troilus's fortunes, Diomedes is the most fully represented in classical Greek and Latin tradition,[7] although he is not portrayed as being a particular enemy of Troilus. Calchas is also quite frequently referred to as a skilled diviner,[8] but he is not said to have a daughter of any importance to the Troy story and he is clearly a Greek, rather than a Trojan defector. An archer called Pandarus is shown by both Homer and Virgil fighting on the side of Troy, yet little is otherwise said of him in either the *Iliad* or the *Aeneid* and there is no evidence at all of any friendship between him and Troilus.[9] Nor is he involved with any of the women in the Troy story. In the *Iliad* neither Briseis, Achilles's slave-concubine, nor Chryseis, the daughter of Chryses the priest of Apollo have anything to do with either him or Troilus.

Chaucer and Boccaccio knew some at least of the classical Latin writers that mention Troilus and they both certainly knew of 'the gret Omer'. But for them, as for other medieval writers the ultimate authorities for the story of the Trojan war were the supposed eyewitnesses, Dictys of Crete and Dares the Phrygian. The *Ephimeridos Belli Troiani Libri* of Dictys and the *De Excidio Troiae Historia* of Dares are both thought to have Greek originals, probably dating from the first century A.D., although their extant Latin versions are, respectively, of the fourth and sixth centuries.[10] Dictys's chronicle is much longer than that of Dares, but Troilus is mentioned in it only once – when he and another son of Priam, who have been captured by the Greeks, are put to death on the orders of Achilles (Book IV, par. 9). The Latin version at this point emphasises Troilus's youth and personal attractiveness, as does the equivalent passage in a Greek papyrus fragment of around 200 A.D.:—

'No small grief came upon the Trojans when Troilus died, for he was still young and noble and handsome.'[11]

Troilus, however, plays a far more prominent part in Dares's chronicle. He is shown early on arguing strongly and successfully against his brother Helenus's objections to the proposed abduction of Helen (ch. 7). Like other heroes he is briefly described in a portrait, which emphasises his good looks and bravery (12); and he is named with Hector as a leader of the Trojan army (20 and 23). After Hector's death his prowess leads him to be recognized by the Greeks as his brother's successor (29 and 30), and he continues to give them a great deal of trouble until he is killed by Achilles and the Myrmidons (31–3). Diomedes also appears among the portraits in Dares and is said to be 'stocky, brave . . . hot-tempered, impatient and daring' (13).[12] He is mentioned, furthermore, as one of the Greeks who are wounded by Troilus in chapter 31, but the two heroes are not said to have any personal cause for enmity. Briseis is not involved with either of them and her portrait places her amongst the Greeks, although the description of her eyebrows as 'joined above her lovely eyes' gives her a characteristic in common with Joseph of Exeter's Briseis, Benoit's Briseida and Chaucer's Criseyde. Dares does not link her with Calchas either, but he does portray the seer as a Trojan who goes over to the Greeks after hearing the response of Apollo's oracle at Delphi (15). And again as in Benoit,[13] Calchas reassures the Greeks of ultimate victory despite the temporary Trojan successes under Troilus (30); but his actions here do not otherwise impinge directly upon the latter's fortunes.

A later version of Dares which is thought to have had some influence upon Chaucer is the verse *Frigii Daretis Yliados*, composed by Joseph of Exeter in the mid 1180's.[14] Certain features of the main characters – such as Diomedes's ancestry, Troilus's giant-like spirit and Briseis's stature are to be found only in their portraits here (Book IV, 61–4, 124–7 and 156–62) and later in Chaucer's *Troilus* (v, 799–840).[15] Joseph also places considerable emphasis upon Troilus's prowess as a warrior and laments his death in a passage of characteristically florid apostrophe (Book VI, 325–31).

But, so far as is known, the first to portray Troilus as the lover of Calchas's daughter was Benoit de Sainte-Maure, whose *Roman de Troie* was probably composed between 1155 and 1160.[16] Benoit's main source was as he indicates in his prologue 'the history that Dares has written' (91), but he also makes use of Dictys during the later stages of his work (24397f.). He also amplifies these sources in various ways – as with the account of Achilles's love for Polyxena (17489f.) – and he devotes almost a tenth of the poem to the new story of Troilus's love for Briseida, which as Lumiansky argues, 'is skilfully integrated with Troilus' fighting role and with Diomedes' activities as one of the chief Greek heroes.'[17]

A French prose redaction of Benoit's *Roman* appeared in the middle of the thirteenth century,[18] but a more influential version was the Latin *Historia Destructionis Troiae*, completed in 1287 by Guido de

Columnis.[19] The *Historia* is considerably shorter than the *Roman*; Guido's treatment of the subject is occasionally more learned and often more rhetorically extravagant; and his treatment of the story of Troilus and Briseida is much less coherent than Benoit's.[20] Yet the *Historia* exists in a large number of manuscripts[21] and because of being written in Latin and in what its modern editor describes as a 'discursive, easily readable, novelistic style',[22] it became more widely known than its original.

It seems probable, however, that Boccaccio and Chaucer, indebted as they both were to the Northern French romance traditions, would have had recourse to Benoit as well as Guido, together with their other sources for the Troy story.[23] Excerpts from both versions are therefore included in the following appendices, in which rather more space will be given to the *Roman* in recognition both of its importance within the tradition and the superiority of its presentation of the tale of Troilus.

Appendix B

Benoit de Sainte-Maure, *Roman de Troie* (excerpts)[1]

[After a summary of the poem's contents the narrative begins with a description of Jason's quest for the Golden Fleece and the first destruction of Troy. Then follow accounts of the rebuilding of the city by Priam son of Laomedon, his attempts to regain his sister Hesione from the Greeks, Paris's abduction of Helen, and the Greek preparations for war. The main Greek leaders are introduced, among them Diomedes, whose portrait follows those of Agamemnon, Menelaus, Achilles, Patroclus, the two Ajaxes and Ulysses, his frequent companion and colleague.]

Diomedes (5211–24)

Diomedes was also most mighty, large, squarely-built and very tall; his expression showed great ferocity and he frequently broke his promises. He was very bold, contentious, and experienced in battle – was most proud and arrogant, and had made himself greatly feared. It would have been very hard to find anyone who would willingly oppose him; nothing could restrain his temper and he was an extremely difficult master to serve.[2] But for love's sake he often endured great suffering and engaged in many a conflict.

[The last of those on the Greek side to be introduced is the daughter of Calchas.]

Briseida (5275–88)

Briseida was charming and neither short nor too tall. She was lovelier, fairer and whiter than a lily or the snow upon a branch; but her eyebrows were joined, and that somewhat flawed her beauty.[3] She had marvellously beautiful eyes, and was very eloquent and most well-mannered and prudent in conduct. She was greatly loved, and she herself loved greatly, but her heart was not constant. Nonetheless she was very timid, modest, generous and compassionate.[4]

[Troilus has already been mentioned as one of Priam's five sons and a knight of great promise (2943–8). Although the youngest of the princes he is said to be 'no less bold than Hector', and during the Trojan council that precedes the abduction of Helen he vehemently and successfully argues against taking notice of his brother Helenus's warnings (3987–4018). When Benoit turns to the Trojan leaders he places Troilus's portrait after those of Priam, Hector and Helenus and immediately before that of Paris.]

Troilus (5393–446)

Troilus was marvellously handsome; he had a cheerful expression, a rosy complexion, a bright beaming face, a broad forehead, and was highly endowed with knightly qualities.[5] He had the most lovely fair and naturally lustrous hair, with sparkling eyes that were full of high spirits and had never been surpassed in beauty. Whenever he was in a friendly mood his gaze was so very gentle that it it was a delight to look at him – but one thing I can tell you for certain: he had a different appearance and expression for his enemies. His nose was finely shaped and proportioned and his carriage well-suited to bearing arms. He had a well-formed mouth and fine teeth that were brighter than ivory or silver, a square chin and a long straight neck as befitted a soldier. His shoulders were well-set, long and sloping; his chest well-shaped beneath the laces of his hauberk, his hands well-formed and his arms handsome. He was slender about the waist and his garments sat well upon him; he was broad about the hips and was a marvellously fine knight. He had straight legs, well-arched feet and limbs that were finely formed in every way; and he had a large stride, so that he cut a very handsome figure. He was tall, but that suited his fine physique.

I do not think there can now be throughout all the world such a valiant man so devoted to joy and pleasure and less likely to give offence to others – or one who was so magnanimous and devoted to the pursuit of fame and deeds of honour. And he was neither haughty nor insolent, but cheerful, gay and loving. He was much loved, and he himself loved dearly and endured great suffering for that reason. He was the handsomest young knight among the youth of Troy and the most valiant, except for his brother Hector who was the true commander and leader when it came to the conduct of battle, as Dares assures us. The latter was the paragon of knighthood and Troilus was most worthy to be his brother, and was well-fitted to be, by virtue of his valour, courtliness and generosity.

[After the portraits of the Trojans follows a catalogue of the Greek ships, and it is then shown how Achilles is sent by the Greeks to seek advice from Apollo at Delphi.[6] Here he meets the Trojan Calchas.]

Calchas at Delphi (5817–44)
You may now hear exactly how Calchas, the wise and famous seer and son of the Trojan Testor, had that day arrived there in person. Calchas was a man of the highest intelligence; he brought gifts for Apollo and had come to entreat the god to have mercy on the people of Troy, and to find out what they should do and how they should conduct themselves. The King and people of that country had sent Calchas there to place their offerings upon the altar, listen to the god's response and find out what was going to happen to them as a result of that invasion. And this was the god's answer: 'Make sure' he said, 'to go at once early tomorrow to the Greek army's ships. You will accompany them to Troy, for you are wise and will thus offer them guidance. Your intelligence will be of great use to them; but let them never return from there until they have taken Troy and avenged themselves upon her people. So it must be, for that is my will.'

[Calchas meets Achilles in the temple and goes with him to join the Greeks at Athens. He informs them of what Apollo has said and assures them of their victory and his loyalty (5845–920).]

The Greeks welcome Calchas (5921–7)
The Greeks were already cheerful and high-spirited, but now Calchas has given them confidence and encouraged them greatly. They welcome him and entertain him with great delight, and are now determined to go ahead.

[The departure of the fleet is however delayed by a storm, and Calchas's first service to the Greeks is to advise them to sacrifice to Diana, in order to appease her and gain a favourable wind. They do so and are enabled to set out for Troy (5928–6000).

The actions of both Diomedes and Troilus are given some attention during the early stages of the campaign. Shortly after the Greeks have landed Diomedes is sent with Ulysses on a mission to request the surrender of Helen in return for leaving Troy in peace; but his own speeches tend rather to inflame the situation (6211–510). He is subsequently mentioned among the Greek commanders during the second and third battles (8283–7; 10565–8). Troilus on the other hand is shown helping Paris to cover the Trojan retreat at the end of the first battle (7573–81). He also makes an impressive appearance before the second battle, at which point Hector urges him to avoid recklessness (7749–80) – and he is said to accompany Hector in leading the Trojans out of the city for the third (10576–8).

The third battle also sees the first encounter between the two heroes, and at the end of it Diomedes captures Troilus's horse, having first had his own killed beneath him by the Trojan (10725–84). They are again mentioned as being involved in a 'fierce struggle' during the fourth battle (11285–90).

Calchas is shown giving the Greeks encouragement during the seventh battle (12775–8), and during the truce that is subsequently agreed upon for the burning of the corpses and the exchange of prisoners he attends a parley between the combatants.]

Calchas asks for Briseida (13086–120)
The wise and courtly Calchas had a much loved daughter who was beautiful, courtly and well-taught. She was greatly renowned and her name was Briseida. Calchas asked Agamemnon, Ajax and the other Kings to request her from Priam; for from that moment on he did not want her to live with the Trojans any longer, as he knew that Fortune was too hostile to them. Hence rather than have her perish along with them he wished her to come out and join him among the Greeks.

This request was well-framed and eloquently supported, but the Trojans denounced Calchas, saying that he was viler than a dog. 'That wretch is the very dregs of shamefulness and baseness. For having lived in wealth and high rank amongst us he deserted us and went over to you.' King Priam swore and vowed that if he ever had him in his power he would make him suffer an evil end by having him broken and torn apart by horses. 'And if the girl had not been noble, good, wise and beautiful she would have been burnt and dismembered because of him.' But, to cut a long story short, Priam surrendered her to them. 'She may leave and be on her way,' he told them, 'for I hate nothing so much as that old traitor – nor do I want anything of his to be or remain within my city.'

[There follows an encounter between Hector and Achilles, during which they challenge each other but are prevented from coming to blows (13121–260). Then the story turns to the love between Troilus and Briseida.]

Troilus and Briseida (13261–340)
Although others might have been joyful and happy, Troilus was in the throes of rage and grief – and that was because of Calchas's daughter, for his love for her was indeed no light matter. He had given her his whole

heart and was so aflame with love for her that he had no thought for anything else. She in return had yielded him herself, her body and her love, as most people knew well. When the truth of the matter was made known to her – that through force of necessity she would have to depart to the Greek camp, and that there was no question of staying any longer, she was deeply afflicted with sorrow and grief. Her eyes flow with tears and her heart utters sighs. 'Alas,' she says, 'what a cruel fate it is when I am thus made to abandon the city in which I was born! The meanest maid-servant would be deeply disgraced by living in the Greek camp; and I know of no king, duke or count there who would ever honour or serve me. Now from henceforth tears will bathe my face each day without pause. Ah, Troilus, my sweet and lovely friend, what devotion have I given you! Nevermore in your life will anyone love you at all better than I. I declare that Priam is doing a great injustice in banishing me from his city. God grant I may never live to see the dawn. Death is what I desire, seek and implore.'

Troilus, who could not be more grieved, comes to her that night. There is now no question of being comforted and they both weep bitterly, for they know that the next day they will be far apart from each other and will no longer be allowed the opportunity to make love together. I assure you that whilst they are able to they both embraced each other as often as they can; but the sorrow afflicting their hearts makes the tears flowing from their eyes run down to their mouths. Between them there was neither ill-temper nor disdain, disagreement nor disharmony. Those who are doing this to them are causing them much pain and affliction, and may God never give them joy of that. Anyone who causes two lovers to be parted as the Greeks did should pay the penalty for his crime as they were later to do, dearly. Troilus hated them before this, but he then made them realize they had done something to him that he would not let them forget for a long time. They would never be able to protect themselves from his vengeance.

They spent that night together, but found it lasted a very short time. Their farewells were most sorrowful, and lamentations and sighs were poured forth. And the next morning when day had fully dawned the lady made her preparations. She had her most precious possessions packed and her clothes and gowns wrapped up, and she adorned herself with the finest garments that she had. She had a tunic of silk worked in gold, finely and richly embroidered, trimmed with ermine and reaching to the ground; and that was most magnificent and lovely and suited her so well that, when she was dressed in it, nothing in the world became her so beautifully.

[There follows a description of the fabulous materials and decorations on Briseida's mantle, which had been sent to Calchas by an Indian colleague (13341–409).]

Briseida's departure from Troy (13410–821)
Being thus finely arrayed she takes leave of many people who are deeply sorry for her. The ladies and the queen are full of pity for the young woman, and Lady Helen weeps bitterly for her sake. And she being by no means ungracious, shares their tears and lamentations, for her heart is

sorely afflicted and no-one seeing her could fail to feel pity for her. A palfrey is brought out for her, and at no time, I think was a maiden ever given a better mount. Her escort was supplied by the sons of the King and more than three of them came forth with her. Her bridle is taken by Troilus who loved her so much and so wonderfully well. But now all that will cease and be no more – hence all are weeping and wailing.

Yet although the lady is stricken with grief, she will be made happy again in time. She will soon have forgotten her sorrow, and her heart will be so altered that the Trojans will mean little to her. If she is sorrowful to-day, she will be made happy again by one who has never yet seen her. Soon she will have granted him her love, and soon she will be consoled by him. A woman will never be too downcast. So long as she is able to look about her, her sighs thereafter will be brief. A woman's sorrow is short-lived, for whilst one eye weeps the other smiles. Their hearts alter very quickly and the wisest of them is foolish enough. Having loved for seven years, she will forget within three days. None of them ever know what it is to suffer grief. Their wisdom is clearly manifest: they think that, whoever may have seen them, they can never at any time have committed any misdeed so hateful that they should be condemned for it. Their greatest delusion is that they never believe themselves to be in the wrong; and whoever trusts and believes in them is betraying and deceiving himself.

I fear indeed that I may be reproached for this[7] by her who possesses such goodness and excellence, glory and merit – integrity, wisdom and honour – virtue, moderation and purity – and noble generosity and beauty. Through her virtues the misdeeds of many women are erased. In her all knowledge abounds, and there is none to compare with her in the whole world. Noble lady of a noble king[8] – may you ever enjoy happiness free from trouble, grief or sorrow!

Solomon who was so wise in spirit has written that 'He who can find a strong woman should give thanks to his Maker'. He calls her strong because he well knew most of their weaknesses; and a strong woman is she who resists being overwhelmed with foolish desires.[9] Beauty and chastity are, it seems to me, a most powerful combination, and nothing beneath the heavens is more highly prized. It very often happens that through the importunings of suitors the best of them[10] are overcome, and it is a wonder how any of them that can be spoken to freely manage to resist. If one of them is found to be fair and true she should be cherished more than an angel from heaven, for precious stones and fine burnished gold are not to be compared to such a treasure. We could add a great deal more here, but this is not the place for it; so let us return to our subject.

The lady thought she would die when she had to part from him she loved and cherished so dearly. And she never ceased imploring him not to forget her, for she would never in her life be mistress to anyone else. She would preserve her love for him, and no-one else would ever possess it, nor would anyone have joy of her.

'Fair lady,' he said, 'I beg you, if you ever loved me, let it be shown now! I do not wish our love to fade, and for my part I assure you it will not diminish in any way. My heart will always remain true to you, and I shall never desert you for another.' Such were the pledges they gave each other before taking their leave.

171

They escorted her until they were outside the city, and there they handed her over, as they had to, to those who were most eager to receive her. Diomedes came to meet them with King Ajax, son of Telamon, King Ulysses, King Ajax, son of Oïleus, Menestheus, the lord and ruler of Athens, and over sixty more knights, of whom the lowest in rank was a mighty count. The lady weeps bitterly, and no-one can console her for her great grief is for Troilus who is going away our of reach of her love. There will be no more joy or happiness for him, and he sadly and pensively departs.

And she is led away by the son of Tydeus;[11] but he will have to go through a great deal before receiving a single kiss from her – let alone sleeping with her.

'Fair lady,' he said, 'he who has been granted your love will have good cause to be proud – and in return for serving you the rest of my life, I should like to win your heart and possess you. Were it not that this is too soon, and we are so close to camp and I see you are so distressed, preoccupied, fearful and grief-stricken – I should beg from you the great honour of accepting me as your very own knight and friend. And I should, if you wished, be ready to endure great trials before attaining that. But I greatly fear that your heart is filled with hatred for me and my countrymen. I know you will always have affection for the people amongst whom you have been brought up, and no-one should ever blame you for that. But I have often heard tell that people who have never seen or got to know each other have quite often happened to fall deeply in love. Fair lady,' said Diomedes, 'I have never had to do with love before, nor had a lady, nor been a lover. But now I feel love drawing me to you. It is no wonder that anyone gazing upon your beauty should become inflamed with desire. And you may indeed be certain of this: that I rest my hopes of happiness upon you. I shall never look for any greater joy once I am certain of possessing your love and may enjoy the delight of holding you in my arms and kissing your eyes, mouth and face. Sweet friend, do not be offended by anything I ask of you or say to you, and do not regard it as dishonourable. You will, I know, be begged and importuned for your love in various ways, and the men that will ask for it are the flower of the world's chivalry – the wealthiest, the fairest and the noblest that there are. But you may trust fair lady, in my assurance that if you take me as your lover you will gain nothing but honour as a result. He who is granted your love must be of great merit and renown – so, fair lady, do not spurn the devotion with which I offer to serve you. Answer this affection and desire of mine by accepting me as you knight – and I shall be your true and honourable friend from now on all the days of my life. I have seen many a maiden and known many a lady, but I have never before entreated any of them to love me thus. You are the first of them and will also be the last. If I love you, may God prevent me striving to win anyone else's favour. I should never do so, I am sure – but if I could win your love I should maintain it without behaving wrongly in any way; and on no occasion would you hear anything said of me to displease you. I shall strive my very best to deliver you from the heavy grief and lamentation with which I find you so burdened and afflicted – and to delight you with my embraces and kisses. In that way I shall bring you such comfort that you will become happy once again. I am eager to serve you, and should be most happy if you would allow me to. I am ready to do so from this moment on – and may God grant that you do not forbid me. For he that loves, woos and serves one who hates him is wasting all his efforts.'

Briseida was wise and honourable and answered him briefly, saying: 'Sir, on this occasion it is neither fit nor just for me to pledge myself to love you, and you would ever after think me too flighty and foolish if I did so. You have told me your desire, and I have heard and understood it well – but I do not know you well enough to grant you my love so soon. That is how many people have been misled. Many a woman has been deceived by those who are full of treachery, lying and false – for such men will lead a trustful heart astray. It is very hard to decide whom one should trust in love – since for each one that gains joy through doing so there are six that find sorrow. I do not want to fall from bad to worse – for anyone who finds within his heart such grief, distress, misery and affliction as I have will set little store by love, happiness or joy. I have abandoned my dearest friends, leaving them behind in a place where I never expect to dwell again, and where I was known and loved and held in high esteem. I had all kinds of wealth and possessions freely at my disposal there; but now I am an utter outcast and hence hold myself of less account. And, with due respect, it would not be at all fitting for a woman of my nobility to embark upon a wild love-affair in the Greek camp; for if she had any widsom at all she would take care not to incur reproach. Ladies whose conduct of affairs within their chambers is most discreet and unobtrusive cannot prevent themselves being talked about a great deal, and I shall now be amid throngs of people, without the company of other ladies – so I do not want to do anything that could be wrongly interpreted. I am not going to do so, nor do I wish to. But I know you to be of such noble blood and in my opinion most valiant, discreet and knowledgeable – and I would not have you believe anything that is not the honest truth. There is no lady beneath the heavens who is so noble, renowned and beautiful that she could refuse you if she were at all inclined to love – and I am not refusing you either. But I do not intend or desire to love you or anyone else at the moment, although you may be assured that if I decided to do so I should give no-one else preference over you. But I had not thought of doing that, nor wanted to – and God grant I never may!'

Diomedes was wise and honourable, and paid good heed to these opening speeches of hers, which were by no means too harsh. And this was what he then said to her regarding his desire: 'Fair lady, you well know that all my hopes rest with you. I shall love you devotedly and place myself at your mercy until such time as you choose to take pity upon me and accept me as your lover. Since love will have me yield to you, I shall neither refuse nor deny him and resolve from now on to attend upon his will and pleasure. If he rewards me with your favour I shall ask nothing further of him, and if I do not trust in that, I shall never be a proper servant of his. I want always to be one of his followers, and if I can kiss your lips just once there will be no-one amongst the army before Troy who will be happier than I.'

Diomedes would have said much more, but they were already close to the tents and he no longer had time to talk to her. Yet before they came to the point of parting he entreated her a hundred times to let him be her lover. Then, without anyone knowing or seeing it, she gave him one of her gloves, which greatly delighted him – nor did she seem to have any regrets about it.

Then Calchas appeared, having come out to meet them. He greeted her warmly, they exchanged many kisses and embraces, and he was moved to tears. Whilst the old man was speaking to his daughter he kissed and caressed her again and again.

'Sir,' she said, 'tell me about this strange conduct of yours – acting in such a way as to bring your name into disrepute henceforth and for ever – helping your enemies to destroy your friends and native country – and abandoning your great inheritance, your wealth, treasure and privileges in order to become an impoverished exile. How will your heart ever be at peace if you become party to such a deed? What has happened to your clear, noble and powerful intelligence? Where has it gone? You have been most harshly condemned, and so indeed you ought to be. They had raised you above all lords, bishops, fathers and rulers, and that has now ended in great disgrace. And one should shun disgrace more eagerly than one flees or avoids death. Everyone, we know, must die, for that is our common lot – and if a man dies respected, his body is treated with honour and his soul departs into a state of bliss. But anyone who lives in infamy in this world will be treated with deep disgrace in the next. The horror and darkness of Hell await him, you may be sure. Sir, my heart is deeply distressed to see how you have thus earned the hatred of Pluto and Proserpina[12] and are thus facing such trouble, degradation and harm. When you took it into your heart not to return to the city or come back to us, why then were you so heartless as to join our deadly enemies here, to do us harm and try to bring about our destruction? You would have done better to go and stay on an island in the midst of the sea until this siege had come to an end. Lord Apollo was doing a great wrong if he gave you that sort of reply or ordered you to do this. May that prophecy, that sacrifice and that moment be accursed for bringing such great shame upon you. He who loses his honour in this world has little reason to hold his life dear.' Then she began to weep, and her heart was so wrung with grief that she could not speak another word.

Calchas replied to the young woman: 'My daughter,' he said, 'I never asked that this should be my fate. I well knew I should be greatly blamed for doing so – but I could not object on this occasion or defy the gods and flout their wishes, for that could soon have brought me into trouble. From the moment that Apollo commanded it, I was bound to obey and come over to this side. I never did anything with such reluctance and should not be condemned for it, for if I could have had my way, matters would have gone very differently. No-one has any notion of the pain this gives my heart both night and day. But had I been so foolish or been one of those seeking to defy the will of the gods or do anything at all against their wishes, I have not the slightest doubt that they would have inflicted a revenge that would ever after have brought me distress, trouble, terror and danger. And furthermore, I well know that I shall see the Trojans slaughtered and annihilated – and in that case it is better for us to survive elsewhere than be killed there along with them. They will be conquered, made captive and killed, for so the gods have decreed, and it cannot be long before that happens. And I have never ceased to think and worry about how I could bring you out here to me. Now that I have you, all is well for me, and I shall never have reason for grief or regret.'

The lady, attracted much attention and the Greeks greatly admired her and all called her most beautiful. Diomedes escorted her until she dismounted at a tent which had belonged to that mighty Pharaoh who had drowned in the Red Sea.

[Here follows an account of how Calchas had obtained the tent from a grateful brother-in-law and of the herbs and flowers with which it is strewn (13822–45).]

Briseida among the Greeks (13845–66)

When the lady reached the tent at which she was helped to dismount by her companion whose face kept changing colour because of her, he reluctantly took leave of her. But the noble princes and lords came there to see her, asking what news she brought, and she answered them all courteously, concisely and intelligently. They welcomed her and made much of her and all cheered her greatly. Thus she feels better than she expected, for she finds many things that are to her liking. And by the time she has seen a fourth evening there she will have neither the will nor the desire to return to the city. Their minds are indeed quickly changed and lack both sincerity and constancy, and their hearts are most vain and fickle. Hence those who are faithful and true pay dearly for that, and often receive pain and distress as a result.

[The three months' truce comes to an end and preparations are made for the eighth battle. Troilus is already playing an important part in this[13] when Diomedes appears on the battlefield with more than three thousand followers.]

Diomedes captures Troilus's horse (14286–352)

Diomedes comes forward to fight for the lady with Troilus, and thrusts him from his saddle. He takes his charger by the bridle and calling a young man who is a servant of his he holds it out to him, saying: 'Go quickly at once to Calchas the Trojan's tent and tell his fair daughter that this charger is sent her from me. I have won it from a knight who has been striving hard to win her favour. And tell her also that I beg her not to be offended by what I say, for my life is wholly in her hands.'

The servant quickly galloped away. He dismounted before the tent and entered that pavilion, of which the pegs, pole and the knob on top were all of fine gold – as well as the eagle which was extremely beautiful. The son of Cariz of Pierrelee greeted the lady on behalf of his knightly master.

'My lady,' he said, 'he sends you this prize as a love-token, and you may be sure that you are never far from his mind. I am able to tell you that a short while ago he won it from Troilus, who used to strive so hard for your favour, and threw him down in the dust. Such was the charge he led there before my eyes that the pride of the enemy was humbled, and he overthrew a hundred of them – of whom the healthiest looks pale and wan. He sends you this, and takes such pains on your behalf, and is wholly and fully at your command.'

The lady held the horse by a ring of gold set with crystal, saying: 'Tell your lord that I say he shows a poor sort of love for me. For if anyone seeks to please me by following my wishes or is a friend of mine, he should, as he hopes to win my favour, neither mistreat nor harm Troilus; and thus he may gain my love and esteem. I am sure that if he loves me at all he will treat my friends better, for he should show tenderness to all of them. But if anyone is left to report it, before ten days have passed I shall hear much about how Troilus has exacted payment for this prize with his sword; and his loss will be fully made good. It will be no dishonour for him thus to redeem his own, for there is no knight like him beneath the heavens. I well know that he will pursue his prey, and it will not matter to him who sees it – and anyone who means to hinder him could well pay dearly for doing so. Go back, return to the battle, greet your lord from me and tell him that I should do wrong to hate him since he loves me. I should never be right to hate him, but neither shall I do him the favour of granting him my love.'

[The Trojans meanwhile have taken the offensive, and Polydamas captures Diomedes's horse, which he presents to Troilus (14415–21). Troilus then energetically re-enters the battle, hoping that Briseida will come to hear of his exploits, and succeeds in unhorsing Achilles (14428–78). In the later stages Hector is wounded, and the eighth battle ends with a six months' truce being requested by Priam and agreed to by the Greeks (14567–83). During this interim Diomedes once again turns to the direct pursuit of Briseida's love.]

Diomedes and Briseida (15001–185)
Although others may be enjoying peace, repose and happiness, the son of Tydeus has none at all,[14] for he remains so wakeful on account of love that he finds no rest in his bed. He can neither sleep nor close his eyes, and has no peace night or day. He often broods and sighs – is often made joyful and often sad – is often vexed and often gladdened. And love's oppression makes him often change colour and frequently break out in a sweat when he was not hot and did not feel so. Love's darts often have such effects, and those who are in any way ensnared by him frequently show as much in their faces. His attacks are most fierce and he makes them suffer extreme agony. And there can be no rest at all for anyone who is aflame with true love as Diomedes is, for he can now have neither happiness nor peace. His anxiety is great, for he has no certainty at all of every being able to possess her. His hopes of happiness rest with the daughter of Calchas of Troy, and he fears that he may never, night or day, be able to lie beneath a coverlet with her – yet that is what he means to strive for, and that is what occupies all his thoughts. And if she will not grant him her consent to do so, he will most certainly die. He often goes to see her, but she is much too clever. She well understands from his sighs that he is entirely devoted to her, and she thus makes herself thrice as difficult for him.

A woman will always behave thus; if she sees that you love her and are suffering agonies because of her, she will keep treating you disdainfully, and will then soon after turn upon you a gaze that shows neither rejection nor disdain. You will have paid most dearly for your happiness before she deigns to grant it to you. It is a very hard thing to love when one's love is not returned, and it happens a great deal; yet one must consider it a marvel that it should ever be so.

He who never could beg is now made to, and it is a hard thing indeed for him to have to do. Diomedes now has to entreat favour, for he is so much in love that his suffering and affliction could never be greater. Often he goes to implore her pity, and often tells her that night and day he is continuing to sacrifice his health to love; he is losing his appetite and his sleep, and melancholy, tears and sighs are making him pale and troubled. It is most humiliating to entreat her thus, but I do not think that anyone who does so and is truly in love can be at all lacking in dignity. In his speeches such a person will say much less than he needs to gain himself favour, and will never consider how much he has forgotten to say. He thus remains silent about things that would favour him and put him in a better position. So Diomedes behaved, for on many occasions he forgot what it was that he most wanted to say. And despite all his efforts he had to endure such suffering a long while before being able to obtain any joy or pleasure from her.

One day he went to beg her to look at the charger that had belonged to her lover. He had been very fully informed of what had happened when his man had presented it to her, and he was very hurt and offended as a result. And he certainly meant to call her to account for it before they had finished. If the lady had dared to do so and not been in fear of shame and reproach, she would willingly have sent it back to him; but she could soon have found herself in a worse position and earned far too much hatred from the Greeks as a result. When she saw him she chided him in this way: 'My lord,' she said, 'too much great a generosity can impoverish, ruin and injure a person, and many have thus been reduced to penury. The other day during the great battle, when he who has no love for us took your noble steed away and never made you amends for it, you would have been at such a loss if you had then had this charger – for I think you could have used it. You gave it away too soon. I was afraid you might be at a loss without it, and if your need had been known, you could soon have had it back. It is no bad thing to make gifts that can be recovered; and over there they are no fools. Anyone who seeks to deprive them of their heritage and drive them out of their country is taking on a mighty task, for they are noble and valiant knights. My lord,' she said, 'I shall lend you a horse, for I cannot do otherwise and you will not be able to find another like it. Since you have lost your own, you will be well placed when you have this one – so I shall make you a loan of it. But those people are keen in pursuit, and if you do not look after it, they will have it back. You may be sure that they will put every effort into doing so. He who has captured yours is neither afraid nor abashed, and there can be no-one of such valour.'

'My lady,' said Diomedes, 'there can be no mistaking his great valour in full battle and in tournaments. But it can be no cause for wonder that a knight should lose his charger. He that truly seeks to devote himself to soldiering and undergo mighty struggles will win and lose on many occasions. I am indeed neither too abashed nor too dismayed by that for I have enough of them. But if you are entrusting it to me I shall look after it to the best of my ability. I should have to be very hard-pressed before I let myself part with it, and more than three of them would first have to pay for it dearly. From now on I can be sure that the great suffering I have endured for you (to whom my heart is drawn in yearning, without gaining any joy, relief or consolation) and the patience I have shown will be wholly transformed into joy. Moreover, I shall keep imploring you to grant me your favour. That is what I look for and entreat; that is what I yearn for and desire; and with that my sighs will come to an end. My happiness will be made perfect when you are mine, and the decision about that is in your hands. Sweet friend, do not let your aid arrive too late! It would be a disaster for me if you were to listen to another suitor, for if I cannot place my faith in you I do not think I shall ever bear or wield a shield or lance again. It would be better for me to be dead and gone than live any longer, for my life would be too miserable. Dear friend, let your heart find room for me. You are so lovely and honourable and wise that I have no thoughts for anyone other than you, noble lady. Now let it be just as you wish and just as you may command. I can do no more than yield and abandon myself to you.'

The lady is quite content, and is thoroughly pleased and delighted with the man she has thus ensnared. She bestows upon him her right sleeve of fine new silk, to serve as a pennant. He who has thus devoted himself to her is now happy; and now that vein which makes others commit those crimes that are often described and recounted is inflamed within him.[15] From now on Troilus may be sure that any further trust in her will be doomed. As far as she is concerned their love has been obliterated – and that was later to be paid for dearly.

[Another brief skirmish between Diomedes and Troilus takes place during the tenth battle (15638–58). During the same battle Hector is killed, and Troilus is shown mourning his death (16399–400) along with other noble Trojans, 'for he loved no-one in the world more than him.' Later the Trojans commemorate Hector's death with a festival and some of the Greek leaders attend as spectators. Here for the first time Achilles sees Polyxena who is to be the cause of his death.]

Achilles and Polyxena[16] (17545–89)

Now hear how destiny works. In what follows you will learn just how he came to suffer the anguish of true love, for he never saw a day dawn so unluckily for him. Destiny is indeed powerful in its workings, and many may find it very harsh and stern. Great woes arise from slight causes. The great beauty and the appearance of the maiden that Achilles beheld kindled his heart with a flame that he would in no way ever be able to put out. He had inscribed and portrayed her upon his heart; he dwells upon her charms – her most beautiful bright eyes, her forehead and her lovely hair which is so fair that it looks like fine pure gold. There is nothing about her that escapes him or fails to give him a mortal wound. The radiant beauty of her face strikes a freezing chill into his heart. Her nose, her mouth and her chin kindle him with such a flame that he will be inwardly ablaze from now on, and Love will grip and gnaw him. Her lovely body and her breast give him such torment that there will be neither night nor day when he does not feel the rod of Love more than fourteen times. From now on he will be so afflicted that he will not know what to do for the best. From now on he will have to stay awake whole long nights without closing an eye. Love has soon humbled his pride; his shield and his hauberk of fine mail would be of little use to him here, and his keen blade of steel would be of no avail – for strength, courage and daring are powerless in the face of Love.

Achilles gazes at the girl and thinks her most beautiful – and so she is, without a doubt. None so lovely was ever seen, nor ever again will be.

[Achilles then returns to his tent. His sufferings for love, his use of a 'faithful friend and confidant' (17747–8) to negotiate with the Trojans, and his attempts to persuade the Greeks to abandon the siege are the subject of the narrative until the start of the twelfth battle (18473).

In the thirteenth battle Troilus leads the Trojans on to the offensive (19281–93, 19366–9),[17] and during the two months' truce that follows the Greeks, considering their recent setbacks and the refusal of Achilles to fight, take stock of their situation. Diomedes reminds them that despite Hector's death Troilus, who is 'no less mighty than his brother', remains a powerful force to be reckoned with (19900–18), and both he and Ulysses are in favour of seeking peace. Calchas, however, dissuades the Greeks from doing so by reminding them of what the gods have ordained (19925–54).

Subsequently in the fourteenth battle Troilus 'avenges his brother' by routing the Greeks (20008–24), and during the fifteenth he inflicts a severe wound on Diomedes, speaking to him in the following terms as he is carried from the field.]

Troilus taunts Diomedes (20080–102)
'Now go and stay with your woman, old Calchas's daughter – for she, they say, by no means hates you. I would have spared you for love of her if I had thought of it earlier. But nonetheless her lack of constancy, her treachery and wrongdoing, and the way she has deceived me have brought you to this pass. Her sins and her betrayal of my love have alighted upon your head. Now we are both here I shall send her this message through you: that although you have taken my place, there will be many others who find a welcome there before the siege comes to an end – and you will have to be quite vigilant. Although you as yet have no partner in her favours she will not call a halt as long as the game appeals to her. For if she can manage to be pleased with so little, her hosts will all benefit by it. And that will be the sensible thing to do if she knows what is best for her.

[Troilus also wounds Agamemnon and the Greek losses come to exceed those of the Trojans by far. A six month truce is, however, granted and the wounded Greek leaders are attended to (20103–201).]

Briseida grants Diomedes her love (20202–340)
When Diomedes was wounded and the daughter of Calchas came to know of it she did all she could to console herself, but she could not disguise the state of her heart sufficiently to prevent laments, tears and sighs emerging from it nevertheless. She made it clearly apparent that she loved him from her heart, more than any other person alive. She had never until that day given much sign of loving him, but now she could not conceal it from him, and she suffers much grief and affliction. And she does not let the

179

fear of gossip stop her going to see him in his tent, for from now on her concern is solely for him – from now on she loves him and is devoted to him, but is in great fear of losing him.[18] The wound is very dangerous, the Greek army is most anxious about it, and thus her eyes flow with tears. Nor despite old Calchas and his reproaches, threats and warnings does she refrain from going to see him frequently. From now on it can be seen that she has turned everything – her affections, her heart and her thoughts – in his direction. But she also well knows that she is acting despicably. She has abandoned Troilus most unjustly and treacherously, and knows that she has behaved very badly and greatly wronged a man who is fair, noble and valiant and superior as a soldier to all of them. And she says to herself in her thoughts:

'Nothing good will ever be written or sung of me. I never at any time wished such a thing to happen. I behaved wrongly and stupidly, I think, when I betrayed my lover, who never deserved that of me. I have not acted as I should towards him. My heart indeed ought to have been so firmly attached to him that I should never have given heed to anyone else; but I was false, fickle and foolish in listening to that man's speeches. Whoever wishes to maintain their loyalty should never give heed to speeches, for by such means the wisest and most prudent people have been misled. From now on I shall be giving those with little love for me a great deal to gossip about. The ladies of Troy will make me the subject of their talk. I have brought the most odious disgrace upon women and upon noble ladies, and my treachery and misdeeds will always be laid to their charge. That ought to weigh heavily upon me, and so indeed it does; my heart is surely most fickle and treacherous. For I had the best lover any woman ever bestowed her love upon, and I ought to have loved all those he loved, and loathed and shunned those who sought to do him harm. It shows just how clever I am, that in defiance of reason and justice I have given my entire devotion to someone he hates above all others, and I shall always be thoroughly despised for doing so. And what good would it do me to repent? I shall never be able to make amends by that means. Let me then be true to this man who is a most valiant and worthy knight. I shall never be able to return to Troy nor leave him, for my heart is too firmly bound to him, and it was for his sake that I did what I did. Yet it would not have been so if I were still within the city, for then my heart would never dream of faltering or changing. But here I have been without any true friends or advisers and hence lacking the kind of reassurance that might have eased my grief and affliction. I might have been plunged in melancholy lamentation and despair and remained so until I died without ever receiving comfort. I am sure I should have died a long time ago, had I not taken pity upon myself. Although I have acted rashly I have got the better of the problem – for, whereas my heart had been deep in grief, I can now be happy and content. Let those who failed to console me complain about this. One should never go on enduring pain and suffering simply through fear of what people will say. If the whole world is happy and my heart is full of grief and woe, that will be no help to me at all, for my heart will ache and bleed because of my distress. For anyone who loves while his heart is at all restless, troubled, fearful or regretful cannot be wholly involved in what he is doing. I often find myself at ease one moment and troubled the next. Often things seem indeed to go according to my wishes; and often, again, my eyes grow full of tears. Thus it is now, and I can do no more about it. May God grant Troilus happiness! Since I can no longer cherish him, nor he me, I shall yield and surrender myself to Diomedes. I should dearly love to be able to forget what has been done in the past, for the memory of it sorely afflicts my heart. But whether I wish to or not, I must from now on devote all my energy and thought to making sure that Diomedes remains in love with me – so that he may have joy and pleasure from it and I from him, since that is how things must be. Now I feel my heart bold and eager to do what would give him pleasure, and he will meet no further resistance. I have led him on with promises so far that it is now time to grant his wish, his pleasure and his desire. God grant I may gain joy and happiness from it!'

[These words are the last to be heard from Briseida in the poem. Troilus meanwhile goes on to distinguish himself in the next battle, the sixteenth of the war.[19] His subsequent entry into Troy is described as follows.]

Troilus in triumph (20595–607)
The Trojans made their way homewards, joyful, happy and triumphant. In this sixteenth battle Troilus had captured a hundred noble knights and a hundred very fine horses. It was a sad fate for them, and they would have been better dead. King Priam was much delighted at the losses that had been sustained by his enemies that day; he is sure that they will all be made to suffer if Troilus lives any longer.

[The ladies of the court attend to Troilus. His mother speaks of her fears for him and of how her life depends upon his, and she implores the gods to protect him. Troilus comforts her, and then begins to speak of Briseida again.]

Troilus denounces Briseida (20666–82)
Then he bitterly condemned his mistress who had left him and granted her love to his enemy. He spoke of ladies as traitors and young women as liars – saying it was wrong to trust them since there were very few one could truly love without fear of deception or betrayal. 'There may be some who can make a joke of it, but I cannot; the daughter of Calchas has deceived me.'

Now she may often hear herself spoken of; the ladies despise her heartily, feel great hatred towards her and wish her the worst of ill luck. They no longer love her as they did, for she has brought shame upon all of them and will always be notorious for doing so.

[Troilus once more makes a major contribution to Trojan victory in the seventeenth battle (20832–7, 20861–4). During the eighteenth battle he drives the Myrmidons back to their tents, thus shaming Achilles into re-entering the conflict (21004–118). An encounter takes place in which Troilus wounds Achilles and captures his horse (21129–77), and the battle ends with Troilus yet again acknowledged as the victor (21188–9). Before the start of the nineteenth battle Achilles orders the Myrmidons to concentrate solely on helping him to take revenge upon Troilus (21292–

320). As the battle begins Troilus drives the Greeks back to their tents once more, but the Trojan advance is brought to a halt by the emergence of the Myrmidons (21383–96).]

The death of Troilus (21397–463)

To support the Myrmidons the Greeks quickly resumed the attack and such combats, slayings and onslaughts took place there that no-one could properly describe them to you. And the Myrmidons did not mean to forget what their leader has asked them to do. They seek out Troilus in the midst of the fray and concentrate their attack upon his company alone. Then they clash and exchange blows with lances and bare blades. Heads are smitten through there, and hands, feet and arms are slashed; it was an awesome struggle.

Troilus grows mightily enraged when he sees those who seek his death surrounding him. He draws his sword of keen-edged steel, then sets about them, cutting them down and venting his fury upon all of them indiscriminately. He advances into the very thick of them and it is all over for anyone he comes to blows with. No-one, Dares tells us, ever saw anyone inflict such slaughter and butchery, and the blood flowed in torrents. He had overcome, slain, cut down or wounded all of them and put them to flight when his horse was killed. It had been wounded by two lance-thrusts and could no longer remain on its feet. It collapsed in the middle of the field, and Troilus fell with it. He had no comrade or fellow with him, and before he could rise to his feet Achilles was upon him. Alas, what sword-blows then rained upon him! Then Achilles set about removing his helmet. He resisted strongly and gave them a fierce struggle. But what good does that do? It is no use to him at all, for treacherous Achilles has cut off his head before anyone can come to his aid. He has done a deed of great brutality and baseness and could well suffer for it.[20] May he be made to repent of it! He tied the knight's body to his horse's tail and then dragged it along behind him for all on the battlefield to see.

The news spread quickly, and when the Trojans have heard it they all pause in dismay – wailing, shouting, weeping and lamenting; and in the midst of the battle many of them fall fainting. Paris heard about it, as did Aeneas, King Memnon and Polydamas – and they are seized with such grief and sorrow that not one of them can think of anything else.[21] Now their affliction is renewed and their strength has been diminished. From now on it will be a struggle for them.

[Memnon rescues Troilus's body, and the Trojans, hard-pressed now by the Greeks, at length bring it back to Troy, where it is lamented over by Hecuba (21702–51) and mourned by the princes and ladies of the city. Hecuba subsequently takes revenge upon Achilles for Troilus and Hector's death by luring him to the temple of Apollo with the promise of marriage to Polyxena. There she has him ambushed and killed by Paris (21838–22330).

After Troilus's death Calchas continues to act as adviser to the Greeks, interpreting omens and showing them how to placate the gods and achieve victory (25572–5, 25722–34, 26375–97, and 26932–61).

Diomedes meanwhile continues to play an important part in the siege – being chosen to accompany Ulysses to discuss peace proposals with the

Trojans (25326–7). Like Ulysses and other Greek leaders he also experiences difficulties in returning home after the fall of Troy (27932–28046 and 28113–46),[22] but he eventually succeeds in overcoming the opposition of his wife and regaining his kingdom (28238–52). Of Briseida this author says nothing more.]

Appendix C

Guido de Columnis, *Historia Destructionis Troiae* (excerpts)

Portrait of Diomedes (Book VIII – Griffin, *ed. cit.*, p. 84)
Diomedes was of great height, broad-chested, square-shouldered, fierce-looking, deceitful in his promises, active in war and eager for victory. He was widely feared, since he was very aggressive, and was highly impatient with his servants for he was an extremely hard master. He was indeed very lustful and endured much torment because of the violence of his passion.

Portrait of Briseida (Book VIII, p. 85)
Briseida, the daughter of Calchas, was most graceful in her beauty. She was neither tall nor short nor too thin, and had a skin of milky whiteness, rosy cheeks and golden hair. But her eyebrows were joined, and because the hairs grew very thickly at the place where they met this seemed a slight blemish. She excelled in the eloquence of her speech and was very readily moved to compassion. Her charms brought her many suitors, and she granted her favour to many, but she did not remain constant in heart towards her lovers.

Portrait of Troilus (Book VIII, p. 86)
Troilus indeed, although mighty of body was made yet mightier by the greatness of his spirit. He was high-tempered and bold, but maintained a great deal of moderation in that respect. Women found him highly attractive and he, though retaining some discretion, found delight in them. Indeed, for both strength and energy in war he was equal or next to Hector. Moreover in the whole kingdom of Troy there was no young warrior of such strength or so famous for his great daring.

[Guido gives little attention to Diomedes and Troilus as rivals in the early stages of the war.[1] The lovers' sufferings on hearing about Briseida's coming departure and return to Calchas are described in rather more florid terms than those employed by Benoit. Briseida's tears are said to be so copious that water could be wrung from her garments, and her more violent reactions are portrayed as follows.]

Briseida's grief (Book XIX, p. 163)
Furthermore, she rends her delicate face with her nails, and her golden hair, which is no longer held by a headband, she tears from the milk-white skin of her head. And when she scores her rosy-coloured cheeks with her sharp nails, torn lilies seem, by way of comparison, to be mingled with torn roses.

[The lovers' last night together is described, and the author then turns to consider the implications of what is to come.]

The inconstancy of women (Book XIX, p. 164)[2]
But Troilus, what youthful credulity makes you so deluded as to trust in Briseida's tears and deceitful endearments? Indeed all women naturally tend to lack any kind of firm constancy – for if one of their eyes is weeping the other will be smiling to one side, and their instability and

fickleness always lead them to deceive men. And however much they display love for some men, as soon as others pay court to them they quickly revise and alter such passing shows of affection. And if it so happens that no-one appears to pay court to them, they will themselves look for someone secretly and with furtive glances as they walk abroad, or whilst they continually flaunt themselves at windows or linger in public places. Thus indeed no hope is vainer than that which is placed in or offered by women. Hence any young man may deservedly be thought foolish (and more so one of mature years) if he puts his trust in the flattery of women or relies upon such false assurances from them.

[Briseida's departure is then described. Little space is given to the initial stages of Diomedes's wooing, but a fuller account is given of Briseida's reproachful address to her father and his reply (Book XIX, pp. 165–6). She is shown being welcomed and given assurances of protection by the Greek leaders, and the narrator then describes her reactions and their implications.]

The inconstancy of women again (Book XIX, p. 166)[3]
And that day had not yet passed towards evening before Briseida began to alter her recent resolve and her heart's former purpose. And already she is beginning to be much readier to remain with the Greeks than she had so far been to stay with the Trojans. Now the love she has in her heart for noble Troilus begins to grow cool, and in thus short a time, thus hastily and suddenly, she becomes changeable and fickle in every way. What then can be said of the constancy of women whose sex is noted for their failure of resolve at moment of sudden weakness, or for their fickle alteration of it within a very short time? It is not fitting for a man to try to describe their fickleness, for their inconstancy of purpose is worse than one can say.

[When Diomedes overthrows Troilus and captures his horse in the seventh battle Briseida receives the prize 'gladly' and instructs the messenger bringing it to tell Diomedes that she cannot hate anyone who loves her so sincerely (Book XX, p. 169). Diomedes's love-sickness and Briseida's delaying tactics are briefly described just before the eighth battle (Book XXI, p. 171), during which Troilus and Diomedes come near to settling their rivalry in single combat but are separated by Menelaus (Book XXI, p. 173). During the eleventh battle Troilus is said to have killed a thousand Greeks and beaten the rest back to their tents; and in the twelfth he unhorses Diomedes, wounds him severely and upbraids him about his love for Briseida – although his actual words are not recorded (Book XXVI, p. 197). Guido then briefly concludes his portrayal of Briseida in the following terms.]

Briseida decides to grant Diomedes her love (Book XXVI, p. 198)
Meanwhile Briseida, against her father's wishes, often goes to see Diomedes who is lying in bed as a result of the wound he has suffered. For although she knows that he had been thus gravely wounded by her lover Troilus a short while ago, she nonetheless has a great deal to think about. And bearing in mind that there was no further hope of rejoining Troilus, she sets her whole heart, in the fickle and inconstant way that women have, upon Diomedes, and wholly alters the course of her affections. And

185

she makes up her mind that she will no longer put him off with promises, but will yield herself to him entirely as soon as he is well on the road to recovery. She is in a ferment of passion for him, and is inwardly aflame with fierce desire.

[Troilus continues to play a leading and successful part in the war (Book XXVI, pp. 199–202), and is finally killed by Achilles in the manner Benoit describes (Book XXVI, pp. 203–4). Immediately after the death of Troilus the narrator accuses Homer of being unduly favourable to the Greeks by praising Achilles, who killed both Hector and Troilus in a treacherous way.]

The narrator reproaches Homer (Book XXVI, pp. 204–5)
Likewise he [Achilles][4] did not slay the mighty Troilus by means of his own bravery, but did not scruple to kill him once he had been assailed and overpowered by a thousand other men and offered no resistance. And he thus struck him down more as if he were a dead man than a living one. And is this Achilles, whom you showed adorned with many noble qualities, worthy of praise for shamelessly dragging at his horse's tail the son of a noble king – a man who was so famed for his nobility and valour and whom he himself had neither captured nor overcome? Indeed if nobility had prompted him and valour inspired him, he would have been moved to pity and never stooped in that savage way to such dishonourable deeds. But he could not be moved to behave thus, for it was indeed not in his nature.

[The narrator furthermore says of Achilles that he never killed a man of valour except through treachery, and that he is worthy of praise only if that provides a title to fame (Book XXVI, p. 206).

Diomedes continues after Troilus's death to play a leading role in the conduct of war and diplomacy (Bks. XXVIII–IX, pp. 213, 216, 223 and 225–8). Once the city has fallen Calchas, as in Benoit, warns that Polyxena must be killed, to appease the gods and enable the Greeks to return home (Book XXX, pp. 235–6). Again as in Benoit, Diomedes has difficulty in regaining his kingdom, but at length succeeds in doing so (Book XXXII, pp. 249–51 and 252).]

ABBREVIATIONS
NOTES
BIBLIOGRAPHY

Abbreviations

Aen	Virgil, *Aeneid*
ASI	*Archivio storico italiano*
Branca *CT*	V. Branca, *Il Cantare trecentesco*
Branca *MW*	V. Branca, *Boccaccio, the Man and his Works*
Canz.	Petrarch, *Canzoniere*, ed. G. Contini
Chau R	*Chaucer Review*
Cl. Prol	Chaucer, *Prologue to Clerk's Tale*
Cl T	Chaucer, *Clerk's Tale*
Cons. Phil.	Boethius, *Consolation of Philosophy*
Conv.	Dante, *Convivio*
Dec.	Boccaccio, *Decameron*
De Cas.	Boccaccio, *De Casibus Virorum Illustrium*
DVE	Dante, *De Vulgari Eloquentia*
ELH	*Journal of English Literary History*
ESt	*English Studies*
Fab.	Hyginus, *Fabulae*, ed. H. I. Rose
Fam.	Petrarch, *Le Familiari*, ed. V. Rossi and U. Bosco.
Filoc.	Boccaccio, *Filocolo*
Filostr.	Boccaccio, *Filostrato*
Fkl. T.	Chaucer, *Franklin's Tale*
Fri. T.	Chaucer, *Friar's Tale*
G. and M.	N. E. Griffin and A. B. Myrick, *The Filostrato* (parallel text)
Genealogia	Boccaccio, *Genealogie Deorum Libri*, ed. V. Romano
GDLI	*Grande Dizionario della Lingua italiana*
Gen. Prol.	Chaucer, *General Prologue to the Canterbury Tales*
Gordon	R. K. Gordon, *The Story of Troilus*
GSLI	*Giornale Storico della letteratura italiana*
Her.	Ovid, *Heroides*, ed. and tr. G. Showerman
HF	Chaucer, *House of Fame*
Historia	Guido de Columnis, *Historia Destructionis Troiae*, ed. N. E. Griffin
Inf.	Dante, *Inferno*
LGW	Chaucer, *Legend of Good Women*
Libro	Binduccio dello Scelto, *Libro de la Storia di Troia*, ed. E. Gorra
MAe	*Medium Aevum*
Merch. T.	Chaucer, *Merchant's Tale*
Met.	Ovid, *Metamorphoses*
Mk. T.	Chaucer, *Monk's Tale*
MLT	Chaucer, *Man of Law's Tale*
MPh	*Modern Philology*
OCD	*Oxford Classical Dictionary*, ed. N. G. L. Hammond and H. H. Scullard
Opere	*Tutte le Opere di Giovanni Boccaccio*, ed. V. Branca
Par.	Dante, *Paradiso*
PF	Chaucer, *Parliament of Fowls*

PL	J. P. Migne, *Patrologia Latina*
PQ	*Philological Quarterly*
Purg.	Dante, *Purgatorio*
Roman	Benoit de Sainte-Maure, *Roman de Troie*, ed. L. Constans
RR	Guillaume de Lorris and Jean de Meun, *Roman de la Rose*, ed. F. Lecoy
Rv. T.	Chaucer, *Reeve's Tale*
SA	*Sources and Analogues of Chaucer's Canterbury Tales*, ed. W. F. Bryan and G. Dempster
SP	*Studies in Philology*
Spec	*Speculum*
Summa Th.	Aquinas, *Summa Theologica*
TB	N. Tommaseo and B. Bellini (ed.), *Dizionario della Lingua italiana*
TC	Chaucer, *Troilus and Criseyde*
Tes.	Boccaccio, *Teseida*
Theb.	Statius, *Thebaid*, ed. and tr. J. H. Mozley
TPAPA	*Transactions and Proceedings of the American Philological Association*
VN	Dante, *Vita Nuova*
WBT	Chaucer, *Wife of Bath's Tale*
ZfRPh	*Zeitschrift für Romanische Philologie*

Notes

INTRODUCTION (i)

1 *De Mulieribus Claris*, CVI, par. 7 (*Opere*, X, ed. V. Zaccaria, pp. 444–5) – my translation. This part of the work was probably written in 1362.

2 *Rime* (ed. V. Branca), esp. nos. iii, iv and vi.

3 *Caccia* I, 12.

4 *Filoc.* I, 1; IV, 9–74; and V, 4–32 (*Opere* I, ed. A. E. Quaglio).

5 Cp. F. Torraca, 'Giovanni Boccaccio a Napoli' (ii), 63, and Branca *MW*, 23. The first four chapters of the latter work (of which Book I is a revision of the *Profilo biografico* in *Opere* I, 3–203) are the most up to date guide to Boccaccio's early years and his life in Naples.

   For a less than enthusiastic view of the conduct of some Neapolitan nobles see Petrarch, *Fam.* V, 6; and for a grimly comic portrayal of certain parts of the city where even the bucket on a well is likely to go missing see Boccaccio, *Dec.* II, 5.

6 According to J. K. Hyde the population of the city around 1340 was less than half the average size of Northern Italian cities such as Milan, Florence, Venice and Genoa (c. 80,000–100,000), and was also smaller than that of Palermo (c. 50,000). See Hyde, *Society and Politics in Medieval Italy*, 153–4 and map 5.

7 The Norman House of Hauteville from the late 11th c., and the Hohenstaufen from the end of the 12th c. to the later 13th. For an account of Angevin rule in Naples and Sicily during the reign of Charles I see S. Runciman, *The Sicilian Vespers*.

8 E. G. Léonard, *Les Angevins de Naples*, ch. X. On the development and layout of the town see ibid. 287f. and Torraca (i), 156–7.

9 Cp. J. Larner, *Culture and Society in Italy, 1290–1420*, 108–9.

10 Léonard, 501. On the painters at Robert's court see also Larner, 109–10. During this period Giotto is also said to have worked in the Castel dell'Uovo and the Church of the Incoronata, although none of his Neapolitan paintings have survived.

11 See esp. *Filoc.* IV 13f. and 74.

12 Robert was deeply involved in Italian Guelf politics (esp. as an opponent of Henry of Luxemburg) and in attempts to recover Sicily from the House of Aragon.

13 Léonard, 281.

14 R. Caggese, *Roberto d'Angiò e i suoi tempi* I, 637.

15 Léonard, 290. Larner considers that 'In the fourteenth century Naples, compared with the rest of Italy, was more prosperous than it is today' (15).

16 Caggese I, 679.

17 Léonard, 281.

18 Ibid.

19 Caggese I, 544–6 and 554.

20 *Par.* IX, 127–32.

21 Hyde, 128. On the extent of the florin's power at this time see also ibid., 157–64 and Larner, 18 and 25–6.

22 The Peruzzi company, for example, were able to pay a dividend of 40% in 1308 (Caggese I, 569).

23 Caggese I, 569–70 (my translation).

24 Ibid., I, 571f.

25 Ibid., I, 584–6. Each of the 'big three' Florentine companies also took on a third of the loan that was regularly contracted against the income of the State (ibid., I, 591).

26 Ibid., I, 570.

27 Ibid., I, 574. Perhaps the most politically successful of these was Boccaccio's early friend and subsequent enemy, Niccolò Acciaiuoli, who became Grand Seneschal to Robert's successor Joanna I (see Léonard, 366–8 and Branca *MW*, 23–4, 28–9, and 103–7).

28 Such titles, as Branca says (*MW*, 12), were 'empty of substance, but signs of esteem and of fondness, with which Florentine merchants . . . loved to decorate themselves and boast.'

29 Notably from Lewis of Bavaria and Frederick of Sicily (see Torraca (i), 147 and Branca *MW*, 11). The first evidence of Boccaccino's presence in Naples is a document of 30 Nov. 1327 authorising Florentine companies to export grain (R. Davidsohn, *Forschungen zur älteren Geschichte von Florenz* III, item 907, pp. 181–2). He is also mentioned as a *familiaris* of Robert in a document of 2 Feb. 1328 (ibid., item 911, p. 182).

30 On the circumstances of Boccaccio's birth see Branca *MW*, 5–8. Precise documentation concerning his arrival in Naples is lacking, but for some conjectures (mostly based on references in his work) see Branca *MW*, p. 15 n. 30.

31 Branca *MW*, 17–19. Boccaccio's later regrets about having spent so much of his youth in training for this profession are expressed in the *Genealogia Deorum Gentilium* XV, 10 (tr. C. G. Osgood, *Boccaccio on Poetry*, pp. 131–2).

32 See esp. Boccaccio: *Comedia Ninfe* xxxv, par. 32; *Amorosa Visione* xiv, 22–33; and Ep. XII to Francesco Nelli (in *Giovanni Boccaccio: Opere in Versi*, ed. P. G. Ricci, pp. 1166–7). Robert is described in similar terms by Giovanni Villani (*Cronica* XI, cxxxvii and XII, x). This aspect of his reputation is also scathingly represented through the words of his elder brother in Dante's *Par.* VIII, 76–84.

33 Osgood, 51 and 98. Cp. Branca's comments on the *Amorosa Visione* passage (*Opere* III, p. 641).

34 Villani's *Cronica* (XII, x) describes him at the time of his death as 'the wisest king there has been in Christendom for 500 years, with regard to both natural wisdom and academic learning – a great master of theology and eminent philosopher . . .' (my transln.).

35 Léonard, 282. For later writers' praise of Robert and his reign see B. Croce, *History of the Kingdom of Naples* (tr. Frenaye), p. 52 and n. 10–12.

36 Robert had been one of the leading opponents of Henry of Luxemburg's attempt to establish Imperial power in Italy (1310–13).

37 A book of *Moralia* (probably by Graziolo de' Bambaglioli) is also ascribed to him, as is a haphazard collection of *Apophthegmata* (Caggese II, 364).

38 Caggese II, 368 (my transln.).

39 Léonard, 283 and 285–6. For Petrarch's opinion of Robert at this time see *Fam.* IV, 4 and *Africa* I, 19–20, and for further evidence E. H. Wilkins, 'The Coronation of Petrarch', *Spec.* XVIII, esp. 180–5. Admiration for Robert's learning and dialectical skill had even reached England as early as 1319 – see R. Weiss, 'The translators from the Greek of the Angevin Court of Naples', *Rinascimento* (1950), 207 n. 2, and Larner, 117.

40 Caggese II, 368. See also Weiss (1950), 206–8.

41 Caggese II, 410, 411. Measures were also taken to protect the university from competition, although the teaching of medicine was permitted at Salerno and of decretals at Bari.

42 Like Dante, Cino had been a supporter of Imperial claims in Italy.

43 A satirical *canzone, Deh, quando rivedrò* is in *Le Rime di Cino da Pistoia*, ed. G. Zaccagnini, and the circumstances of its composition are discussed by E. Treves, *GSLI* LVIII, 122–39.

44 Although these were not, as Branca points out (*MW*, 39 n. 7), obligatory for students of canon law.

45 See the note on the *Filostr.* passage below, p. 202. Branca (*MW*, 32) also notes that *Rime* XVI, XLVI and LXXI are decorated with 'Cino-inspired traceries'.

46 Branca, *MW*, 36–7. See also Torraca (i) 193–6 and R. Weiss, 'Notes on Dionigi da Borgo San Sepolcro', *Italian Studies* X, 40–2 (for the attribution of two further works to Dionigi).

47 Branca *MW*, 34.

48 Tr. Osgood, 112. Andalò is cited by Boccaccio at least 14 times in the *Genealogia* (ed. Romano, 868). Boccaccio's interests in the study of arithmetic, geometry and astrology, were also furthered by his fellow-Florentine Paolo dell'Abbaco (see Branca *MW*, 34 and *Genealogia* XV, 6).

49 On the identification see *Opere* I, 917 n. 22. Andalò's teaching is also referred to explicitly and admiringly in *De Cas.* III, 1 and in Boccaccio's last vernacular work, the *Esposizioni* (v, 1, 162).

50 Branca *MW*, 10–11, 51 and 105–6. For details of their careers see Torraca (i), 176–9 (on Barbato) and 179–84 (on the more politically successful Barrili). See also N. F. Faraglia, 'Barbato di Sulmona e gli uomini di lettere della corte di Roberto d'Angiò', *ASI* (1889), 313–60.

51 Petrarch even asserts that Barbato knew Greek (*Fam.* XXIV, 12), although, according to Weiss (1950), such evidence as there is indicates the contrary (210).

52 Ed. Ricci, 1100–1, 1142–9 and 1190.

53 He was sent to crown Petrarch on Robert's behalf in Rome, but fell among thieves on the way from Naples. Cp. Osgood, 180.

54 Osgood, 88–9.

55 For the strange story of Leontius Pilatus and his translation of Homer see *Genealogia* XV 6 and 7 (tr. Osgood, 114–15 and 120), Branca *MW*, esp. 115–19 and C. C. Coulter, 'Boccaccio's Acquaintance with Homer', *PQ* V (1926), 44–53.

56 R. Weiss (1950), 201.

57 Ibid., 205.

58 Ibid., 206 and esp. 216f. (on Niccolò da Reggio, translator of Galen).

59 Weiss considers that 'the translators probably cared little for polite letters, while it is unlikely that the humanists had more than a superficial knowledge of Greek medicine' (ibid., 210; see also 223–5).

60 Caggese II, 372.

61 Ibid., I, 679.

62 C. C. Coulter, 'The Library of the Angevin Kings at Naples', *TPAPA*, LXXV (1944), 143.

63 The most important of these collectors, it appears, was the Greek translator Azzolino de Urbe of Otranto, about whom see Caggese II, 371 and Weiss (1950), 213–14.

64 They included Biblical texts and commentaries and works by Boethius, Gregory and Augustine; see Coulter (1944), 148.

65 Ibid., 150–2.

66 A quaternion *De Viris Illustribus* (probably the one by Jerome), a copy of Seneca (works unspecified), and the fourth decade of Livy (Coulter [1944], 152–3).

67 Not a great deal is known about Paolo's life; his association with the King and court is attested by documents of 1324 and 1332, and he died in 1348. On his relationship to Boccaccio see *Genealogia* XV, 6 (Osgood, 113–14) and Branca *MW*, 33–4. For a more detailed account of his work and influence see Torraca (i), 197–232; cp. also N. Faraglia (1889), 320–6, Caggese II, 383f., and Léonard, 282.

68 Torraca (i), 216.

69 Ed. Romano II, 883.

70 The commentary, according to Torraca ([i], 228–9), shows Paolo's acquaintance with a wide range of classical Latin prose and verse, together with much familiarity with the encyclopaedic works of (for example) Solinus and Isidore, and some knowledge of the ideas of the ancient Greek philosophers.

71 Ibid., (i), 239 (my transln.).

72 The narrator, for example, finds himself at the end of the *Caccia* becoming, like Actaeon in reverse, 'transformed from a stag into a human and rational being' (XVIII, 11–12).

73 For example, the stories of Fileno (IV, 2–5) and Idalogo (V, 6–12). Quaglio (*Opere* I, 969, n. 10) also cites III, 24, III, 28 and IV, 31 as examples of the influence of the *Metamorphoses*.

74 Branca, *Opere* II, 4–5 and *MW*, 42.

75 Notably the references to Jupiter (III, 76–7) and Hercules (III, 80) – transformations that contrast ironically with the change that Fortune is to wreak upon Troiolo (III, 94). The major Ovidian influence upon *Filostr.* would appear, however, to be that of the *Ars Amatoria* (cp. Branca, *Opere* II, 6 and 9).

76 Such as the Franciscan friar Paolino Minorita of Venice; see *Genealogia* XIV, 8, Branca *MW*, 35, and (on the influence of Paolino's *Compendium* or *Chronologia Magna* upon the *Filocolo*) A. E. Quaglio, 'Tra Fonti e Testo del *Filocolo*'. *GSLI* CXL, 490–513.

77 Branca *MW*, 45 and A. E. Quaglio, *Opere* I, esp. 55. (Introdn. to *Filoc.*).

78 Torraca (i), 238.

79 *Filoc.* V, 9, pars. 4–5.

80 Ibid. I, 45, par. 6.

81 For example III, 33, par. 9 and IV, 45, par. 6

82 A Greek source for the story is claimed by Boccaccio in his gloss to *Tes.* I, 2, and a concise survey of attempts to identify or account for this is given by P. Boitani, *Chaucer and Boccaccio*, 41–4 (see also Branca *MW*, 49). On the names of the two heroes see P. Savj-Lopez, 'Sulle Fonti della "Teseide" ', *GSLI* XXXVI (1900), 76f.

83 For example:
   (i) Theseus's campaign against Creon in *Tes.* II (cp. *Theb.* XII).
   (ii) the meeting in the grove outside Athens in V, 33f. (cp. *Theb.* I, 390f.).
   (iii) the description of the Temple of Mars in VII, 30f. (cp. *Theb.* VII, 34–69).
   (iv) the long account of Arcita's funeral in XI, 7f. (cp. *Theb.* 28–248, and for details see *Opere* II, 898 n. 3).

84 See Limentani's introduction, *Opere* II, esp. 232 and, for an excellent summary of Boccaccio's dealings with Statius, his 'Boccaccio, "traduttore" di Stazio', *La Rassegna* VII, esp. 234–7. For a list of the *Teseida*'s numerous quotations from and allusions to the *Thebaid*, *Aeneid* and *Metamorphoses*, see Boitani, 61–71.

85 Boitani, 9–10.

86 For example, the description of the Temple of Venus in VII, 50f., and the references to those heroes such as Narcissus who were unable to accept Theseus's invitation in Bk. VI because undergoing metamorphosis or similar existential crisis (st. 61–3). See also Boitani, 21 and 39–40.

87 Coulter (1944), 143.

88 The *De Sancta Fide* 'in vulgare Gallico', for the use of his heir the Duke of Calabria (ibid., 147 and 153). Coulter also notes (146) that among the more expensive items listed as having been purchased in 1335 is a French historical work, at 12 *tari*.

89 Branca *MW*, 37–8 and 40 n. 19. For a more sceptical discussion of the question see Torraca (i), 242–4.

90 Branca's introduction to *Filostr.*, *Opere* II, 5–7. See also n. 23 on Appendix A, below, p. 213.

91 For example, some of the events of Arcita's exile and return in *Tes.* III–V; see Savj-Lopez (1900), 63–6.
92 On the relationship between the French romance, the *cantare* and *Filocolo* see Quaglio's introduction to *Filostr.*, *Opere* I, 47–8, and A. Balduino, *Cantari del Trecento*, 33–4.
93 Branca *CT*, 29–30.
94 Branca (ibid., 42–3) cites as an example the description of the Emir's garden in *Il Cantare di Florio*, ott. 102–3.
95 Ed. Mills (1973), lines 505–16 and 793–801 especially.
96 Including, in the late 14th century, the story of Troy. For a list of titles see Branca *CT*, 95–7.
97 Although Boccaccio's friend and collaborator, Antonio Pucci (d. 1388), is known to have composed at least six *cantari*.
98 Also for his later narrative, the *Ninfale fiesolano*.
99 Branca *CT*, 56–7 n. 4.
100 For example, in *Filostr.* I, 11; II, 71; and V. 44 – and in *Tes.* I, 125; VII, 93; and XII, 77.
101 Branca *CT*, 59.
102 See esp. *Tes.* VIII, 94–110 (cp. Branca *CT*, 22–4 and 86–7).
103 Branca *CT*, 57 n. 1, 89 and 92.
104 P. Rajna, 'Il Cantare dei Cantari e il Serventese del Maestro di tutti l'Arti', *ZfRPh* II, 430 (st. 26).
105 Branca *CT*, 57 (my transln.).
106 On Fiammetta and her *senhal* in Boccaccio's work see Branca *MW*, 29 and 38 n. 2.
107 Ch. VIII (ed. Pernicone), p. 155.
108 She also makes an important contribution to the storytelling in the later *Comedia Ninfe* (esp. xxxiv–v), and a lady of the same name is queen for the fifth day of the *Decameron*.
109 Cp. esp. the account of Dante's reactions on first seeing Beatrice (*VN* II).
110 Cp. the description of the lover's state in the *Prologue* to *Filostr.* as also in IV, 20–1, 29, 35 and 116. In *Tes.* see esp. the account of how Palemone and Arcita fall in love with Emilia in III. See also Boitani, 35–7 and n. 56.
111 See n. 45 above, and p. 202 n. 18, below.
112 *DVE*, chs. 10, 13 and 17; II, chs. 2 and 5. Dante's *Ep.* III (IV) addresses Cino as *frater carissime*.
113 Barbi, nos. xciv–vii and cx–xv.
114 *Avvegna ched el m'aggia più per tempo*, ed. Zaccagnini, 61–3.
115 Ibid., 256–8.
116 The sonnet, *Piangete donne* (*Canz.* xcii).
117 See Branca *MW* 9–10 and 14 n. 19.
118 Ibid., 34–5.
119 The *Trattatello in Laude di Dante* (c. 1350–55).
120 The *Esposizioni sopra la Comedia di Dante* (1373–4). On Boccaccio and Dante in general see also E. Cavallari, *La Fortuna di Dante nel Trecento*, ch. VII, and R. Hollander, *Boccaccio's Two Venuses*, 10 and 128 n. 8.
121 See *Caccia* II, 17; IV, 12 and 19f; VIII, 32; IX, 1–2; X, 19; XVII, 57; and XVIII, 49. Some of these allusions perhaps hint at the narrator's own progression towards eventual transformation.
122 *Filostrato* I, 26.7 and 38.7; II, 72.6.
123 Ibid., II, 33, 63, 105 and 135; II 16 and 56.
124 Ibid., II, 33, and 80; III, 1, 16, and 56; IV, 54 and 56; V, 17 and 24.
125 *Filoc.* III, 65, par. 6 and IV, 16, par. 9.
126 Ibid., III, 67, par. 12. Cp. *Inf.* XXVI, 119–20.
127 Ibid., V, 50, par. 1 and 63, par. 1.

128 For example:
   II, 67, par. 2.
   III, 7, par. 9; 18, par. 13; 27, par. 1.
   IV, 2, par. 3; 4, par. 1; 35, par. 5; 81, par. 2; 85, par. 13.
   V, 6 (the episode); 51, par. 5.
129 Ibid., V, 97, par. 6.
130 See Boitani, 37–9 and, for examples, his list on pp. 67–71.
131 Thus, for example, even Branca (*CT*, 56 n. 2) identifies the address to the reader in *Tes.* VIII, 4 as characteristic of the *cantari*, without, apparently, noticing the reminiscence of Dante, *Inf.* XXXIV, 26.
132 *Tes.* XII, 84–5. Cp. Dante, *DVE* II, the end of. ch. 2: 'Arma vero nullum Latinum adhuc invenio poetasse'.

INTRODUCTION (ii)

1 *Genealogia* XV, 6 (tr. Osgood, 116).
2 See G. Mathew, *The Court of Richard II*, 16–17 and 25, on the family connexions between Plantagenets and Angevins, and p. 9 above on the marriage of Lionel of Clarence to Violante Visconti.
3 Italian ingredients appear to be favoured in the royal cook-book, the *Forme of Cury* (see Mathew, 24–5). On Italian influence upon English painting in the later 14th century see Mathew, 39–4, and in more detail M. Rickert, *Painting in Britain: The Middle Ages*, esp. 147–53 and 206–7.
4 A. Beardwood, *Alien Merchants in England, 1350 to 1377: Their Legal and Economic Position*, 8 – quoted in H. Schless, 'Transformations: Chaucer's Use of Italian', 192–3. Schless also points out that 'Walter de Bardi exemplifies the level to which Italians could rise in the English court, with services to the crown in areas in which Chaucer had regular interests'.
5 See M. M. Crow and C. C. Olson, *Chaucer Life Records*, 40.
6 On the reasons for this see G. B. Parks, *The English Traveller to Italy* I, 290–1.
7 For the evidence see *Life Records*, 29–30. Schless (190) appears to favour the idea, whilst F. N. Robinson (*The Works of Geoffrey Chaucer*, 2nd edn., xx and xxi) is sceptical about it. Cp. also M. McKisack, *The Fourteenth Century*, 267. On Chaucer's previous experience of foreign travel see *Life Records* 29 and 44–53, and, for evidence of his having travelled to Spain in 1366, ibid. 64–5.
8 The mission to Genoa was to negotiate about facilities for Genoese merchants in England. For the relevant documents see Life Records, 32–3 and for further information and references about dealings between England and Genoa ibid., 39. The extension of the journey as far as Florence may, it is suggested, have been occasioned by Edward III's involvement with Florentine financiers (from whom he had raised a loan the previous year), or by business connected with ships that a Florentine partnership had undertaken to provide for the King (ibid., 39–40).
9 See Parks I, esp. 511–13 and 521f., and, with regard to Chaucer in particular, 'The Route of Chaucer's first Journey to Italy', *ELH* XVI (1949), 174–87. Merchants and couriers, according to Parks, might travel faster and cover the distance from Genoa to London in 20–30 days.
10 *Gen. Prol* A, 465. Cp. Parks I, 351f.
11 *Gen. Prol* A, 671. Cp. Parks I, 337f.
12 *Cl. Prol* E, 26f. Cp. Parks I, 423f.
13 Cp. Parks I, 384f., McKisack, 346, and R. A. Pratt, 'Geoffrey Chaucer Esq., and Sir John Hawkwood', *ELH* XVI (1949), 188–93.
14 Cp. Parks I, 395f.

15 A speculation that Branca, among others, finds it pleasant to entertain; see *MW*, 184 and 192–3 n. 10.

16 R. A. Pratt, 'Chaucer and the Visconti Libraries', *ELH* VI (1939), 191–9. Cp. Boitani, 72 and n. 1.

17 Such works are at least listed as being present later on in the history of the Pavia library. See Pratt (1939), 196.

18 *Life Records*, 40–2. Cp. Robinson, xxi.

19 See p. 9, above, and V. B. and L. J. Redstone, 'The Heyrons of London', *Spec* XII, 193–4.

20 *Life Records*, 32–3 and 37–8.

21 The *Livre de Troilus* by 'Beauvau, Seneschal of Anjou', ed. L. Moland and C. d'Héricault in *Nouvelles françoises en prose du xiv Siècle*, 117–304. See also H. Hauvette. 'Les plus anciennes traductions francaises de Boccace' in *Études sur Boccace*, 170–85 – although Hauvette here (175–6) attributes the work to Louis de Beauvau, writing much later than Chaucer. The main arguments for and evidence of Chaucer's indebtedness to the French version are in R. A. Pratt, 'Chaucer and *Le Roman de Troyle et de Criseida*', *SP* LIII (1956), 509–39.

22 The parallels noted by Pratt (1956), 513–36, are worth attention from this point of view. They appear to occur with far greater frequency in *TC* I, IV and V than they do in Books II and III. Yet even in Book I of *Troilus* Chaucer's rendering of *Filostr.* is not only, as we might expect, less laboured and more imaginative than Beauvau's, but it is often literally closer – viz: *thynges* (134); *upon cas* (271); *wo comynge* (375); *with pitous vois* (422); *ye standen* (428) and *Grekes* (483). He also at times attends to phrases from Boccaccio that Beauvau has ignored – viz: *forknowynge wise* (79, tr. *antiveduto saggio*); *But how it was* (492, tr. *E qual si fosse*); *man of so gret sapience* (515, tr. *il provveduto*). And his grasp of Italian is on occasion decidedly firmer, as well as quicker, than that of the French translator – cp. 429 and 472.

   Further evidence of Chaucer's assimilation of Boccaccio's work by the time he came to *Troilus* is provided by the echoes of *Teseida* in the poem – a notable example being the transference of the episode in *Tes.* XI 1–3 to the end of *TC* V (1807–27). See R. A. Pratt, 'Chaucer's Use of the *Teseida*', *PMLA* LXII (1947), 608–13.

23 See Mathew, 4 and 65, and P. Gathercole, 'Boccaccio in French', *Studi sul Boccaccio* V (1968), 275–97.

24 The earliest French translation of *Tes.* exists in a manuscript of the second half of the 15th century – see Hauvette, 203–13 and Gathercole (1968), 290.

25 On the presence of Dante in the *House of Fame* see J. A. W. Bennett, *Chaucer's Book of Fame*, esp. 49–51, 53–64, 74–8, 100–3, 136–8 and 139–40. For the *Parliament of Fowls* see D. S. Brewer's edn. 45–6 and Bennett, *The Parlement of Foules*, 42–3, 63–4, 68–9 and 75–8.

26 Thus the poet's declarations of intent in the poems to *HF* combine echoes of both poets; see Pratt (1947), 604. And Dante's Earthly Paradise is momentarily present amid the surroundings of Boccaccio's Temple of Venus in *PF*, 201–3; see Bennett, *Parlement of Foules*, 74–105.

27 For discussion of this see Boitani, 72–3.

28 See Pratt (1947), 608–13 and 620 (on *TC* and *LGW*), and Robinson, *Works*, 851 and 723 (on *LGW* and *Fkl. T.*)

29 See the discussion of Chaucer's treatment of *Tes.* VII in Boitani, ch. IV, esp 78–80 and 97. The portrayal of Saturn as a baleful elder statesman may perhaps reflect Chaucer's response to the rather bureaucratic detachment with which Boccaccio's Mars and Venus envisage and apportion their dealings with the two heroes.

30 'Conjectures regarding Chaucer's Manuscript of the *Teseida*', *SP* XLII (1945), 745–63.

31 Boitani, ch. VI. It is also pointed out here (116 n. 8) that Chaucer probably had a 50% chance of obtaining a text with the *chiose*, since 6 out of the 12 surviving 14th century MSS of *Tes.* contain them.
32 *The Origin and Development of the Story of Troilus and Criseyde*, ch. IV.
33 *The Indebtedness of Chaucer's Works to the Italian Works of Boccaccio*, 1–12.
34 *Design in Chaucer's Troilus*, 60–1.
35 G. Dempster and J. S. P. Tatlock, 'The Franklin's Tale', in *SA*, 377 and n. 1.
36 Though of course, as Pratt and Young point out, 'the *Filocolo* had no demonstrable influence upon Chaucer's plan' in *CT* (*SA*, 13). Chaucer may also have been interested in a similarly framed collection in Boccaccio's *Comedia Ninfe* XVII–XXXIX (cp. G. Dempster, *SA* 339–40).
37 Cummings, 176–80; W. Farnham, 'England's Discovery of the *Decameron*', *PMLA* (XXXIX (1924), 123–39; H. G. Wright, *Boccaccio in England*, 114 and n. 3; and E. Reiss, 'Boccaccio in English Culture of the Fourteenth and Fifteenth Centuries', in G. Galigani (ed.), *Il Boccaccio nella Cultura inglese e anglo-americana*, esp. 15–17. The question is also discussed by Pratt and Young in *SA* 13–20 (see esp. 14 n. 3) and by Ruggiers, 153–4.
38 *Rv. T* (*Dec.* IX, 6); *Cl. T.* (*Dec.* X, 10); *Fkl. T.* (*Dec.* X, 5) and *Shipm T.* (*Dec.* VIII, 1 and 2). Analogous features are also to be found in *MLT* (*Dec.* V, 2) and *Merch. T.* (*Dec.* VII, 9).
39 See esp. M. Copland, 'The *Shipman's Tale:* Chaucer and Boccaccio', *MAe* XXXV (1966), 11–28 and R. Guerin, 'The *Shipman's Tale:* The Italian Analogues', *ESt* LII (1971), 412–19. A tentative inclination in this direction is also evident in Ch. I (esp.) of M. F. Bovill's *The Decameron and the Canterbury Tales* (Oxford B. Litt, thesis, 1966).
40 For references to Dante see *HF*, 450; *LGW*, 360; *Mk. T.* B, 3651; *WBT* D, 1126–7; and *Fri. T.* D. 1520. For Petrarch see *CLT* E, 31, 1147; and *Mk. T.* B, 3515. More emphasis has been placed recently upon the importance of Dante to Chaucer; see: Bennett, *Chaucer's Book of Fame*; Reiss, 21; and T. Pisanti, 'Boccaccio in Inghilterra tra Medioevo e Rinascimento', in G. Tournoy (ed.), *Boccaccio in Europe*, esp. 197–200.
41 On the story of Zenobia in *Mk. T.* see Root, *SA*, 632–6, and, on Chaucer and the *De Casibus*, ibid. 615–16 and 626–8 – also Wright, 5 and Reiss, 19–20. On the sources of the *Clerk's Tale* see J. B. Severs, *SA*, 288 and Wright, 116–22.
42 As Beauvau appears to have been in assigning the *Filostrato* to Petrarch (see Moland and d'Héricault, ci).
43 Cp. Mathew, 7 and 179 n. 5.

FILOSTRATO

Prologue

1 A number of such questions are discussed during the assembly at Naples that is presided over by Fiammetta in *Filoc.* IV, 15–72.
2 A mountainous province of the Kingdom of Naples, N and NE of the capital, around Campobasso.
3 Branca draws attention to 'the solemn opening with *Dico*, favoured by Dante (*Conv. passim*) and Boccaccio (*Dec.*, Intr. VIII).' He also notes that the whole of the following passage (up to 'most bitter complaints') takes its tone from Dante's *VN* 'in speaking with almost mystical fervour of tears and weeping eyes.'
4 Lamentations i, 1. The verse is also quoted by Dante when announcing the death of Beatrice in *VN*, xxviii.

5 Marti's repunctuation is followed here. Branca and others have a comma before *s'udirono* – which would mean that there is no finite verb for the preceding relative construction (dep. on *le mie voci*).

6 i.e., after the lady's departure.

7 *il vostro nome di grazia pieno*. Branca (*Opere* II, 4) sees here a clear allusion to the name *Giovanna* (Cp. *Par*. XI, 80–1 and *Filoc*. IV, 1, par. 13 and 27, par. 2), and hence further evidence that *Filostr*. has nothing to do with 'Fiammetta'.

8 An indirect allusion to Boccaccio's use of his main sources, esp. Benoit and Guido. Cp his reference to such authorities in the prologue to *Tes*., above, p. 104.

9 *Compuosi*. Among the meanings of *comporre* in Boccaccio's time both 'bring together' and 'compose' (in literary or musical form) are attested, and both may be involved here.

10 i.e., Criseida.

11 i.e., the verses still.

Part I

1 The metaphor is found frequently in Provencal *canso* and 13th century Italian lyric (see for example A. R. Press, *Anthology of Troubadour Lyric Poetry*, 240–1; K. Mahn, *Gedichte der Troubadours* I, 131; and G. Contini, *Poeti del Duecento* I, 363, 466 and 498. It also recurs in *Inf*. XV, 55–6 and again in *Filostr*. IV, 143 and IX, 3, as later in *Filoc*. V, 30 par. 2, *Tes*. XII, 86 and *Comedia Ninfe*, xvi, 37–9.

2 Cp. Benoit, *Roman de Troie*, 5817f. and p. 168, below.

3 As Branca points out, Briseida in the *Roman* is, on the other hand, a *pucele*.

4 The image of Pallas Athene, which was stolen by Diomedes and Ulysses (see *Aen*. II, 162–70), with disastrous results for Troy. The theft is also referred to by Dante in *Inf*. XXVI, 63.

5 Cp. the description of Beatrice in *Purg*. XXX, 31. The phrase is repeated here in st. 38.

6 Cp. Benoit's account of how Achilles fell in love with Polyxena (*Roman*, 17545f.).

7 Cp. Andreas Capellanus, *De Amore* II, viii, rule 13: *Amor raro consuevit durare vulgatus*.

8 Or possibly: 'finding out what she felt' (Marti).

9 Or perhaps: 'dry or rotten material that is ready for it' (Marti).

10 The lover makes a similarly obliging offer at the end of a ballata in Dante's *VN*, xii.

Part II

1 On the possible antecedents of Boccaccio's Pandaro see K. Young, 42–66 and G. and M. (introduction) 41f.

2 Troiolo's language in much of this stanza recalls several of Francesca da Rimini's assertions about the power of love in *Inf*. V, 100–5. Marti notes especially the use of *offende* ('afflicts') as a rhyme word here and in *Inf*. V, 102.

3 lit.: 'I have hardly held back my hand from'.

4 lit.: 'it seems to me that the pain little burns (*cuoca*) her'. Griffin and Myrick's rendering of the passage is very different, viz.: 'foolish is he that does not ravish her. And little in my opinion does the punishment vex her.' But such a notion seems somewhat crude, even for Pandaro.

5 G. and M. take *ne* in the previous line to mean 'of him', and translate: ' "Art thou aware of him?" . . . "No more of one man than another" '.

6 Or possibly, taking *come* earlier in the stanza to mean 'as' (rather than 'since'), the line could mean: 'since the affections change as the thoughts do'.

7 i.e., the will of God.

8 Marti compares *Inf.* II, 72 (Beatrice's words to Virgil). But there is also a strong (and verbally closer) resemblance to Virgil's explanation of his motives in *Purg* VII, 24.

9 Marti suggests that *la più gente* could also mean 'even the noblest'.

10 An exact quotation of St. Lucy's words to Beatrice in *Inf.* II, 106.

11 The imagery here again recalls *Inf.* II (cp. st. 63 and 72), where the pilgrim's response to Virgil's reassurances are described (127–32). It is not only inherited from Boccaccio by Chaucer (*TC* II, 967–70), but also, as Sapegno points out, derives from Provencal lyric, and recurs frequently in later Italian. Cp. *Tes.* IX, 28.

12 Pandaro's energetic practicality is reflected in this swift transition from the conditional to the indicative.

13 *riman.* G. and M. read *rimarrà* and translate: 'it will not be my task to content thee'.

14 *Come saggio.* 'In the manner of a poet, in the ancient meaning of the word – that is, according to the rules of rhetoric by which the verse-letter that follows is in fact governed' (Marti). Dante refers to his forerunner, Guinizelli, as *il saggio* in 1.2 of the sonnet in *VN* xx.

15 The stanza develops an untranslatable *bisticcio* (quibble) on the words *salute* ('greeting', 'well-being') and *salutare*.

16 G. and M. (introduction, 69) note a parallel between this expression and that in Phaedra's letter to Hippolytus (*Her.* IV, 1–2).

17 Marti's interpretation is followed here. G. and M. render the passage: 'and that my sore distress, discreetly amiable and gracious one, who dost not wish that I perish in my misery for loving thee so much, will turn, delectable lady, to sweet joy'.

18 A further echo of the exchanges between Dante and Virgil in *Inf.* II. Troiolo's language at this point is very close to that in which Dante concludes his request for reassurance about the purpose of the pilgrimage (*Inf.* II, 36).

19 Branca, on the other hand, takes the line to mean: 'came to meet him, meanwhile, on the way'.

20 Marti's reading is followed here, as it seems more consistent with Criseida's inconsistency. G. and M., on the other hand, give the lines a precisely opposite sense: 'I must put aside (*dar lato a*) the pity I felt for thee, whereby thou wilt gain but little satisfaction from me'. *Dare lato a qc.* seems to have had the sense both of 'abstain from' and 'yield to' during the late 13th and early 14th centuries.

21 This seems to refer particularly to the wish Troiolo has expressed at the end of his letter (st. 106).

22 *aguale.* G. and M. read *avale*, and translate: 'what is wished can do little good'.

23 G. and M. translate: 'The power to do will perhaps sometime take the place of (*farà luogo a*) good intentions'. The sense of 'give place to' seems however to be better attested in 14th century Italian, and can be found also elsewhere in Boccaccio (*Dec.* X, 6: 'Intra tante cose abbiate *fatto luogo al* lusinghevole amore').

24 Presumably the offer made at the opening of st. 105.

25 Probably the flames of love.

26 A nearly exact echo of Virgil's words in *Purg.* III, 78 – where, however, concern with a somewhat different kind of progress is being voiced. Boccaccio also alludes to the passage in *Filoc.* IV, 81, par. 2.

27 *Traiamo omai a capo questa tela* – lit.: 'Let's now draw to an end with this

cloth.' Branca compares a similarly phrased metaphor of weaving in *Par.* III, 96.

Part III

1 The invocation to the lady in this stanza recalls Dante's appeal to Apollo in *Par.* I, 22–7, esp. in its use of the rhyme words *regno* and *degno*.
2 Cp. Troiolo's renewal in II, 80, and the description of how Palemone and Arcita receive Theseus's suggestions in *Tes.* V, 99.
3 Cp. Pandaro's view of his own role in II, 32.
4 Branca suggests that Boccaccio may have had in mind here the cough by which the Lady of Malehaut makes her presence known to Lancelot during his meeting with the Queen (H. O. Sommer [ed.], *Vulgate Version of the Arthurian Romances*, III, 261).
5 The reference to the skills of poets here may be a reminiscence of *Par.* XXIII, 55–60, and for the appeal to the reader's imagination in such circumstances see *Tes.* XII, 76 (Branca cites also *Filoc.* IV, 120, par. 1). Another 'inexpressibility topos' of this sort recurs in st. 86.
6 For the contrast between lovers and misers cp., for example Andreas Capellanus, *De Amore* II, viii, rule 10, and *RR* (ed. Lecoy), 2199–2212.
7 Or possibly: 'during the night when she had him close to her (*da presso*)' (Marti).
8 The speech in this stanza and the following one is usually assigned to Troiolo (G. and M., 271, Gordon, 66), but it makes better sense to take *poi cominciava* to mean 'began again', 'continued' and assume that Criseida is still speaking. This reading is supported by the masc. inflexion of *tutto* in line 5 of this st., and by the first line of st. 69.
9 Troiolo is addressing Venus as a planetary deity.
10 Branca sees here an allusion to the myths of Proserpina and Eurydice that figure frequently in Boccaccio.
11 i.e., Spring.
12 Cp. for example, *Met.* II, 401f. and 846f., IV, 611, and VI, 103–14.
13 The love of Mars for Venus (cp. *Met.* IV, 172–89) is also mentioned by Arcita in *Tes.* VII, 25.
14 As Branca points out, 'the myth of Hercules in love is recurrently invoked by Boccaccio, following Ovid, in defence of lovers'. He cites *Amorosa Visione* XXVI, *Fiammetta* (ed. Pernicone) 21–2 and *De Casibus* I, 18. Hercules is also cited, among other examples, in exoneration of Dante's lustfulness in the *Trattatello in Laude di Dante*, red. I, par. 173 (*Opere* III, p. 480). His love for Iole is mentioned in *Tes.* VII, 62, the *chiose* to *Fiammetta* (ed. Pernicone, p. 203) and the *Genealogia* XIII, 1. The transforming power of love is thus exemplified at this stage in the poem by Jupiter (76), Mars (77), Hercules (here) and Troiolo himself (90–3) – although in the last instance a further and more brutal change is to be effected by Fortune (94).
15 Cp. Petrarch, *Canz.* xiii, 5, and lxi, 1–4.
16 lit.: 'bless'.
17 Cp. st. 33 and n. Branca also compares here the opening of Cecco Angiolieri's sonnet, *Sed i' avessi mille lingue in bocca* (*Canz.* cv, ed. C. Steiner, pp. 109–10).
18 i.e., the power of a hundred tongues ('the first') and the wisdom of all the poets ('the second').
19 lit.: 'forests'.
20 lit.: 'birds'.
21 i.e., Criseida.

22 Forms of *volgere* ('turn') recur 3 times in this final stanza – viz.: *volse* ('turned'), *volgendo* ('turning') and *rivolse* (lit.: 'turned back').

Part IV

1 In Benoit's *Roman* Antenor is captured during the 5th battle (12551–5), some time before Calchas's request for the return of Briseida, which is made during the truce after the 7th battle (13086–120). In Guido's *Historia* the two events are much closer together (Griffin, 159–61).
2 In both the *Roman* (12843–13020) and the *Historia* (Griffin, 160) it is the Greeks who request a truce at this stage.
3 i.e. as grief-stricken parent.
4 Marti's suggested reading (*fello* as equiv. to *lo feci* and foll. by full stop rather than comma) is adopted here. Alternatively (taking *fello* as adj.) the lines could read: 'and like a traitor, as soon as the bright daylight etc.'.
5 Cp. esp. *Aen.* IX 435–7 and *Met.* X, 190–5.
6 Presumably to enable Troiolo to sleep.
7 Cp. Dante's description of the Minotaur, *Inf.* XII, 22–4.
8 Cp. the first line of the *canzone* in *VN* xxxi.
9 'Denunciations of Fortune are very frequent in the early works of Boccaccio, who refers to himself as "Fortunes foe" (*inimicus fortunae*) in the letters of the period; whilst in his mature works, from the *Decameron* to the *Esposizioni*, Fortune is considered in scholastic and Dantean terms as Providence's "general minister and guide" [*Inf.* VII, 78]' (Branca, *Opere* II, 858–9, my tr.). See also *Tes.* VI, 1f., and n. 1, below.
10 *Salute*. Troiolo's language in this stanza has a markedly stilnovistic character.
11 Protesilaus is said to have been the first of the Greek invaders to set foot on Trojan land and the first to be killed. Cp. *Roman*, 7123f. and 7511–30; and *Historia* (ed. Griffin), 120, 121, 125.
12 *sincero* here may carry the sense of 'not tinged with any unhappiness' (*TB*, 9).
13 *Novus amor veterem compellit abire* (Andreas Capellanus, *De Amore* II, viii, rule 17) – although the notion was and is proverbial.
14 i.e., 'this constant love'.
15 This may, as Marti suggests, be an allusion to the lovers in *Inf.* V. Cp. notes 18 and 19, below.
16 *abito*. The word is probably to be understood in the sense both of 'disposition' (*GDLI*, 5) and of 'appearance' (*GDLI*, 3).
17 *divisatamente*. GDLI (1) cites this passage. G. and M. on the other hand translate: 'in set terms'.
18 An obvious echo of *Inf.* V, 121–3; cp. also Boethius *Cons. Phil.* II, pr. iv.
19 A further reminiscence of Francesca's words in *Inf.* V (100).
20 G. and M. 'if I love' is probably a misprint.
21 i.e., 'this grief' (cp. st. 66).
22 *La fama velocissima*. Cp. Virgil's 'Fama, malum qua non aliud velocius ullum' (*Aen.* IV, 174). For the subsequent allusion to Rumour as bringing 'false and true reports alike', see ibid., 188.
23 lit.: 'two desires to weep'. Cp. *Tes.* III, 80 and *VN* xxxix (sonnet), 5–6. Briseida's grief in *Historia*, 163 (see above, p. 184) is also described in broadly similar terms.
24 Or possibly 'it', i.e. her face (thus G. and M.).
25 Cp. *VN* xxxix, 4.
26 *'l tuo ben*, lit.: 'your happiness'.
27 Cp. III, 28.

28 Such anatomizing of the lover's distress in stilnovistic terms had, as Marti notes, by now become commonplace. Branca points to parallels between this scene and that in *Filoc.* II, 21.
29 Or perhaps 'him' (thus G. and M.).
30 i.e., by returning her to Calchas.
31 A further allusion, perhaps, to *Inf.* V; Cp. st. 54.
32 Branca (*CT*, 71–2) dismisses this crucial shift in Criseida's tone as clumsy and bathetic, but Chaucer (judging from *TC* IV, 1254f.) does not appear to have done so.
33 Or possibly: 'I could not imagine'.
34 lit.: 'besieged'.
35 Cp. Andreas Capellanus, *De Amore* II, viii, rule 14: *Facilis perceptio contemptibilem reddit amorem, difficilis eum carum facit haberi.*
36 *questa pace*, lit.: 'this peace'. Dante uses the phrase several times as a figure for Paradise (*Par.* X, 129 and XV, 148).

Part V

1 Cp. the role of Diomedes in *Roman*, 13517f. (above, p. 172).
2 In both the *Roman* (13427f.) and Binduccio's *Libro* (cap. cclxxvi – Gorra, p. 407) this moment occasions an antifeminist digression (see above pp. 170–1).
3 In the *Roman* (13857f.) Briseida's attitude changes more quickly, and in the *Historia* (166) quicker still. See above, pp. 175 and 185.
4 Cp. *Inf.* III, 103–5. Boccaccio makes a similar allusion to Dante's souls on the banks of the Acheron in *Tes.* III, 3.
5 The quibble is in the original: 'O di *partenza* sia stato al *partito*'.
6 lit.: 'vetch' (sometimes used as fodder).
7 *tregua* (*TB*, 3).
8 *gioia*. G. and M. read *noia* and tr.: 'woe'.
9 On Sarpedon see *Roman*, 6685–94, 18784–818 and 19141f.; and *Historia*, 182, 190 and 193.
10 lit.: 'the desire formed by his thought'.
11 lit.: 'the keys'.
12 *Stella mattutina*. Both this expression and *rosa di spina* ('rose among thorns') later on in this stanza probably derive from the diction of the *cantari* (cp. Introduction, p. 7, and Branca *CT*, 17–18). See also *Tes.* VII, 93 and XII, 77.
13 *Or siam noi per lo foco / venuti qui*. G. and M. translate: 'Look you now, have we come hither to escape the hot pangs of love'. But, as Marti's note confirms, Pandaro is speaking of a rather more homely activity – presumably like nowadays calling on a neighbour to borrow a cup of sugar.
14 Troiolo's description of his loss in this stanza and those that follow recalls the narrator's language in the *Prologue* (see above, pp. 21–2 and cp. also st. 61 and 70).
15 *storia*.
16 Marti's suggested reading of *ma'* for *ma* is adopted here.
17 Cp. *Prologue*, p. 23.
18 This stanza and the three that follow are closely modelled on st. 1–2 and 4–5 of Cino da Pistoia's *canzone, La dolce vista e 'l bel guardo soave* (ed. Zaccagnini, 215–17). On Boccaccio's indebtedness to Cino see Introduction, above, pp. 3–4 and 8.
19 G. and M. translate *ignuda* as 'naked', but for the sense given here, see *GDLI ignudo*, 6.
20 Cp. *Prologue*, p. 21, and *Tes.* IV, 32.

Part VI

1 G. and M. read *mormorando* and tr.: 'whispering'.
2 *Or prova.* G. and M. read *Aoperava* and tr.: 'made use of'.
3 Cp. *Roman*, 13859–61 and p. 175, above.
4 *artista (GDLI, 5).* Cp. *Par.* XVI, 51.
5 Diomedes's initial attraction to Criseida has been briefly described in V, 13, but this is the first and only occasion on which Boccaccio shows him speaking to her. Contrast *Roman*, 13532f. and 15001f., and *Libro*, caps. cclxxviii–xxxi (Gorra, pp. 408–11).
6 In this stanza and the two that follow Boccaccio's Diomedes adopts rather more aggressive tactics than those of his predecessors in the *Roman*. *Historia* or *Libro*. Boccaccio may perhaps have been influenced here by Calchas's justification of his actions in reply to Briseida's reproaches (*Roman*, esp. 13803–8).
7 Cp. *Roman*, 13575–7, and p. 172, above.
8 On Diomedes's ancestry and associations with Thebes see *Iliad* VI, 222; Apollodorus, *The Library* I, viii, 6; and *Theb.* VIII 342–766.
9 Cp. *Par.* XXV, 4–5, where Dante is speaking of his banishment from Florence.
10 Here as in 29 and 30 the closing couplet of the stanza signals the change in Criseida that has been foretold in V, 14.
11 *mani.* Possibly 'in the handiwork of Hector' (G. and M.), but see *GDLI* IX p. 717, col. 2 for the sense given.

Part VII

1 i.e. around sunset, the 6th of the canonical hours.
2 *rivera.* G. and M. have 'shore', which is possible, but the meaning of *campagna, contrada (TB, 4)* is more likely. Cp. *Ninfale fiesolano*, st. 62, and the reference here to 'countryfolk' (*villani*) in st. 11.
3 i.e., waiting in vain.
4 Cp. what is said about the effects of jealousy in the *chiose* on the Temple of Venus (*Tes.* VII, p. 132, above).
5 Ominous dreams of this sort are often, as Branca points out, introduced into Boccaccio's tales of unhappy love – cp. *Filoc.* IV, 74; *Dec.* IV, 5 and 6, and esp. IX, 7.
6 Diomedes's ancestor was Meleager whose story is told in *Met.* VIII, 260–546.
7 Branca cites suicide-attempts by desperate lovers in *Filoc.* II, 21, par. 17; III, 18, par. 30–2; and III, 63 pars. 12–16; also *Fiammetta* VI.
8 Cp. perhaps the way souls pursue each other in *Inf.* XIII, 109–29 – a passage which Boccaccio also seems to have had in mind when describing the vision in *Dec.* V, 8.
9 Marti's proposed emendation (*intera / niente*) is adopted here. The usual reading is *intera- / mente*, which splits a word between verses and gives an adverb of very uncertain meaning.
10 Marti suggests that this could mean either that Criseida had become proud and haughty (as the Greeks were reputed to be), or simply that she was now on the Greek side.
11 i.e., because of persuasion from Calchas ('the first reason') or generosity on his part ('the third').
12 i.e., as lover or as soldier.
13 *Gli occhi dolenti.* The same words begin the *canzone* in *VN*, ch. xxxi. Cp. the reminiscence of the same line in IV, 28.
14 Cp. the narrator's invocations in *Prologue*, p. 22, above.

15 Troiolo's behaviour here and in the following stanza once again recalls that of the narrator in *Prologue* (p. 21, above) – cp. also st. 60 and V, 70. As Branca points out, Boccaccio seems to be thinking of the landscape between Naples and Sannio, since there would not have been mountains around the Greek camp.

16 i.e. Criseida.

17 Deiphebus was the 3rd son of Priam (*Roman*, 2939). His portrait is combined with that of Helenus in the *Roman* (5382–9). Like Troilus he supports the plan to abduct a Greek noblewoman (ibid., 3931–42), and he accompanies Paris to Greece (ibid., 4175). His death precedes that of Troilus (*Roman*, 19087–139). Cp. *Historia*, 44, 63 and 190–3.

18 Polyxena was Troilus's sister (cp. III, 18) and the third daughter of Priam (*Roman*, 2955–8). Her beauty is spoken of in the *Roman*, 2958, 5541–76 and 17552–73 (see above, p. 178). Cp. *Historia*, 45, 87 and 183f.

19 Cassandra, like Polyxena (see above, n. 18) was one of Troilus's sisters and the second daughter of Priam (*Roman*, 2953–4). Apollo (cp. st. 88 and 90) had endowed her with the gift of prophecy, but she was fated never to be believed (cp. *Aen*. II, 246–9). Benoit refers to this gift in his portrait of her (*Roman*, 5532–6). He also shows her arguing against the plan that leads to the abduction of Helen (4143–66) and lamenting its outcome (4883–936). Cp. *Historia*, 45, 66–7, 79 and 87.

20 Marti's suggested alternative reading of *di* (imperative) for *di'* (2 pres. indic.) is adopted here.

21 *È gentilezza dovunque è virtute* – an exact quotation of line 101 of the *canzone* in *Conv*. IV.

22 lit.: 'checkmate'.

23 'With this stanza', notes Branca, 'culminates Boccaccio's first passionate expression of belief in the superiority of nobility of soul over nobility of blood'. He also notes the recurrence of the notion in *Amorosa Visione* XXXIII and *Dec*. IV, 1. The inappropriateness of such praise at this stage, however, would seem to lend the passage a certain irony.

24 Despite the use of the 2 pl. form here Troiolo is probably not addressing all the Trojan ladies as Marti suggests. He does indeed mostly use the 2 sg. form to his sister, but he also addressed her in the plural in st. 99 (perhaps, as here, for the sake of rhyme).

Part VIII

1 Cp. *Roman*, 16007–858 and *Historia*, 175f.

2 *Credien* (GDLI, *credere*, 14).

3 Cp. Florio's description of himself as 'a poor pilgrim of love' in *Filoc*. IV, 16, par. 9, and the presentation of Love himself thus disguised in *VN*, ch. iv.

4 *mal volentier*. G. and M. assume that *mal* modifies *ama*, and translate: 'he who loveth ill, willingly believeth . . .' But *male* is well attested in the sense of 'not' or 'hardly' (GDLI, *male* [advb.], 15). Cp., for example, *Inf*. XVIII, 52.

5 *intelletto*. For this meaning of the word cp. the *canzone* in *Conv*. IV (93).

6 Cp. the apostrophe in *Purg*. VI, 118–20.

7 *ferventi*. Thus GDLI, 1, but sense 4 'inspired by zeal' may also be involved here.

8 That is, when Pandaro prevented him from taking his own life (VII, 33f.).

9 *che può che gli pare*. G. and M. read: *che può tutto voltare*, and translate: 'who can change all'.

10 GDLI *contrario* (noun), 9. G. and M. read: *per contrario*, and translate: 'on the contrary'.

11 Cp. the descriptions of the encounters between Troilus and Diomedes in the *Roman* (pp. 175–9, above), *Historia* (169–70, 173 and 197–8) and *Libro* (caps. cccxxiii and cccxcviii – Gorra, 417–18).

12 lit.: 'selling their intemperate love most dearly'.

13 Cp. Benoit's account of this episode (pp. 181–2, above), and Guido's comments on Achilles (p. 186 above).

14 Boccaccio's antifeminism here is, especially when compared with Guido's (pp. 184–5, above), of a fairly light-hearted kind, and the following stanzas, like the moralizing finale that Zerlina leads in *Don Giovanni*, sound like a cheerful repetition of *l'antichissima canzon*.

15 The same image is found in Troiolo's first speech (I, 22).

Part IX

1 On voyaging as a metaphor for poetic composition see esp. Curtius, *European Literature and the Latin Middle Ages*, ch. 7.

2 See n. 1 on I, 2, above.

3 Cp. the close of both *Filoc.* (V, 97, pars. 2–4) and *Tes.* (XII, 86), and n. 1, above.'

4 i.e., Troiolo's. Cp. *Prologue*, p. 23 above.

TESEIDA

Prologue

1 Square brackets indicate editorial summary of the narrative. Curved brackets are used for references to stanzas and for Boccaccio's own rubrics.

2 Cp. the reference to sources in *Filostr. Prologue* (p. 23, above). On the sources of *Tes.* see Introduction (p. 6, above).

3 Ricci cites in this connexion the passage in *Filoc.* V, 24, par. 5, where Venus prophesies to the Neapolitan lady Alleiram (Mariella) that 'the praises already spoken of your beauty in verses of love will take a different name from yours'. Cp. also *Rime*, V, 12.

4 Boccaccio here draws a traditional comparison between ploughing and writing. Cp. the *Indovinello veronese* in *Early Italian Texts*, ed. Grayson and Dionisotti, 1–3, and Petrarch's reference to the 'plough-share of the pen' (*Canz.* ccxxviii, 5). The Knight's remarks about having weak oxen to plough a large field (*Kn. T.*, A, 886–7) are in the same tradition, if not actually influenced by Boccaccio's metaphor.

Book I

1 Boccaccio's gloss refers to the mythical origins of the fountain of Hippocrene on Mt. Helicon. This was said to have sprung from the ground when it was struck by the hoof of Pegasus the winged horse born of the blood of Medusa the Gorgon.

2 i.e., the laurel tree into which Daphne the nymph pursued by Apollo ('Phoebus') was transformed (see *Met.* I, 452–567).

3 i.e., Venus.

4 lit.: 'in each world', including, presumably, the Earth, the Heavens and Hell.

5 The force of Boccaccio's encyclopaedic interests is made engagingly apparent here.

Book II

1 i.e., Greek. The term is used in this sense a number of times in *Tes.* (VII, 5; VIII, 55 and XI, 3).
2 In the following stanzas (10–14) Boccaccio summarizes most of the action of Statius's *Thebaid* (I–XII, 463).
3 The account of the widows, their appeal to Theseus and the latter's campaign against Creon is based upon *Theb.* XII, 464–809.
4 *teatri*, thus interpreted by Boccaccio's gloss.
5 On the death of Capaneus at Thebes see *Theb.* X, 827–936.
6 Boccaccio's gloss refers to the belief that the souls of the unburied would have to wait on the banks of the Acheron for a hundred years (*Aen.* VI, 325–30).
7 'That is, the plea' (gloss).
8 'That is, Athenian' (gloss).
9 No 'Arcita' is mentioned by Statius, although, as Savj-Lopez (1900) points out, the adj. *arquitenens* or *arcitenens* is found in *Theb.* IV, 478 and *Achill.* I, 68. The name may perhaps derive, as H. and R. Kahane suggest (*Spec.* XX, 415–25) from that of the Byzantine epic hero, Digenis Akritas. 'Palaemon', on the other hand, is mentioned once in *Theb.* VIII, 435, and the name is also given to Melicerta, son of Athamas of Thebes, when he is transformed into a sea-god (*Met.* IV, 542). Limentani (1960, 232) notes the resemblance of the following episode to *Theb.* III, 14f.
10 Limentani compares the attitude of the two princes with that of Dante's Farinata in *Inf.* X, 35–6.
11 The legendary founder of Thebes (see *Met.* III, 129f.)

Book III

1 Cp. the references to Thrace and its climate in the description of Mars's temple in VIII, st. 30, and at the beginning of Boccaccio's gloss on the passage (p. 126, above).
2 Cp. the description of souls on the banks of the Acheron in *Inf.* III, 103–5. The same passage is alluded to during the portrayal of Troiolo's grief in *Filostr.* V, 17.
3 'That is, the sign called Taurus' (gloss). Cp. the references to Jupiter's transformations in Troiolo's hymn to love (*Filostr.* III, 76).
4 'Jupiter, which is a benevolent planet, was in Pisces . . . whence it sheds a more benign and powerful influence than it does from any other' (gloss).
5 'That is, Venus' (gloss).
6 'Phaeton was the son of Phoebus (Apollo) and Clymene' (gloss). Apollo's love for Daphne has already been alluded to in I, 1 (see note).
7 Cp. the God of Love's attack on the dreamer in *RR* 1679f.
8 A further reference to Apollo's love for Daphne (Cp. I, 1 and III, 16). On Apollo as physician see *Met.* I, 521–4.
9 Cp. the sonnet in *VN*, ch. xxvi (7–8).
10 Pirithous is associated with Theseus in II, 4. On their friendship cp. *Theb.* I, 475–6 and VIII, 53–4.
11 lit.: 'two desires to weep bitterly'. Cp. the description of Criseida's grief in *Filostr.* IV, 96.
12 'In this conclusion to the third book there is no hint of the epic. Instead we are presented with a scene of fourteenth-century life' (Limentani).

Book IV

1 Arcita's choice of alias may, perhaps, have a certain grim appropriateness. Pentheus succeeded Cadmus as King as Thebes and was driven mad by Bacchus (*Met.* III, 701f.). The lover's change of name is a common romance device, and is found also, for example in *Filoc.* III, 75, pars. 4–6.
2 Arcita seems to be alluding in particular to the strife-ridden history of Thebes.
3 On the association of Bacchus with Thebes see *Theb.* I, II and *Met*, III, 528, 701f. He was the son of Zeus and Semele, daughter of Cadmus (cp. *Met.* III, 310–15 and 520).

Book V

1 'One of the three furies of Hell' (gloss). She also appears on the walls of Dis in *Inf.* IX, 48. On her association with Oedipus, see *Theb.* I, 46–113.
2 Cp. *Met.* II, 846–7.
3 Cp. *Met.* III, 115–26. The warriors then, as Boccaccio's gloss says, all killed each other except for the five who then helped Cadmus build the city of Thebes.
4 Actaeon was the grandson of Cadmus; cp. *Met.* III, 138–252.
5 Cp. *Met.* IV, 464–542.
6 Amphion was the son of Zeus and Antiope and a King of Thebes (cp. *Met.* VI, 177–9, 271–2). For the story of his wife Niobe and her children see *Met.* VI, 204–312.
7 Juno's hatred was caused by Jupiter's love for Semele, daughter of Cadmus (*Met.* III, 253f.).
8 Agave was the mother of Pentheus. She and her sister Autonoe tore him to pieces during a Bacchic ritual (*Met.* III, 708f.).
9 i.e. Eteocles and Polynices, whose pyre burnt with a double flame (see *Theb.* XII, 431–2). The rivalry between them has already been alluded to in II, 11 and 29.
10 Cp. II, 12f.
11 The god of gardens and of fertility in general.
12 'In his youth Theseus abducted the daughter of Tyndareus, Helen, who was later abducted by Paris. But his mother returned her to her brothers, Castor and Pollux, without her having been touched by Theseus; and so he was pardoned for that offence' (gloss). Cp. Hyginus, *Fab.* 79.
13 Cp. I, 137 and IV, 35.

Book VI

1 On the views about Fortune in Boccaccio see n. 9 on *Filostr.* IV, 30, above. As Limentani points out, the whole of this passage (st. 1–5) is indebted to Dante's portrayal of Fortune in *Inf.* VII, 77–96. Cp. also Arcita's lament in IV, 80.
2 On the death of Opheltes and the mourning for him see *Theb.* V, 499–753 and VI, 1–248.
3 For the story of Narcissus see *Met.* III, 351–510, and for that of Erysichthon and Ceres, *Met.* VIII, 738–878.
4 The winner of the competition was to be the god who created the most noble object by striking the ground with a rod. Neptune produced a horse and Pallas Athene an olive-tree. 'Jupiter thus declared that Pallas should name the city, since what had sprung up after her blow (namely the olive-tree) signified peace and tranquillity, whilst the horse born of Neptune's blow signified war' (gloss). Cp. Hyginus, *Fab.* 164.

Book VII

1 i.e., Greece (cp. n. 1 on II, 10, above).
2 The most striking example of the Centaurs' violence is the battle between them and the Lapiths at the wedding of Pirithous and Hippodame (*Met.* XII, 210–535). Theseus himself fought against them on that occasion.
3 'Greek' (gloss).
4 Cp. V, 57 and n., above.
5 The people of Thrace.
6 Cp. Hyginus, *Fab.*, Pref. 1.
7 On the net which Vulcan designed to entrap his wife Venus with her lover, Mars, see *Met.* IV, 171–89. Neptune's pity for them is described in *Odyssey* VIII, 344–58 and is referred to in Bersuire, *Ovidius Moralizatus* IV, fol. xxxviii.
8 The ensuing description is based on the account of the temple of Mars in *Theb.* VII, 34–69.
9 'Just as ambassadors are often exchanged between two lords who are far apart, so that each may know the other's intention – such is the function of prayer between us and God. And so the author pretends it has a human shape in order to express what he means' (gloss).
10 Boccaccio describes the climate of Thrace in similar terms in his gloss on, I, 15.
11 i.e., the gloss on I, 15.
12 i.e., Vulcan – cp. n. 7, above.
13 i.e., Venus.
14 i.e., Arcita's prayer.
15 See *Met.* X, 503–738.
16 Cp. *RR* 1376–80. Here as elsewhere in the description of the surroundings of Venus's temple there are affinities with the garden portrayed in *RR* 629f. (cp. also *Dec.* III, Intr.). Boccaccio's gloss says that lustful people are often aroused by the sight of rabbits, as also by sparrows and doves (see st. 57). The pun on *cunnus / cunniculus, conno / coniglio,* and *con / conin* probably accounts for the presence of rabbits in such contexts as this; as B. Rowland points out: 'the pursuit of small furry animals is associated with the hunt of Venus' (*Blind Beasts,* esp. 65 and 89). Venus and other figures representing carnal love are sometimes attended by rabbits or hares in Renaissance art (see G. de Tervarent, *Attributs et Symboles dans l'Art Profane,* cols, 231 and 241).
Doves are rather more frequently associated with Venus, and Fulgentius asserts that this is because 'birds of this kind are passionate in mating' (*Opera,* ed. Helm, 40). Sparrows of course proverbially have this reputation (cp. Pliny, *Natural History* X, 36 and Juvenal, *Satires* ix, 54f.).
17 'There are few who are or know how to be courteous' (gloss). Limentani refers to Dante, *Purg.* XIV, 109–11, although complaints about declining standards of courtesy are commonplace among romance writers and courtly poets (cp. the opening of Chrétien's *Yvain,* 18–32).
18 Cp. the deformation of *nostra imagine* that confronts Dante's pilgrim in the circle of false diviners, *Inf.* XX, 19–24.
19 For the story of Priapus and Vesta see Ovid, *Fasti* I, 415–40.
20 See Ovid, *Fasti* II, 155–92 and *Met.* II, 409–507.
21 As Boccaccio's gloss recognizes, there were two Atalantas (Arcadian and Boeotian), about whom similar stories are told (cp. *Met.* VIII, 380 and 425–7), and X, 560f.). Parthenopaeus was the son of Atalanta (the Arcadian, acc. to Boccaccio) and Meleager, and as the gloss says, 'he was later killed at Thebes' (see *Theb.* IX, 877–907).
22 i.e., Semiramis (cp. Orosius, *Historiarum Adversam Paganos Libri VII,* ed.

Zangemeister, I, 4, pp. 43–4). She is also the first of the lustful souls to be mentioned in *Inf.* V (52–60).

23 Cp. *Met.* IV, 55–166.

24 Cp. *Her.* IX, 5–6 and n. 14 on *Filostr.* III, 80, above.

25 Byblis was in love with her brother Caunus (see *Met.* IX, 453–665).

26 Probably an allusion to the often quoted line of Terence: *sine Cerere et Libero friget Venus*, 'without Ceres (food), and Bacchus (wine) Venus remains cold' (*Eunuchus*, 732).

27 A reference to the Judgment of Paris; cp. esp. *Her.* XVI, 51–83 – also *Roman*, 3860–921 and *Historia*, 61–2.

28 A tradition at least as old as Plato's *Symposium* lies behind this notion – cp. Hollander, *Boccaccio's Two Venuses*, 6of. and 158–60 (n. 144). Boccaccio may well have been influenced in this particular instance by Albericus, the '3rd Vatican mythographer' (see Bode, *Scriptores Rerum Mythicarum*, 239), who here follows Remigius of Auxerre (ed. Lutz, I, 180). Such indebtedness is frequently apparent in Boccaccio's later work and is often acknowledged in the *Genealogia* (see Romano's edn., e.g. pp. 265, 270 and 867). Cp. also the *chiose* to *Fiammetta* (ed. Pernicone, p. 174).

29 Cp. Apuleius, *Met.* IV, 28.

30 See n. 4 on V, 57.

31 The opposition between Diana and Venus is portrayed in the *Caccia*, esp. cantos XVI–XVII, and as Limentani points out it is a *topos* that also recurs in Boccaccio's later work. Cp. esp. the rivalry between the two goddesses in the *Ninfale fiesolano*, and see also Hollander, 191 n. 167.

32 Cp. Diana's reconciliation to the marriage of Florio and Biancifiore in *Filoc.* IV, 122 par. 2.

33 Cp. the description of Tiresias prophesying the future of Thebes by such means (and, moreover, speaking of the need for a human sacrifice) in *Theb.* X, 589–615.

34 Cp. the description of the flame in which the soul of Ulysses burns in *Inf.* XXVI, 85–8.

35 Cp. the description of the breaking of a branch from the tree in which the soul of Pier della Vigna is imprisoned in *Inf.* XIII, 40–4.

36 The simile is based, as Limentani points out, on *Theb.* IV, 494–9 (and for Boccaccio's treatment of it see Limentani (1960), 234–5). There may also be some reminiscence here of the simile that introduces the hunt in the wood of the suicides in *Inf.* XIII, 112–14.

37 i.e., African.

38 i.e., from the hunter(s). The phrase *mosso per lungo romore* here is the equiv. of *longo motum clamore* in *Theb.* IV, 495.

Book VIII

1 i.e., the trumpet, which (acc. to the gloss) 'was first found in Tyrrhenia or Tuscany'. Limentani cites *Aen.* VIII, 526 and *Theb.* VI 404.

2 Cp. the first of the *Febus-el-Forte cantari*, 46, 3. These six *cantari*, as Limentani points out, often show affinities with the language of *Tes.* Cp. also Limentani, *Dal Roman de Palamedés ai Cantari di Febus-el-Forte*, xvii, xxiv–v and xxxvi–vii.

3 The Straits of Messina.

4 See Introduction, above, p. 7. For beliefs about the ills that may befall those who are thus endowed see G. Joseph, 'Gifts of Nature, Fortune and Grace in *Phys.*, *Pard.* and *Pars. T.*', *Chau. R.* IX, esp. 237 and n. 2.

Book IX

1 *Erinyes* (pl.) is the name given to the ancient Greek spirits of punishment, but Demeter Erinys, the earth goddess, also represented the powers of vengeance (*OCD*, 407). Cp. the reference to 'cruel Erinys' in *Theb.* VIII, 686–7.
2 Limentani believes this scene to have been inspired by the portrayal of Tisiphone in *Theb.* VIII. Boccaccio may also perhaps have recalled the way she is shown emerging from Hell at Juno's behest in *Met.* IV, 432–511 (cp. also *Theb.* I, 88–122).
3 'That is, ... Pluto' (gloss).
4 Cp. *Met.* IV, 492–8.
5 A river flowing S. of Athens (cp. *Theb.* VIII, 766).
6 'Since they could not see her' (gloss).
7 The following episode appears to be modelled on the account of how Apollo deprives Polynices of victory (and ensures it for Amphiaraus) in *Theb.* VI, 491–512.
8 i.e., Ganimede, who became 'the constellation that is called Aquarius' (gloss). Cp. *Met.* X, 155–61.
9 i.e., Pisces – also associated with Venus in *Purg.* I, 19–21.
10 See *Met.* II, 1–400.
11 On the power of planetary influence and its limitations see *Summa Th.* I, cxv, 4 and *Purg.* XVI, 67–84.

Book X

1 Idmon also appears as physician in *Theb.* III, 398.
2 These properties were associated with the four 'humours' of the body – viz.: blood (hot and moist); choler (hot and dry); phlegm (cold and moist); and melancholy (cold and dry) – as also with the elements of air, fire, water and earth. On Apollo as physician see III, 25 and n., above.
3 The hostility of Juno towards Thebes is a recurrent motif in *Tes.* (cp. III, 66; IV, 16; V, 56; IX, 44; and X, 95, 97), as it is in the *Thebaid* (cp. I, 12, 256 etc.). See also *Met.* III, 261f. and IV, 421f., 543f. The temple in which Arcita's ashes are ultimately placed is dedicated to Juno (XI, 69).
4 Juno is also (see n. 3, above) 'the goddess of marriage' (gloss). Cp. VII, 83 and Hollander, 192 n. 170.
5 As in VIII, 96f. and IX, 11–12.
6 *intelletto* (*GDLI*, 5).

Book XI

1 'That is, the planets' (gloss).
2 'Certain philosophers think that the heavens as they revolve make the sweetest of sounds, which we below are unable to hear' (gloss). The allusion is, of course, to the 'music of the spheres' – cp. Cicero, *De Republica* I, 7; Dante, *Par.* I, 78, 82; and Lewis, *The Discarded Image*, 112. On the sources for the episode as a whole (st. 1–3) see G. Velli, 'L'apoteosi di Arcita', *Studi e problemi di critica testuale* V, 33–66.
3 Cp. the dream of Scipio in Cicero, *De Republica* I, 7; Boethius *Cons. Phil.* II, vii; and Dante, *Par.* XXII, 133–53 and XXVII, 79–87.
4 Cp., for example, *Filostr.* VIII, 1 and Benoit, *Roman*, 16317–498. As Limentani

shows, from this point on up to the extinguishing of the pyre Boccaccio follows *Theb.* VI. For a detailed list of correspondences see *Opere* II, 898 n. 3, and Limentani (1960), 237–40.

5 *Canto* in transferred sense, as in the phrase, *con canto e riso.*

6 Cp. Ovid's epitaph for Phaeton in *Met.* II, 327–8. Limentani cites *Inf.* XIV, 51 (Capaneus), although there is very little resemblance, and certainly not enough to warrant the sombre parallel between Arcita and Capaneus that Hollander draws (191, n. 166). In any case 'as you are now so once was I' is a common enough formula in epitaphs and medieval mortality lyrics. Cp. D. Gray, *Themes & Images in the M. E. Religious Lyric*, 200 and 289, n. 64.

Book XII

1 Cp. Boethius, *Cons. Phil.* IV, met. 6, esp. 34f.

2 'That is, because of man's mortality' (gloss).

3 On Phoroneus as law-giver see Hyginus, *Fab.* 145 and 274.

4 Thus Ricci (p. 414). His interpretation of *cerchiata* is somewhat better attested than Marti's rendering ('well-turned').

5 'She was fifteen years old' (gloss).

6 See *Filostr.* V, 44 and n., above.

7 'Since poetry began to be written in the vernacular' (gloss).

8 Cp. *DVE* II, 2 and Introduction, pp. 6 & 9, above.

9 For the imagery of voyaging here see the notes on *Filostr.* IX, 3 and 4, above. Dante also uses the term *pileggio* ('voyage') to describe his poetic undertaking in *Par.* XXIII, 67.

10 lit.: 'the Bear'. 'Sailors set their course by the pole-star, which . . . is in the tail of the Little Bear' (gloss).

FILOCOLO

1 *Filocolo* IV, 19–70.

2 *da perfettissimo amore*, 'a conventional term to describe love that is fulfilled through marriage' (Marti).

3 *armeggiando.* This may refer to the kind of jousting that took place in streets and squares during festivals (*GDLI, armeggiare,* 1). On jousting at Naples in Boccaccio's time see *Fiammetta* V (ed. Pernicone, p. 125) and, less favourably, Petrarch, *Fam.* V, 6. Cp. also Torraca (i) 159 and (ii) 20–1, and Branca *MW*, 21.

4 *darmi questi stimoli* (*TB, stimolo,* 3).

5 Cp. Ovid, *Ars Amatoria* I, 469–74. The image also recurs, as Quaglio points out, in *Ex Ponto* IV, x, 3–6. On the influence of Ovid in *Filoc.* see Introduction, p. 6 and n. 80–1.

6 *leanza.*

7 lit.: 'I shall get him off my back' – but this appears to be less of a colloquialism in Italian than it is in English (*GDLI, dosso,* 5).

8 The final battle in the civil war between Caesar and Pompey was fought at Pharsalus in 48 B.C. Cp. Lucan, *Pharsalia*, esp. VII, 617–46 and 847–72. Thessaly appears to have had a reputation for sorcery – cp., for example *Met.* VII, 223f. and *Pharsalia* VI, 435f.

9 *I vaghi gradi della notte passavano.* Among other meanings, *vago* can have the senses of 'mobile, wandering' (*TB*, 1) or 'graceful, charming' (*TB*, 4). Hence the reference could be to the movement of time, discernible from the position

of the stars and planets (lit.: 'the shifting phases of the night went by) – or to 'the charming hours of the night' (Miller).

10 *liberalità.* The adj. *liberale* is subsequently translated as 'generous', and in both cases the notion of noble conduct is implicit.

11 *villania.* The adj. *villano* is subsequently translated as 'churlish'.

12 *lealmente* – cp. n. 6, above.

13 *cortesia (GDLI,* 2).

14 *cortese (GDLI,* 6).

15 *cortesia (GDLI,* 3).

16 The allusion is to Lucius Aemilius Paullus, the Roman consul who brought the 3rd Macedonian War to an end by defeating Perseus at Pydna (168 B.C.). Out of the spoils he is said to have kept only Perseus's library. This example and those that follow are taken from Valerius Maximus's *Factorum ac Dictorum Memorabilium Libri IX,* Bk. IV, chs. iii–iv. This work (publ. shortly after 31 A.D.) was translated into Italian during the 14th century and was provided with a commentary by Boccaccio's friend Dionigi of Borgo San Sepolcro (cp. Introduction p. 4 and n. 46, above, and Branca *MW,* 79 n. 5). On the arguments for attributing a translation of Valerius to Boccaccio himself see the recent article by M. Casella in *Studi sul Boccaccio X* (1977–8), 109–21.

17 Valerius Maximus (IV, iii, ext. 2) ascribes the quotation to Sophocles. Xenocrates was a follower of Plato; for the story of his resistance to the blandishments of Phryne see ibid. IV, iii, ext. 3.

18 Both Attilius Regulus and Valerius Publicola are praised in Valerius Maximus's chapter on poverty (IV, iv, 5–6 and 1).

19 An oath was not held to be binding if it had certain evil consequences – cp., for example, Ambrose, *De Officiis* I, 10 (*PL* LXXVI, col. 357) and Aquinas, *Summa Th.* 2a 2ae 89, 7 ad 2. It was of course invalid if it ran contrary to justice, 'either because it is a sin, as when a man swears to commit murder, or because it impedes a greater good' (*Summa Th.* 2a 2ae 89, 9 ad 3). On the theory of vows and promissory oaths in general see *Summa Th.* 2a 2ae, 88–9. Contravention of a previous lawful oath or the fulfilment of its conditions by fraud would also, as Miller points out, render it void.

20 Miller cites James iv, 4.

21 Cp. Boethius, *Cons. Phil.,* esp II pr. and met. v, and III pr. and met. 3 – also Dante *Conv.* IV, xi–xiii. Boccaccio's wording here is close to that of Dante in *Par.* XI, 82.

22 For the story of Diogenes, the Cynic philosopher, and his rejection of Alexander's patronage see Valerius Maximus IV, iii, ext. 4.

APPENDIX A

1 See Proclus's summary of the *Cypria,* 1. 162 (in A. Severyns, *Recherches sur la 'Chrestomathie' de Proclos* IV, 84).

2 A. C. Pearson (ed.), *The Fragments of Sophocles* II, 253–5.

3 See M. R. Scherer, *The Legends of Troy in Art and Literature,* 3–4 and 53; A. M. Young, *Troy and her Legend,* 9809; and W. H. Roscher, *Ausführliches Lexicon der griechischen und römischen Mythologie* V, cols. 1220–30. For further evidence of the early and widespread popularity of the subject see A. M. Young, 92, 141, 148 and n. 24. Lycophron (3rd cent. B.C.) implies that Achilles's motive for the killing was unrequited love for Troilus – see *Alexandra,* 307–13.

4 *Epitoma* III, 32. See Apollodorus, *The Library,* ed. Sir J. G. Frazer, II, 201–3 and notes.

5 Plautus (*Bacchides,* 953–5) alludes to the belief that Troilus's death was one of

the three signs of the fall of Troy (the others being the loss of the Palladium and the removal of the lintel from the Phrygian gate). The 1st Vatican mythographer appears considerably later (5th cent.?) to be drawing upon this tradition when he adds to his description of Troilus's death: 'It was said of him that if he reached the age of twenty, Troy could not be overthrown' (G. H. Bode, *Scriptores Rerum Mythicarum*, 66).

6 The scene is portrayed (along with, for example, the exploits of 'plumed Achilles' and 'blood-stained' Diomedes) in the temple of Juno at Carthage. This appears to be the only reference to Troilus in the *Aeneid* and it is cited by Boccaccio in *Genealogia* VI, 28 (Romano, 308–9).

7 Cp. esp.: *Iliad* V; *Odyssey* III; *Met.* XIII, 68, 100–2, 238–42, and XIV, 457–511.

8 Cp. esp.: *Iliad* I, 69f. and II, 300f.; *Aen.* II, 100, 122–4 and 185; *Met.* XII, 11–23; and Hyginus *Fab.* 98.

9 On the antecedents of Boccaccio's Pandaro see n. 1 on *Filostr.* II, 1, above.

10 For Dictys see the edn. of W. Eisenhut and for Dares that of F. Meister. Both works are translated by R. M. Frazer Jr, *The Trojan War*. On the dating of the two texts see N. E. Griffin, *Dares and Dictys*, 17f., and R. M. Frazer Jr, 3 and 7–13.

11 R. M. Frazer Jr's transln.

12 Ibid.

13 See *Roman*, 19925–54.

14 Recent editions are those of G. B. Riddehough (Harvard Ph.D. dissertation, 1950) and L. Gompf, *Joseph Iscanus: Werke and Briefe*. The poem has been translated by G. Roberts, *Joseph of Exeter, the Iliad of Dares Phrygius*.

15 R. K. Root, '*Chaucer's Dares*', MPh XV (1917), 1–22.

16 These are the dates proposed by Constans in his SATF edn. of the *Roman* (VI, 190), whilst F. E. Guyer, in *MPh* XXVI (1929), 261, argues for a date after 1184.

17 See R. M. Lumiansky, 'The Story of Troilus and Briseida according to Benoit and Guido', *Spec.* XXIX (1954), 728.

18 See *Roman*, ed. Constans. VI, 267–318, and *Le Roman de Troie en Prose*, ed. L. Constans and E. Faral.

19 The standard edition of the *Historia* is that of N. E. Griffin. The work has recently been translated by M. E. Meek.

20 Cp. Lumiansky (1954).

21 There may be as many as 150 altogether – see Griffin, xi–xiv and Meek, xi.

22 Griffin, xvii.

23 For other early 14th century Italian versions of the Troilus story see the *Istorietta Troiana* and Binduccio dello Scelto's *Libro de la Storia di Troia* (in Gorra, *Testi Inediti*, 396–8 and 404–19; see also 161–2 and 167–9).

On Boccaccio's indebtedness to Benoit and Guido esp. see: Young, *Origins and Development*, ch. I; G. and M. (Introduction) 24f.; and V. Pernicone, *Studi di Filologia italiana* II, 93–106. The most recent and thorough investigation and comparison of the various possible sources and analogues is by M. Gozzi, 'Sulle Fonti del *Filostrato*', *Studi sul Boccaccio* V, 123–209.

On Chaucer in relation to Benoit and Guido see Young, *Origins and Development*, ch. III. Recently C. D. Benson has claimed that the 'beginnings of Chaucer's narrator in the *Troilus* can be found in Guido delle Colonne's *Historia*' (*Chau R* XIII, 308–15).

APPENDIX B

1 The edition used is that of L. Constans (SATF, Paris, 1904–12), although occasional reference has been made to the excerpts ed. by K. Reichenberger

(Tübingen, 1963). Square brackets indicate editorial summary of the narrative.

2 Cp. Dares, ch. 13: 'Diomedes was stocky, brave, dignified and austere. No-one was fiercer in battle. He was loud at the war-cry, hot-tempered, impatient and daring' (tr. R. M. Frazer Jr, 144).

3 Both Dares (see below, n. 4) and Joseph of Exeter (IV, 158–9) mention this feature, although neither considers it to be a blemish.

4 Cp. Dares, ch. 13: 'Briseis was beautiful. She was small and blonde, with soft yellow hair. Her eyebrows were joined above her lovely eyes. Her body was well-proportioned. She was charming, friendly, modest, ingenuous and pious' (tr. R. M. Frazer Jr., 144–5).

5 Cp. Dares, ch. 13: 'Troilus, a large and handsome boy, was strong for his age, brave and eager for glory' (tr. R. M. Frazer Jr., 143).

6 This episode is more briefly presented in Dares, ch. 15.

7 *De cest, veir, criem g'estre blasmez.* Reichenberger, on the other hand, reads; *D'icest vers criem j(e) estre blasmez* ('I fear I may be blamed for these lines').

8 Benoit is probably referring to Eleanor of Aquitaine, wife of Henry II of England and formerly married to Louis VII of France (Constans VI, 188–90).

9 For this quotation and Benoit's subsequent commentary see Proverbs xxxi, 10–31.

10 *les meillors.* Reichenberger reads: *les plusors* ('most of them').

11 i.e., Diomedes.

12 The gods of the underworld, here seen as judges of human conduct.

13 Specifically: 13915–19, 14098–101, 14119–22, 14201–4, and 14237–44.

14 Cp. the description of Troilus's state at the time of Briseida's impending departure (13261f.).

15 Constans sees here a reminiscence of *Met.* I, 128.

16 The episode is also briefly presented in Dares, ch. 27. On Boccaccio's possible indebtedness to it in *Filostr.* see: Savj-Lopez, *Romania* XXVII, 450–3; K. Young, 36–40; and G. and M. (introduction), 36–8.

17 Cp. the pattern of events in Dares, chs. 31–2.

18 Gordon (19) makes Diomedes the subject of the passage from 20204 up to this point, but it surely makes better sense to assume that an access of sympathy on Briseida's part (as here) precipitates her decision to accept him (cp. also the use of *lui* in 20211, 20216 and 20218).

19 Specifically: 20462–72; 20493–9; 20539–44; and 20572–6.

20 Dares describes Troilus's death in ch. 33, but does not accuse Achilles of treacherous or reprehensible behaviour. Cp. also Joseph of Exeter's account of the episode (Bk. VI, esp. 325–31).

21 See Dares, ch. 34.

22 Cp. Dictys, Bk. VI.

APPENDIX C

1 Brief conflicts between them are recorded in Bk. XVII, 150 and 152.

2 Cp. *Roman* 13438–94, although Benoit, as Lumiansky (1954) points out, is generally 'a much less vociferous antifeminist than Guido' (733).

3 Cp. *Roman*, 13859–66.

4 Guido has given an account of how Achilles fell in love with Polyxena in XXIII, 183–6 (cp. n. 16 on Appendix B, above). The description of how Hecuba took revenge upon him for Troilus's death is at the beginning of XXVII (207–8).

Bibliography

(of works consulted and referred to in Notes.
For abbreviations used see pp. 188–9)

ALBRICUS LONDONENSIS: *Allegoriae poeticae*. Paris, 1520.

ANDREAS CAPELLANUS: *De Amore Libri Tres*, ed. E. Trojel. Copen-
hagen, 1892, repr. Munich, 1964.
The Art of Courtly Love, tr. J. J. Parry. N.Y., 1941.

APOLLODORUS: *The Library*, tr. Sir J. G. Frazer, London, 1921.

APULEIUS: *Metamorphoses (The Golden Ass)*, tr. W. Adlington, rev. S.
Gaselee. London, 1915.

BALDUINO, A.: *Cantari del Trecento*. Milan, 1970.

BATTAGLIA, S. & SQUAROTTI, G. B. (eds.): *Grande Dizionario della
lingua italiana*. Turin, 1961–

BENNETT, J. A. W.: *The Parlement of Foules*. Oxford, 1957.
The Knight's Tale (2nd edn.). London, 1958.
Chaucer's Book of Fame. Oxford, 1968.

BENOIT de SAINTE-MAURE: *Le Roman de Troie*, ed. L. Constans.
Paris, 1904–12.

BENSON, C. D.: ' "O Nyce World": What Chaucer Really Found in
Guido delle Colonne's, *History of Troy*', *Chau R* XIII (1979), 308–15.

BERSUIRE: *Ovidius Moralizatus (Reductorium Morale* Liber XV, cap.
ii–xv), ed. J. Engels. Utrecht, 1962.

BINDUCCIO dello SCELTO (see GORRA).

BOCCACCIO: (i) *Opere (Scrittori d'Italia*, Bari)
Le Rime, ed. V. Branca, (1939)
Filocolo, ed. S. Battaglia (1938)
Filostrato & Ninfale fiesolano, ed. V. Pernicone (1937)
Teseida, ed. A. Roncaglia (1941)
Fiammetta, ed. V. Pernicone (1939)
Genealogie Deorum Gentilium, ed. V. Romano (1951)
(ii)   *Tutte le Opere di Giovanni Boccaccio*, gen. ed. V. Branca
(Mondadori, Milan)
  I *Caccia di Diana*, ed. V. Branca
    Filocolo, ed. A. E. Quaglio (1967)
  II *Filostrato*, ed. V. Branca
    Teseida, ed. A. Limentani
    Comedia Ninfe, ed. A. E. Quaglio (1964)
  III *Amorosa Visione*, ed. V. Branca
    Ninfale fiesolano, ed. A. Balduino
    Trattatello in Laude di Dante, ed. P. G. Ricci (1974)
  IV *Decameron*, ed. V. Branca (1976)
  VI *Esposizioni sopra la Comedia di Dante*, ed. G. Padoan (1965)
  X *De Mulieribus Claris*, ed. V. Zaccaria (1970)
(iii)   *Opere minori in volgare*, ed. M. Marti (Rizzoli, Milan)
  I *Filocolo* (1969)
  II *Filostrato, Teseida, Chiose al Teseida* (1970)
  III *Comedia Ninfe, Amorosa Visione, Fiammetta, Ninfale
fiesolano* (1971)

IV *Caccia di Diana, Rime, Trattatello in Laude di Dante, Esposizioni, Lettere* (1972)

(iv)   *Opere in Versi* etc., ed. P. G. Ricci (includes excerpts from *Filostr., Tes. & Epistole*). Milan & Naples, 1965.

(v)   *The Filostrato of Giovanni Boccaccio: A Translation with Parallel Text*, ed. N. E. Griffin & A. B. Myrick. Philadelphia & London, 1929 (repr. N.Y., 1967).

(vi)   *Teseida*, ed. S. Battaglia. Florence, 1938.
    The Book of Theseus, tr. B. M. McCoy. Sea Cliff, N.Y., 1974.

BODE, G. H. (ed.): *Scriptores Rerum Mythicarum Latini Tres*. Celle, 1834.

BOETHIUS: *Tractates & Consolation of Philosophy*, tr. H. F. Stewart, E. K. Rand and 'I.T.'. London, 1918.

BOITANI, P.: *Chaucer and Boccaccio*. Oxford, 1977.

BOVILL, M. F.: *The Decameron and the Canterbury Tales: a comparative study* (Unpubl. B.Litt. thesis. Oxford, 1966).

BRANCA, V.: *Il Cantare trecentesco e il Boccaccio del Filostrato e del Teseida*. Florence, 1936.
    Boccaccio medievale. Florence, 1956.
    Boccaccio: The Man and his Works. N.Y., 1976.
    (See also Boccaccio i and ii).

BREWER, D. S. (ed.): *The Parlement of Foulys*. London & Edinburgh, 1960.
    Geoffrey Chaucer (Writers & their Backgrounds). London, 1974.

BRYAN, W. F. & DEMPSTER, G.: *Sources & Analogues of Chaucer's Canterbury Tales*. Chicago, 1941 (repr. N.Y., 1958).

CAGGESE, R.: *Roberto d'Angiò e i suoi tempi*. Florence, 1922–30.

CAVALLARI, E.: *La Fortuna di Dante nel Trecento*, Florence, 1921.

CHAUCER: *The Works of Geoffrey Chaucer*, ed. F. N. Robinson (2nd edn.). London, 1957.
    The Parlement of Foulys, ed. D. S. Brewer. London & Edinburgh, 1960.
    The Book of Troilus & Criseyde, ed. R. K. Root, Princeton, 1926.
    The Knight's Tale, ed. J. A. W. Bennett (2nd edn.). London, 1958.

CINO da PISTOIA (see TREVES and ZACCAGNINI).

CONSTANS, L. (see BENOIT).

CONTINI, G. (ed.): *Poeti del Duecento*. Milan & Naples, 1960.
    Petrarch, *Canzoniere* (with D. Ponchiroli). Turin, 1964.
    Dante, *Rime*. Turin, 1946 (repr. 1970).

COPLAND, M.: 'The Shipman's Tale: Chaucer and Boccaccio', *MAe* XXXV (1966), 11–28.

COULTER, C. C.: 'Boccaccio's Acquaintance with Homer', *PQ* V (1926), 44–53.
    'The Library of the Angevin Kings at Naples', *TPAPA* LXXV (1944), 141–55.

CROCE, B.: *History of the Kingdom of Naples*, ed. H. S. Hughes, tr. F. Frenaye. Chicago, 1970.

CROW, M. M. & OLSON, C. C. (eds.): *Chaucer Life-Records*. Oxford, 1966.

CUMMINGS, H. M.: *The Indebtedness of Chaucer's Works to the Italian Works of Boccaccio*. Cincinnati, 1916 (repr. N.Y., 1965).

Boccaccio, *Filostrato* (verse tr.). Princeton, 1924.

CURTIUS, E. R.: *European Literature & the Latin Middle Ages*, tr. W. R. Trask, N.Y., 1953.

DANTE: *Le Opere di Dante Alighieri*, ed. E. Moore & P. Toynbee (4th edn.), Oxford, 1924 (repr. 1963).

Rime, ed. G. Contini. Turin, 1946 (repr. 1970).

Epistole, ed. P. Toynbee (2nd edn.). Oxford, 1966.

La Vita Nuova, ed. M. Barbi. Florence, 1932.

Il Convivio, ed. M. Simonelli. Bologna, 1966.

De Vulgari Eloquentia, ed. P. V. Mengaldo, Padua, 1968.

La Divina Commedia, ed. N. Sapegno. Florence, 1955–7.

DARES (see FRAZER, R. M. and MEISTER, F.)

DAVIDSOHN, R.: *Forschungen zur älteren Geschichte von Florenz*. Berlin, 1896.

DEMPSTER, G. (see BRYAN & DEMPSTER)

DICTYS (see EISENHUT, W. and FRAZER, R. M.)

DIONISOTTI, C. & GRAYSON, C. (eds.): *Early Italian Texts* (2nd edn.). Oxford, 1965.

EISENHUT, W. (ed.): *Dictys Cretensis Ephimeridos Belli Troiani Libri*. Leipzig, 1958.

FARAGLIA, N. F.: 'Barbato di Sulmona e gli Uomini di Lettere della Corte di Roberto d'Angiò', *ASI* ser 5, III (1889), 313–60.

FARNHAM, W.: 'England's Discovery of the *Decameron*', *PMLA* XXXIX (1924), 123–39.

FRAZER, R. M., Jr (ed. & tr.): *The Trojan War: the Chronicles of Dictys of Crete and Dares the Phrygian*. Bloomington & London, 1966.

FULGENTIUS: *Opera* (incl. *Mythologiarum Libri Tres*), ed. R. Helm. Leipzig, 1898.

GATHERCOLE, P.: 'Boccaccio in French', *Studi sul Boccaccio* V (1968), 275–97.

GORDON, R. K. (ed. & tr.): *The Story of Troilus* incl. Filostr. and excerpts from *Roman*. London, 1934 (pbk. edn., London & N.Y., 1964, repr. Toronto, 1978).

GORRA, E. (ed.): *Testi inediti di Storia troiana*. Turin, 1887.

GOZZI, M.: 'Sulle fonti del *Filostrato*', *Studi sul Boccaccio* V (1968), 123–209.

GRIFFIN, N. E. (see also BOCCACCIO and GUIDO): *Dares and Dictys: An Introduction to the Study of the Medieval Versions of the Story of Troy*. Baltimore, 1907.

GUERIN, R.: '*The Shipman's Tale*: the Italian Analogues', *ESt* LII (1971), 412–19.

GUIDO de COLUMNIS (delle Colonne): *Historia Destructionis Troiae*, ed. N. E. Griffin. Cambridge (Mass.), 1936. Ibid., tr. M. E. Meek. Bloomington & London, 1974.

GUYER, F. E.: 'The Chronology of the Earlier French Romances' *MPh* XXVI (1929), 257–77.

HAUVETTE, H.: *Études sur Boccace, 1894–1916*. Turin, 1968.

HOLLANDER, R.: *Boccaccio's Two Venuses*. N.Y., 1977.

HYDE, J. K.: *Society & Politics in Medieval Italy, 1000–1350*. London, 1973.

HYGINUS: *Hygini Fabulae*, ed. H. I. Rose. Leyden, 1963.
 Myths of Hyginus, tr. M. Grant. Lawrence, Kansas, 1960.
JOSEPH OF EXETER (Josephus Iscanus): *Daretis Phrygii Ilias*, in *Briefe und Werke*, ed. L. Gompf. Leyden & Cologne, 1970.
 The Iliad of Dares Phrygius, tr. G. Roberts. Cape Town, 1970.
KAHANE, H. & R.: 'Akritas and Arcita: A Byzantine Source of Boccaccio's *Teseida*', *Spec* XX (1945), 415-25.
LARNER, J.: *Culture & Society in Italy, 1290-1420*. London, 1971.
LÉONARD, E. G., *Les Angevins de Naples*. Paris, 1954.
LEPSCHY, A. L.: 'Boccaccio Studies in English, 1945-69', *Studi sul Boccaccio* VI (1971), 211-29.
LEWIS, C. S.: *The Discarded Image*. Cambridge, 1964 (pbk., 1967).
LIMENTANI, A.: 'Boccaccio "traduttore" di Stazio', *La Rassegna* (1960), 231-42.
 (ed.) *Dal Roman de Palamedés ai Cantari di Febus-el-forte*. Bologna, 1962. (see also BOCCACCIO ii, II)
de LORRIS, G. & de MEUN, J.: *Le Roman de la Rose*, ed. F. Lecoy. Paris, 1965-70.
LUMIANSKY, R. M.: 'The Story of Troilus and Briseida According to Benoit and Guido', *Spec* XXIX (1954), 727-33.
LYCOPHRON: *Alexandria*, tr. G. W. Mooney. London, 1921.
MARTI, M. (see BOCCACCIO iii)
MATHEW, G.: *The Court of Richard II*. London & N.Y., 1968.
McCOY, B. M. (see BOCCACCIO vi)
McKISACK, M.: *The Fourteenth Century, 1307-1399*. Oxford, 1959.
MEECH, S. B.: *Design in Chaucer's Troilus*. Syracuse, N.Y., 1959.
MEEK, M. E. (see GUIDO)
MEISTER, F. (ed.): *Daretis Phrygii De Excidio Troiae Historia*. Leipzig, 1873.
de MEUN, J. (see de LORRIS & de MEUN)
MILLER, R. P. (ed.): *Chaucer: Sources & Backgrounds* (incl. tr. of *Filoc.* IV, 31-4). N.Y., 1977.
MILLS, M. (ed.): *Six Middle English Romances*. London & Totowa, N.J., 1973.
MOLAND, L. & d'HERICAULT, C.: *Nouvelles françoises en prose du xiv⁰ siecle* (incl. Beauvau's tr. of *Filostr.*). Paris, 1858.
MYRICK, A. B. (see GRIFFIN & MYRICK)
OLSON, C. C. (see CROW & OLSON)
OSGOOD, C. G.: *Boccaccio on Poetry* (tr. of *Genealogia* Preface & Bks. XIV-XV). Princeton, 1930 (pbk. edn., Indianapolis & N.Y., 1956).
OVID: *The Art of Love & Other Poems*, tr. J. H. Mozley. London, 1939.
 Heroides & Amores, tr. G. Showerman. London, 1914.
 Metamorphoses, tr. F. J. Miller. London, 1916.
 Fasti, tr. Sir J. G. Frazer. London, 1931.
 Tristia & Ex Ponto, tr. A. L. Wheeler. London, 1924.
PARKS, G. B.: 'The Route of Chaucer's First Journey to Italy', *ELH* XVI (1949), 174-87.
 The English Traveller to Italy, I: the Middle Ages. Rome, 1954.
PERNICONE, V.: 'Il *Filostrato* di Giovanni Boccaccio', *Studi di Filologia italiana* II (1929), 77-128. (see also BOCCACCIO i)

PETRARCH: *Le Familiari,* ed. V. Rossi & U. Bosco. Florence, 1933–42.
   Rerum Familiarium Libri I–VIII, tr. A. S. Bernardo. Albany, N.Y., 1975.
   Canzoniere, ed. G. Contini & D. Ponchiroli. Turin, 1964.
PISANTI, T.: 'Boccaccio in Inghilterra, tra Medioevo e Rinascimento', in *Boccaccio in Europe,* ed. G. Tournoy. Louvain, 1974.
PRATT, R. A.: 'Chaucer and the Visconti Libraries', *ELH* VI (1939), 191–9.
   'The *Knight's Tale' SA,* 82–105.
   Conjectures regarding Chaucer's Manuscript of the *Teseida', SP* XLII (1945), 745–63.
   'Chaucer's Use of the *Teseida' PMLA* LXII (1947), 598–621.
   'Chaucer and *Le Roman de Troyle et de Criseida', SP* LIII (1956), 509–39.
PRESS, A. R. (ed.): *Anthology of Troubadour Lyric Poetry.* Edinburgh & Austin, Texas, 1971.
QUAGLIO, A. E.: 'Tra fonti e testo del *Filocolo', GSLI* CXL (1963), 321–63 and 489–551. (see also BOCCACCIO ii)
RAJNA, P.: 'Il *Cantare dei Cantari* e il Serventese del Maestro di tutti l'Arti', *ZfRPh* II (1878), 220–54 and 419–37.
REDSTONE, V. B. & L. J.: 'The Heyrons of London', *Spec* XII (1937), 182–95.
REISS, E.: 'Boccaccio in English Culture of the Fourteenth and Fifteenth Centuries', in *Boccaccio nella cultura inglese e anglo-americana,* ed. G. Galigani. Florence, 1974.
REMIGIUS of AUXERRE: *Commentum in Martianum Capellam,* ed. C. E. Lutz. Leyden, 1962–5.
RICCI, P. G. (see BOCCACCIO ii and iv)
RICKERT, M.: *Painting in Britain: the Middle Ages.* Harmondsworth, 1954.
ROOT, R. K.: 'Chaucer's Dares', *MPh* XV (1917), 1–22.
   (see also CHAUCER)
ROSCHER, W. H. (ed.): *Ausführliches Lexikon der griechischen und römischen Mythologie.* Leipzig, 1884–
ROWLAND, B.: (ed.): *Companion to Chaucer Studies.* Toronto, N.Y. & London, 1968.
   Blind Beasts. (Kent, Ohio, 1971).
RUGGIERS, P. G.: 'The Italian Influence on Chaucer', in *Companion to Chaucer Studies,* ed. B. Rowland. Toronto, N.Y. & London, 1968.
RUNCIMAN, S.: *The Sicilian Vespers.* Cambridge, 1958 (pbk. edn., Harmondsworth, 1960).
SAVJ-LOPEZ, P.: 'Il *Filostrato* di Giovanni Boccaccio', *Romania* XXVII (1898), 442–79.
   'Sulle fonti della *Teseide', GSLI* XXXVI (1900), 57–78.
SCHERER, M.: *The Legends of Troy in Art and Literature.* N.Y. & London, 1963.
SCHLESS, H.: 'Transformations: Chaucer's Use of Italian', in *Chaucer (Writers & their Background),* ed. D. S. Brewer. London, 1974.
SCHMIDBAUER, F.: *Die Troilusepisode in Benoit's 'Roman de Troie'.* Halle A.S., 1914.

SERVIUS: *Servii Grammatici qui feruntur in Vergilii Carmina Commentarii*, ed. G. Thilo & H. Hagen. Hildesheim, 1961.

SEVERYNS, A.: *Recherches sur la 'Chresthomathie' de Proclos*, IV. Paris, 1963.

SMITH, W.: *Dictionary of Greek & Roman Biography and Mythology*. London, 1844–9.

SOMMER, H. O. (ed.): *The Vulgate Version of the Arthurian Romances*, III. Washington, D. C., 1910.

STATIUS: *Silvae, Thebaid & Achilleid*, tr. J. H. Mozley, London, 1928.

de TERVARENT, G.: *Attributs et Symboles dans l'Art Profane, 1450–1600*. Geneva, 1958.

TOMMASEO, N. & BELLINI, B. (eds.): *Dizionario della lingua italiana*. Turin & Naples, 1861–72.

TORRACA, F.: 'Giovanni Boccaccio a Napoli', *Rassegna critica della letteratura italiana* XX (1915), 145–245, and XXI (1916), 1–80 (Page refs. are to this version. The work was first publ. in *Archivio storico napoletano*, 1914, and repr. Rome, 1916).

TREVES, E.: 'La Satira di Cino da Pistoia contro Napoli', *GSLI* LVIII (1911), 122–39.

VELLI, G.: 'L'apoteosi di Arcita: ideologia e coscienza storica nel *Teseida*', *Studi e problemi di critica testuale* V (1972), 33–66.

VILLANI, G.: *Cronica di G. Villani*. Florence, 1823.

VIRGIL: *Eclogues Georgics, Aeneid & Minor Poems*, tr. H. R. Fairclough. London, 1916–18.

WEISS, R.: 'The Translators from the Greek of the Angevin Court of Naples', *Rinascimento* (1950), 195–226.
'Notes on Dionigi da Borgo San Sepolcro', *Italian Studies* X (1955), 40–2.

WRIGHT, H. G.: *Boccaccio in England, from Chaucer to Tennyson*. London, 1957.

WILKINS, E. H.: 'The Coronation of Petrarch', *Spec* XVIII (1943), 155–97.

YOUNG, A. M.: *Troy and her Legend*. Pittsburgh, 1948.

YOUNG, K.: *The Origin and Development of the Story of Troilus and Criseyde*. London, 1908.

ZACCAGNINI, G.: *Le Rime di Cino da Pistoia*. Geneva, 1925.

Index of Personal Names

Most of the characters and mythical figures mentioned in the text, Introduction and Notes are included here (except for Troiolo/Troilus, Criseida/Briseida, Pandaro, Arcita, Palemone, Emilia, Theseus, Tarolfo and Tebano) – as are most of the classical and medieval writers, artists and political figures that are referred to, apart from Boccaccio himself.

Benoit de Sainte-Maure, 7 & n.90, 18, 165 & n.16, 166, 167f., 184, 186, 198 n.8 and 6, 201 n.1 and 2, 204 n.19, 205 n.13, 213 n.23, 214 n.2, 215, 218, 219.
(Refs. to *Roman de Troie, passim* in Notes)
Bersuire, Pierre (*Ovidius Moralizatus*), 208 n.7, 215.
Binduccio dello Scelto, 188, 202 n.2, 213 n.23, 215.
Boccaccio di Chelino (father of the poet), 2–3 & n.28–9.
Boethius, 6, 16, 188, 192 n.64, 201 n.18, 210 n.3, 211 n.1, 212 n.21, 216.

Cadmus, 110, 119 & n.3, 124 & n.4, 142, 207 n.1 and 3.
Calchas, 23, 25, 26, 56, 57–8, 71, 79, 83, 84, 92, 99, 164, 168, 169, 170, 174, 175, 176, 179, 180, 181, 182, 184, 202, n.30, 203 n.6 and 11.
Capaneus, 107, 108, 211 n.6.
Cassandra, 86, 95–7 & n.19.
Cecco Angiolieri, 200 n.17.
Centaurs, 124 & n.2.
Ceres, 130 & n.26, 132.
Charles I, King of Naples (1266–85), 1, 2, 4 & n.57.
Charles II, King of Naples (1285–1309), 1 & n.8, 4.
Chaucer, 9–12 & n.1–43, 13–15, 16, 17, 188, 189, 202 n.32, 205 n.4, 213 n.23, 215, 216, 218, 219, 220.
Cicero, 164, 210 n.2–3.
Cino da Pistoia, 4 & n.42–5, 8 & n.111–16, 202 n.18, 216, 220.
Creon, 106, 109, 110, 120, 193 n.83.
Cupid, 111, 121, 129, 131, 141.
Cytheraea, see Venus.

Dante, 2 & n.20, 3 & n.36, 7, 8–9 & n.112–32, 10, 11, 12 & n.40, 188, 189, 194 n.109, 196 n.25–6, 197 n.4, 198 n.10, 199 n.14 and 18, 200 n.1 and 14, 202 n.36, 203 n.9, 207 n.1, 210 n.2–3, 211 n.9, 212 n.21, 215, 216, 217.
(Refs. to *Comedy, VN, DVE* & *Conv., passim* in Notes)
Daphne, 113 & n.6, 205 n.2.
Dares Phrygius, 164 & n.10, 165, 168, 182, 214 n.2–6 and 20–1, 217, 218, 219.
Deiphebus, 86, 94–5 & n.17, 97, 98.
Diana, 130, 133–4, 142, 149, 168, 209 n.31–2.
Dictys Cretensis, 164 & n.10, 165, 217.
Diogenes, 161 & n.22.
Diomedes, 70, 74 & n.1, 75, 76, 83–6 & n.5–8, 89 n.6, 90, 97, 98, 99, 100, 123, 136, 164, 165, 167 & n.2, 169, 172 & n.11, 173, 175, 176–8, 179, 181, 182–3, 184, 186, 198 n.5, 213 n.6, 214 n.18.
Dionigi da Borgo San Sepolcro, 4 & n.46, 5, 6 & n.76, 212 n.16, 220.
Dis, see Pluto.

Edward III of England, 9, 195 n.8.
Erinis, 138–9 & n.1.
Eteocles, 107, 109 (son of Oedipus), 120 & n.9.

Fiammetta, 7 & n.106–8, 104–5, 154, 159, 160–1, 197 n.1, 198 n.7.

Fortune, 22, 23, 35, 36, 39, 45, 51, 53, 56, 60 & n.9, 61, 64, 67, 68, 69, 73, 89, 100, 105, 115, 116, 117, 119, 122 & n.1, 193 n.75, 200 n.14, 209 n.4.
Fulgentius, 6, 208 n.16, 217.

Giotto, 1 & n.10, 5 & n.61.
Graziolo de' Bambaglioli, 8 & n.118, 191 n.37.
Guido de Columnis (delle Colonne), 18, 165–6 & n.19–22, 184f., 188, 198 n.8, 201 n.1, 205 n.13, 213 n.23, 214 n.2 and 4, 215, 217, 218.
    (Refs. to the *Historia, passim* in Notes)
Guillaume de Lorris & Jean de Meun (*Roman de la Rose*), 189, 200 n.6, 206 n.7, 208 n.16, 218.

Hector, 25–6, 29, 57, 58, 85, 98, 144, 164, 165, 167, 168, 169, 178, 179, 182, 186.
Hecuba, 95, 181 (Troilus's mother), 182, 214 n.4.
Helen, 29, 48, 60, 63, 64, 70, 85, 165, 167, 169, 170, 207, n.12.
Helenus, 165, 167, 204 n.17.
Hercules, 55 & n.14, 130 & n.24, 137, 193 n.75.
Hippolyta, 106, 107, 108, 110, 123, 135, 140, 142, 144, 150.
Homer, 164, 186.
Horace, 164.
Hyginus (*Fabulae*), 188, 207 n.12, 207 n.4, 208 n.6, 211 n.3, 213 n.8, 218.

Jeremiah, 21.
Jerome, St, 192 n.66.
Joseph of Exeter, 165 & n.14, 214 n.20, 218.
Juno, 111, 119, 120, 134, 142 & n.3–4, 147, 151, 207 n.7.
Jupiter, 24, 27, 54 & n.12, 55, 67, 69, 99, 112 (Ammon), 119, 136, 140, 193 n.75, 200 n.14, 206 n.3–4, 207 n.7.

Leontius Pilatus, 192 n.55.
Lionel, Duke of Clarence, 9 & n.7, 195 n.2.
Lucan, 6, 9, 211 n.8.
Lycophron, 212 n.3, 218.
Lycurgus, 123.

Mars, 48, 54 & n.13, 55, 92, 105, 107, 110, 111, 124, 125–8 & n.8, 129, 130, 133, 137, 138, 139, 140, 141, 196 n.29, 200 n.14, 206 n.1.
Medea, 157.
Menedon, 11, 15, 16–17, 154, 159, 160.
Menelaus, 61, 70, 123, 139, 167, 185.
Mercury, 142, 144.
Muses, 24, 105, 136, 151, 152.

Narcissus, 123 & n.3, 193 n.86.
Neptune, 123 & n.4, 125 & n.7.
Nestor, 123, 144.

Oedipus, 118, 120.

Ovid, 6 & n.80–1, 16, 154 & n.5, 157, 188, 193 n.73 and 75, 208 n.20, 211 n.5, 218.
(Refs to *Metamorphoses, passim* in Notes)

Pallas (Athene), 26, 55, 77, 108, 123 & n.4, 198 n.4.
Paolino Minorita, 193 n.76.
Paolo da Perugia, 5 & n.67–71, 6 & n.76.
Paolo dell' Abbaco, 192 n.48.
Paris, 60, 63, 167, 169, 182, 204 n.17.
Peleus, 116, 144.
Pentheus (Arcita's alias), 116 & n.1, 117, 118, 119, 120, 207 n.8.
Petrarch, 3 & n.39, 4 & n.51, 8 & n.116, 10, 12 & n.40, 188, 190 n.5, 192 n.51 and 53, 200 n.15, 205 n.4, 211 n.3, 219, 220.
Phaeton, 113, 140 & n.10, 211 n.6.
Phoebus, see Apollo.
Pirithous, 114 & n.10, 115, 123, 144, 208 n.2.
Plato, 209 n.28, 212 n.17.
Plautus, 212–13 n.5.
Pluto, 133, 138 & n.2 (Dis), 141 (Dis), 174 & n.2.
Polynices, 107, 109, 120 & n.9, 210 n.7.
Polyxena, 29, 48, 60, 95 & n.18, 165, 178–9, 182, 186, 198 n.6, 214 n.4.
Priam, 23, 58, 69, 88, 144, 169, 170, 176, 181.
Priapus, 120 & n.11, 130.
Protesilaus, 61 & n.11.

Remigius of Auxerre, 209 n.28, 219.
Richard II of England, 9, 10, 218.
Robert I, King of Naples (1309–43), 1–5 & n.10–18 & n.32–40 & n.58–64, 7, 9, 216.

Sarpedon, 78–9 & n.9.
Saturn, 11, 196 n.29.
Seneca, 192 n.66.
Servius, 6, 220.
Solomon, 171.
Sophocles, 159 & n.17, 164 & n.2.
Statius, 6 & n.84, 12, 16, 189, 206 n.2 & 9, 218 (*Stazio*), 220.

Tisiphone, 118, 210 n.2.
Tydeus, 85, 107, 172, 176.

Ulysses, 8, 123, 167, 169, 179, 183, 198 n.5, 209 n.34.

Valerius Maximus, 212 n.16–18.
Venus, 39, 54–6 & n.9 and 13, 92, 99, 105 & n.3 ('mother of Love'), 111, 112 & n.5 (Cytheraea), 117, 119, 125 & n.7 (Cytheraea), 127 (Cytheraea), 128–33 & n.16 and 28, 138, 139, 140 & n.9, 150, 151, 196 n.26 and 29, 203 n.4, 205 n.3, 209 n.26–8, 209 n.31.
Villani, Giovanni, 3 & n.34, 191 n.32, 220.
Virgil, 4, 6, 164, 188, 199 n.8 & n.11 & n.18 & n.26, 201 n.22, 220.

.

Lightning Source UK Ltd.
Milton Keynes UK
05 July 2010

156566UK00001B/54/A